Overcoming learning and behaviour difficulties

This book asserts that for some pupils, school-based factors play a major role in creating and maintaining learning and/or behavioural difficulties. Not surprisingly, it is often true that the people best placed to identify these factors are the pupils themselves. Current thinking therefore encourages teachers and other professionals to respond to learning and behaviour difficulties through a greater partnership with pupils.

Overcoming Learning and Behaviour Difficulties considers the rationale to partnership and looks at ways in which teachers can empower pupils, giving them greater control over their own learning and behaviour. It focuses upon practical ways in which this can be achieved at pupil, class and whole-school levels, thus overcoming or avoiding problems.

It includes advice on:

* non-directive counselling
* peer support
* contracting
* use of information technology
* self-monitoring schemes
* pupil involvement in school policy and governance
* auditing and enhancing partership.

Kevin Jones is Senior Lecturer in the School of Education at Nanyang Technological University, Singapore. **Tony Charlton** is Professor of Education at Cheltenham and Gloucester College of Higher Education. They are the co-editors of *Learning Difficulties in Primary Classrooms* (Routledge 1992).

Overcoming learning and behaviour difficulties

Partnership with pupils

Edited by Kevin Jones and Tony Charlton

London and New York

First published 1996
by Routledge
11 New Fetter Lane, London EC4P 4EE

Simultaneously published in the USA and Canada
by Routledge
29 West 35th Street, New York, NY 10001

Typeset in Palatino by Datix International Limited, Bungay, Suffolk
Printed and bound in Great Britain by Clays Ltd, St Ives PLC

British Library Cataloguing in Publication Data
A catalogue record for this book is available from the British Library

Library of Congress Cataloging in Publication Data
Overcoming learning and behaviour difficulties: partnership with
pupils/edited by Kevin Jones and Tony Charlton.
Includes bibliographical references and index.
1. Learning disabled children – Education – Great Britain. 2. Problem
children – Education – Great Britain. 3. Teacher–student relationships –
Great Britain. 4. Classroom management – Great Britain. I. Jones, Kevin,
1950– . II. Charlton, Tony.
LC4706.5.G7084 1996
371.93'0941–dc20   96–7568
                                                                              CIP

ISBN 0–415–11866–2
ISBN 0–415–11867–0 (pbk)

Contents

Part IV Classroom-based support

Part V Whole-school approaches

Part VI Enhancing pupils' involvement in schools

Contributors

Graham Bill has worked in primary, secondary and special schools in the UK and with SCEA in Germany. Currently, he heads the Learning Support Service in West Gloucestershire where he works with both teachers and governors in promoting good practice in teaching pupils with special educational needs.

Julian Brown is an educational psychologist with Kirklees Education Authority. He has previously taught in secondary schools, worked for Durham and Doncaster Psychological Services and spent six years as a lecturer in special education at the National Institute of Education, which is part of Nanyang Technological University, Singapore. His current research interests include behaviour management and attributional style amongst low-attaining children.

Tony Charlton is Professor of Education at Cheltenham and Gloucester College of Higher Education. Many of his books and articles reflect his particular interests in behaviour problems and learning difficulties. More recently, his research interests have centred on the effects of broadcast television upon young pupils' social behaviour.

He is co-editor of *The Caring Role of the Primary School* (Macmillan Education, 1988), *Managing Misbehaviour* (1st edn) (Macmillan Education, 1989), *Supportive Schools* (Macmillan Education, 1990), *Managing Misbehaviour* (2nd edn) (Routledge, 1993) and *Pastoral Care Matters: In Primary and Middle Schools* (Routledge, in press).

Paul Cooper has worked in mainstream primary and secondary schools as well as special schools. Since 1989 he has held academic posts at Birmingham University and Oxford University. He is currently a lecturer in education (special educational needs) at Oxford University. A central theme in his work to date has been a recognition of the need for theorists, policy makers and managers to understand the experience of schooling from the perspectives of teachers and pupils. He has published widely on aspects of emotional and behavioural difficulties as well as teachers' and pupils' perspectives on effective teaching and learning.

Philip Garner has worked in mainstream and special schools for fifteen years. He is now a senior lecturer in the School of Education at Brunel University, where he is also the Director of the Centre for Comparative Studies in Special Education.

Malcolm Hanson is Deputy Head of Allington Boys' School, Chippenham, Wiltshire. His experience includes both primary and secondary schools before entering special education to specialise in working with pupils with emotional and behavioural disorders. In a previous post he worked closely with Marlborough Children's Hospital developing individual development plans for emotionally troubled children within the adolescent unit.

Kevin Jones' teaching experience spans primary, secondary and special schools. He is now a senior lecturer in special educational needs at Nanyang Technological University in Singapore. His research interests include the assessment/recognition of learning difficulties, special educational provision in mathematics and co-operative teaching approaches. Additionally, he has investigated the special oral language needs of low attaining mathematicians.

He has written many articles and chapters concerned with special educational needs, and is co-editor, with Tony Charlton, of *Learning Difficulties in Primary Classrooms* (Routledge, 1992).

Ian Leech taught in Gloucestershire for twenty-seven years. During that time he worked in special schools before becoming an information technology advisory teacher. He now lectures in IT at Gloucester College of Arts and Technology. His elder son, who is disabled, runs a small desktop publishing business from home.

Jeff Lewis is a principal lecturer in Rolle School of Education, University of Plymouth, where his major areas of responsibility are special educational needs and pastoral care. He recently contributed a chapter to a volume on children's rights.

Mayling Quah is currently senior lecturer and Head of the Division of Specialised Education at the National Institute of Education, Nanyang Technological University, Singapore. Her research interests include reading problems in the primary years, learning difficulties of children and young adults in regular school settings, strategies for developing language and reading skills and the determinants of achievement in primary-school children. She has written many articles and chapters that deal with various aspects of school learning and problems faced by children and adolescents. She is currently serving as editorial consultant to two journals – *The International Journal of Disability, Development and Education* and *Support for Learning*.

Alison Scott-Bauman works as an educational psychologist, a teacher trainer at Cheltenham and Gloucester College of Higher Education and as an Open University tutor. Her main research interest is in the area of supporting teachers to improve the effectiveness of pupils as learners.

Pamela Sharpe is a senior lecturer at the National Institute of Education, Nanyang Technological University, Singapore. She is currently seconded to the PCF Pre-School Development Unit as Dean of the Early Childhood Institute. She has been in Singapore for ten years and during this time has been involved in the training of pre-school and special needs teachers. She has also conducted research into various aspects of children's learning and development, and, parental involvement in pre-school education.

Amongst her research studies, a central focus has been early intervention for children with learning difficulties, and the role of parents in maximising the potential of their young children.

Susannah Temple's interest and expertise in encouraging and inspiring children is woven from a professional lifetime working with children, families and teachers in various educational contexts, in roles ranging from community worker and advisory teacher, counsellor and psychotherapist, to tutor and trainer. Particularly relevant here are her seven years as a counsellor in primary and secondary schools, and work as a child therapist for the Devon Joint Agencies Child Abuse Team. She holds a graduate diploma in counselling and guidance, and is a Certified Transactional Analyst with educational specialisation.

Rebecca Whittern has been teaching for six years in a large junior school in Gloucester. She is currently completing her M.Ed. studies at Cheltenham and Gloucester College of Higher Education.

Introduction

Recent legislation and current thinking encourage teachers, and other involved professionals, to respond to learning and behaviour problems through a greater partnership with pupils. This book considers the rationale for this partnership and focuses upon practical ways in which this can be achieved at pupil, class and whole-school levels. Chapters show how pupils' academic, social and emotional development can be enhanced when schools more fully involve them, for example, in consultative and decision-making processes.

Understandings of school-based factors which cause learning and behaviour difficulties can benefit from consultations with pupils who encounter these difficulties. They are well placed to make visible certain features of the curriculum and learning environment which cause and maintain such difficulties. In order to participate in this process pupils need to be given a voice and receive reassurance that their contributions will be taken seriously. Contributors to early chapters advise upon ways in which teachers (and associated professionals) can facilitate this process, through the development of their own listening skills and the creation of conditions under which real partnership can flourish.

The main focus of the book is upon ways in which teachers can empower pupils to take greater control over their own learning and behaviour in order that problems can be overcome, or circumvented. Advice is given about ways in which non-directive counselling, peer support and contracting can help to achieve these goals at the individual pupil level. Later chapters examine how support, personal problem solving and information technology can help to address learning and behaviour problems within classrooms and the wider school. Contributors then present examples of ways in which pupils can become involved in self-monitoring schemes, whole-school governance and the determination of school policies. Finally, the editors give consideration to ways in which the quality of partnership can be audited and enhanced.

Part I

Pupil responses to schooling

Kevin Jones and Tony Charlton challenge common responses to learning and behaviour difficulties and draw attention to the multiplicity of factors which may create and sustain them, including factors:

- within pupils (e.g. physical, cognitive and emotional states)
- within the curriculum
- within pupils' learning environment (e.g. classroom management strategies, pedagogy, ethos)
- located within the broader social context (e.g. home, neighbourhood).

The authors claim that a *real* understanding of the factors which cause a particular pupil to experience difficulties can only be achieved through consultation with the individuals concerned. Many pupils are able to make visible sources of learning and behaviour problems which are often overlooked by their teachers. This understanding leads to the suggestion that best responses to learning difficulties and problem behaviours will be achieved through a development of 'partnership with pupils'.

Chapter 1

Sources of learning and behaviour difficulties

Kevin Jones and Tony Charlton

INTRODUCTION

When a simple mechanical device fails to function properly, a skilled engineer is usually able to trace the cause to a single fault and rectify the problem within minutes. In contrast, learning and behaviour difficulties are rarely attributable to single, uncomplicated, causes. They are usually the result of a complex interaction of different factors, some of which are easily visible, while others are 'hidden' amongst features of the setting in which they occur. If professionals merely seek to identify and respond to the causes which, to them, are most visible, they will, at best, produce only temporary solutions to problems. More lasting solutions will also require an in-depth assessment of, and appropriate responses to, less visible factors which cause people to behave in certain ways.

The intricacies of human behaviour also affect the way in which different people attempt to describe the causes of difficulties. The roles which people play, their interests, past experience, knowledge base and theoretical inclination will all affect the way in which they are inclined to analyse and describe causation. Rachel's experiences, described below, illustrate some of these points:

> The first sight of Zell am Zimmer took Rachel's breath away. The majestic snow-covered mountains and valleys of the Austrian Tyrol were every bit as beautiful as they had appeared in the brochures. As the coach drew near the outskirts of the town attractive Alpine houses came into view, many of which were surrounded by neatly stacked firewood which would keep the inhabitants warm throughout winter. Although it was

already early evening, ski-lifts were still plucking people from queues, tugging them up clearings between pine trees, and discharging them on to pistes of varying levels of difficulty. Rachel was filled with a strange mixture of competing emotions. She felt excitement, anxiety and eager anticipation as she watched the progress of the skiers. She had been looking forward to this holiday for over eighteen months.

When she looked out of the window the following morning a small trickle of snow was covering tracks which had been made the previous day. It was a peaceful and quiet scene; a stark contrast to the view from her own bedroom window at home, which faced on to the main street of Kimberley, in Nottinghamshire.

The group assembled in front of their instructor at the bottom of the nursery slope. Despite the fact that the area was relatively flat, 'raw recruits' were skidding past at some speed. Having introduced them to the rudiments of skiing, Jan encouraged members of the group to make their first attempts at the 'snow-plough'. Rachel was excited by the challenge and couldn't wait to master the technique. She was eager to experience the wonderful sensation of gliding down the more advanced runs, which her cousin, Mark, had often described to her.

Rachel was satisfied with her first attempts on the nursery slope and she was pleased to receive warm smiles and positive comments from Jan. She soon got to grips with the snow-plough and could weave around the nursery slope and bring herself to a controlled stop. She was promoted to the next stage on the second day.

The day started much like the previous one. After rising from the warmth of the big wooden bed, she took in the delightfully peaceful scene before savouring a light breakfast of croissants and coffee. The success and enjoyment of the first day made her eager to get going.

The new group gathered around Julie, who instructed them on the intricacies of getting on to a T-bar ski-lift. This seemingly simple act had to be deftly performed with one hand while holding ski-sticks with the other. The first three members of the group managed without mishap, giving Rachel confidence as she shuffled into position. The next T-bar came swinging around towards her. She had prepared herself well; the ski-sticks were already in her left hand, and she was easily able to take hold of the T-bar with the other, positioning herself ready for 'take-off'. She was surprised by the speed at which she was plucked from standing position and hauled quickly up the slope. She went forward without mishap and soon settled back to enjoy the sensation of sliding effortlessly uphill. After a relatively short time, the town of Zell am Zimmer seemed quite a distance below her. When she reached the top she skied from the T-bar and positioned herself alongside other members of the group who were chatting to Volka, their instructor for the next stage.

The short feeder slope, which linked the top of the ski-lift with the 'mini-piste', was slightly greater in gradient than the nursery slope. Each person in the group enjoyed the sensation of zig-zagging down this pretty little clearing. Volka gathered them together at the top of the mini-piste. Rachel came to a halt and then looked down towards the town. For the first time panic swept through her. Previously relaxed muscles tensed up like the taut strings of a violin. The mini-piste, as it had been called, appeared to plunge towards the distant town at an incredibly steep angle. Given the speeds which had been achieved on the relatively flat nursery slope, she feared that this 'mountain' would plunge them into disaster. On a nearby slope, more experienced skiers flicked up snow as they performed skilful turns.

Rachel snapped out of her thoughts as Volka started to give the group new instructions. The wind was starting to get up and Rachel struggled hard to make sense of Volka's broad Austrian accent. She picked out the words 'snow-plough position', 'traverse', and 'turn'. She also heard him say, 'Do not attempt to lean back into the slope of the hill'. She watched avidly as he demonstrated the technique to the group. At the end of the demonstration he side-stepped back to the group and was eager to set the first members off down the piste.

The three people who had been first on the ski-lift were also first to go down the slope. They picked their way cautiously and carefully across the line of the hill and executed shaky, but safe turns at the end of each traverse. Within minutes the first person was standing at the bottom of the slope, waving encouragement to other members of the group. Rachel pushed off with her ski-sticks, determined, but anxious. The tightness in her muscles eased, but her legs now felt like jelly. Her heart was pounding in her chest. She maintained the correct snow-plough position and managed to get across the slope quite smoothly. When she reached the far end she put her weight on her left ski and began to turn. Slowly, but surely, she completed the manœuvre and enjoyed the second 'traverse'. As she approached the next turn her heart began to pound. She put her weight on to her right ski and once again turned to face downhill. This time the turn seemed to fade. Fear caused her to transfer some of her weight on to what now seemed the *safer* ski. The effect was catastrophic. She went into a fast, oblique, downhill run. She thought about flinging herself on to the ground in order to reduce speed, but her body was gripped by fear. She couldn't move. The faster she went the more frightened she became. She was now at the total mercy of natural forces. Everything became blurred. Eventually she crashed into a huge pile of snow which had been piled up to one side of the piste. The enormous force of the impact punched the breath from her lungs. Tears streamed down her face and her skis continued their journey to the bottom of the slope without her. Her pulse was racing and she trembled vigorously. After a few moments she picked up her sticks and hurled them down the slope. Eventually, she stood up, stared down at the snow, and stamped down the slope. No longer was she attracted by the beauty of the Tyrol. Never again would she attempt to ski.

That incident destroyed Rachel's holiday, as well as her confidence in her ability to learn to ski. She complained to the manager of the ski-school and demanded a refund, on the grounds that instructions were unclear and the level of proficiency required on the mini-piste was too high. In her opinion there should have been an intermediate stage between the nursery slope and the mini-piste. When Volka gave his account of the incident to the manager he had quite a different perspective on things, claiming that Rachel had let her emotions take control. He was also of the opinion that she was poorly co-ordinated and that the first instructor should not have allowed her to progress to the second stage so quickly. The manager asked him whether the mishap might have been caused by a freak patch of ice on the slope.

The above incident shows how the three key 'players' were inclined to protect their own interests by looking for causes which were outside their own control. For example, Volka preferred to blame Rachel and Jan, rather than considering whether the incident was also related to his own actions. The truth of the matter is that Rachel's problems were caused by a mixture of interacting factors, some of which resided within her (e.g. co-ordination, emotional state), while others were related to the progression and presentation of instructions and the condition of the piste, to name but a few.

PERCEPTIONS OF THE CAUSES OF LEARNING AND BEHAVIOUR DIFFICULTIES

Learning and behaviour problems which are encountered by pupils in schools are also usually caused by a mixture of interacting factors and, as in the above case, different people (e.g. teachers, pupils, parents, associated professionals) have sometimes differing views about the causes of those problems, depending upon their own interests, experience, knowledge base and theoretical inclination.

It is interesting to note the results of Croll and Moses' (1985) study, which showed that many teachers believe that the main causes of learning and behaviour problems are related to:

- factors innate to the child (e.g. IQ/ability)
- the child's attitude or concentration
- home circumstances.

Thus, like Rachel and Volka, many teachers identified causes which were external to them. Very few considered that problems could be caused by factors which were within their control, such as the curriculum, classroom activities or their own actions. In contrast, Ainscow (1993) claims that many pupils encounter problems because of the inability of a teacher, or a group of teachers, to provide classroom experiences that are meaningful and relevant to the interests, experiences, skills and knowledge of particular children. These opposing views further illustrate the disparate theories of causation which are held by different people.

Pupil learning and behaviour, like that of adults, will be affected by a *range* of interacting factors, some of which reside within *the child*, while others can be traced to an inappropriate *curriculum*, or related to conditions within the *learning environment* (Jones 1992, 1994). A failure to consider adequately any one of these factors, or the interaction between them, is to risk overlooking the very heart of what affects learning for a particular child. Teachers and associated professionals must be wary of the danger of only addressing those causal factors which, to them, are highly visible. While other influential factors might be 'hidden' from their immediate view, they should be aware that others (especially pupils), are likely to be in a much better position to notice them. Effective responses to learning and behaviour problems are only likely to occur when the whole spectrum, rather than just one layer, of causal factors is taken into account.

Despite the fact that pupils are likely to be able to throw light upon causes of learning and behaviour problems which might be overlooked by their teachers, research shows that until recently they were rarely consulted (see Chapter 2). While there has been a growing involvement of parents in the assessment of their child's special educational needs, and a growth in case conferencing, the need to consider the interests and views of pupils has only recently been accorded more importance. This is regrettable, because there is a growing body of evidence which shows that, under the right conditions, pupils can provide useful insights into important matters which affect their learning (see Tisdall and Dawson 1994). In Chapters 3 and 4, Lewis and Scott-Bauman, respectively, discuss ways in which teachers can develop their listening skills in order to help pupils to voice their concerns and opinions, and Leech (Chapter 10) describes how computer technology helped teachers to adapt classroom conditions for learning and allowed one pupil to inform his teachers and parents about his educational and life needs. Furthermore, both Charlton (Chapter 2) and Garner (Chapter 13) emphasise that children, *by right*, should be involved in educational decision-making.

Wade and Moore (1993) provide several examples of insightful comments made by pupils, which further support the argument that if they were considered to be 'partners' in the assessment and planning process, the information which they could contribute would provide a good foundation from which simple changes could be made to overcome, or circumvent, the difficulties they experience. Wade and Moore (1993) claim that many teachers don't appreciate the difficulties which some pupils encounter. For example, in their own study (see Chapter 8 for more details) they found that many children were reluctant to undertake learning activities due to a fear of failure ('I am scared', 'I think I will get it wrong'), feelings and thoughts which were undetected by their teachers.

Jones and Quah (in press) describe the case of Gavin, aged 11 years, who has a mixture of positive and negative learning experiences in school. The negative experiences leave such a marked impression upon him that they overshadow and partially 'block out' (Charlton 1992) the positive ones, leaving him with a poor impression of schooling, which in turn seems to have a detrimental effect upon his learning.

Gavin's comments about different settings reveal certain conditions which appear to affect learning. In some settings, he encounters conditions which contribute towards positive learning outcomes. The following selection of comments reveal the positive influence which good teacher–pupil relationships seem to have upon his learning:

Maths   When I don't know what to do the teacher explains it to me. She doesn't mind me asking. Then I know what to do and it's easy. I can usually do it on my own after that, without any help. The teacher says I try really hard and I am getting good at my work. She makes me work really hard, but I never feel stressed out.

Geography   It is really interesting. Sometimes we see videos, sometimes we make models, sometimes we do writing. We never spend 'hours' on the same stuff. Our teacher is sort of strict. He doesn't let anyone mess about, but he never shouts at you. If we do something wrong he tells us why it is wrong. I like that. It's fair. Even when he tells us off he says he likes us. Most of the time we are really good in his lessons.

Gavin's teachers and parents were able to confirm that in these types of setting he achieves good academic results. From his comments it is also quite clear that he feels both comfortable and 'fired-up' for learning in those settings. Certain characteristics of his relationships with teachers seem to be particularly important to him. An analysis of all his comments revealed that he appears to need conditions in which he:

• feels able to ask for clarification about tasks and activities
• is encouraged to find solutions to his own problems

- is listened to with interest
- is given positive rewards (verbal and non-verbal) for effort, achievement and acceptable behaviour
- is allowed to seek support from other pupils, as well as seeking the advice of the teacher
- receives explanations about undesirable behaviours.

Gavin's comments about those settings within which he is on a slippery spiral of failure illustrate the negative impact which certain kinds of teacher–pupil relationships have upon his learning:

English   We have to keep our books under the tables on a sort of ledge. Mine were missing. I put them there, but someone took them. I got really shouted at. It has happened three times now. I don't know who takes them but I always get the blame. I've had two detentions already and I didn't even do it. I can't concentrate on the lesson because he keeps staring at me, as if I am going to do something wrong.

Science   When I get work wrong the teacher calls me 'idiot'. He's always calling me idiot. And he calls me Gaz bag, he knows I hate that, I'm sure he does. He always tells me I am doing things wrong.

History   The teacher stands at the front and lectures for 'hours'. It's so boring. When we have to do work he doesn't let us ask questions. He never comes round to our desks to talk to us. We call him 'the Robot'.

Art   Someone didn't tidy up and I got the blame. There was some paint on the desk. She just came up to me and made the mess even worse and made me tidy up. She is always picking on me. It wasn't even my mess. I know I do things wrong sometimes cos I don't know what I'm supposed to do. I don't always 'get it' at first, but some teachers let me ask. I usually understand really well after that. But she goes mad if I don't know what to do.

Certain conditions, in the above settings, seem to act as barriers to learning. In particular, and understandably, Gavin does not like to be:

- called names
- scolded for doing things wrong, without being told why
- blamed for things he claims he didn't do
- labelled 'troublemaker' because of a genuine lack of understanding of task requirements
- taught by impersonal and uncaring teachers.

While we do not wish to advocate that teachers should feel compelled to make changes in their own behaviour in response to every single comment offered by pupils, it seems sensible to suggest that conditions for learning could be greatly enhanced if pupils' views were elicited and carefully examined and (where appropriate) responded to. In Gavin's case, relatively simple things (e.g. clarification of tasks, peer support, being listened to with interest) seem to enhance learning. If these supportive strategies were implemented in those settings which he sees as problematic, alongside a reduction in undesirable actions (such as name calling), it is likely that his academic and social learning would improve.

In later chapters in this book, contributors draw attention to other benefits which can arise when pupils are actively involved in the identification of causes of learning and behaviour problems. In Chapter 5, for example, Temple indicates that children are more likely to find solutions to their own problems if they can be helped to assess their own experience, thoughts, feelings, desires and feelings of self-worth. Similarly, in Chapter 7, Brown claims that the most effective behaviour management contracts will be those which are based upon pupil, as well as teacher, assessment. Hanson (Chapter 11) takes this further by discussing a school-wide scheme which encourages pupils to self-manage their own behaviour through self-monitoring. These accounts, together with examples of ways in which pupils can use their knowledge to influence school policy and governance positively (see Chapters 12 and 13), point to the wide-ranging benefits which can arise when good working partnerships are formed between teachers and pupils.

People's explanations about the sources of learning and behaviour problems will also be affected by their theoretical preferences. Charlton and George (1993) suggest that behaviouristic models encourage teachers and other professionals to see problems in the context of maladaptive behaviour being learned (e.g. through reinforcement or modelling of undesirable behaviours) and adaptive behaviours or competencies not being learned. The psychodynamic model, on the other hand, focuses on a pupil's inner experiences; for example the extent to which a succession of rejections (by father, mother and other adults) pose a threat to the ego, and generate anxieties; and the manner in which the pupil handles those anxieties. Similarly, the humanistic model's focus would be upon the manner in which a child perceived experiences and the impact of these perceptions upon its developing 'self' (i.e. self-concept, self-esteem) and consequent behaviour. Thus, as well as eliciting the viewpoints of others (e.g. their pupils), teachers and other professionals should be aware of the impact which their own theoretical leanings have upon their personal theories of causation. They should, perhaps, be open to other explanations which they might otherwise disregard.

MAKING SENSE OF VISIBLE AND HIDDEN SOURCES OF LEARNING AND BEHAVIOUR DIFFICULTIES

Charlton and George (1993) suggest that one way of helping to clarify the complexity of factors which underpin and/or surround learning and behaviour difficulties is to think in terms of *predisposing*, *precipitating* and *reinforcing* causes. For example, although research findings are not conclusive, they suggest that particular types of temperament may predispose young children to later maladjustment (Thomas and Chess 1977). Such predispositions include under- and over-activity, tendency to withdrawal and irregularity of sleeping. Behaviours will also be precipitated and reinforced by what is happening in the environment. Teachers who pay a lot of attention to misbehaviour and ignore good behaviour can unwittingly signal to children that the best way to receive attention is through displays of inappropriate behaviour, thus reinforcing undesirable actions.

Predisposing, precipitating and reinforcing causes of learning and behaviour problems can be found within the *child*, the *curriculum* and the *learning environment* (Jones 1992, 1994). Teachers and other professionals are only likely to understand the spectrum of interacting causes if they add to their pool of knowledge by eliciting information from those (e.g. pupils) who are often best positioned to identify, and make visible, causes within each of these locations. They should also be aware that their own theoretical inclinations encourage them to seek out causes in a particular way. They should, therefore, be prepared to be receptive to other explanations. Furthermore, during their best efforts to trace the sources of learning and behaviour difficulties they should be aware that there are still many unknown causes (Beirne-Smith *et al.* 1994). This fact should not encourage them to put off their search. In partnership with others (e.g. pupils, parents, associated professionals) they should be prepared to attempt to uncover hitherto unrecognised causes of learning and behaviour problems.

The following sections of this chapter will discuss factors within the learner, the curriculum and the learning environment which might predispose, precipitate and reinforce learning and/or behaviour problems. The discussion will consider the extent to which causal factors are visible to teachers, and the extent to which others (e.g. pupils, other professionals, parents) might be equally or better placed to provide essential information about them.

SOURCES OF LEARNING AND BEHAVIOUR DIFFICULITES 'WITHIN THE CHILD'

The most obvious, but sometimes overlooked, 'within-child' factors which can influence pupil learning outcomes are the quality of *hearing and vision*. If problems of hearing or vision go undetected, they are likely to cause considerable difficulties for the pupil concerned. The following indicators, developed by Ainscow and Muncey (1981), can help teachers to identify pupils whose difficulties might be due (in part) to such problems. Children who are observed to have several problems in either area should be invited to discuss the matter with the teachers and if necessary be referred for medical examination, through the appropriate channels. For convenience, the indicators are presented in the form of checklists.

Indicators of hearing loss

As the child works, watch out for the following:

> Tilts head at an angle to hear sound ...
> Shows frequent lack of attention during oral lessons ...
> Fails to respond when questioned ...
> Has difficulty in following directions ...
> Has peculiar voice qualities, often high pitched ...
> Tends to rush words together ...
> Depends on classmates for instructions ...
> Watches the faces (especially mouth and lips) of speakers ...
> Shows defects in speech ...
> Frequent use of 'pardon', 'eh', 'uh?' ...

Indicators of poor vision

Difficulties of vision may be indicated by the following symptoms when working in the classroom:

> Rubs eyes excessively ...
> Shuts or covers one eye ...
> Is sensitive to light ...
> Squints, blinks or frowns when doing close work ...
> Holds reading material too close or too far ...
> Complains of pains, itching or aches in the eyes ...
> Complains of blurred or double vision ...
> Reverses letters, syllables or words ...
> Confuses letters or similar shapes ...

Other less obvious *sensory-processing* factors (e.g. poor visual or auditory discrimination, sequencing difficulties) can also influence learning outcomes (see, for example, Tyler 1990). To give a simple example, a child with specific learning difficulties in the auditory area (e.g. poor level of hearing, difficulties in discriminating between sounds) will experience considerable difficulties in learning when faced with a teacher who relies almost wholly on verbal explanations, without any supportive visual or manipulative resources. Conversely, children are likely to learn much more effectively if their stronger channels (e.g. vision, kinaesthetic sense) are utilised (see Chapter 8).

Since the existence of sensory-processing difficulties might not be so obvious to class or subject teachers the assessment should be carried out by someone with specialist training. This could, of course, be the class/subject teacher, but it is more likely to be a learning support co-ordinator or a visiting professional, who has the skills to locate these potential sources of learning difficulties. However, after completing the assessment, this person should shift the locus of professional responsibility back to the class/ subject teacher who should be encouraged to develop teaching and learning activities which will take advantage of that child's strengths (e.g. good 'visual' and 'kinaesthetic' processing skills). Neither party should forget that the majority of pupils will be able to offer valuable advice upon the impact of the processing difficulty and the appropriateness of particular teaching strategies to their individual learning needs.

While teachers and associated professionals, through classroom observation and testing, might be able to identify and respond to sensory sources of learning and behaviour difficulties, they may have to consult with others (e.g. medical colleagues and/or their written records, parents, pupils) in order to appraise the educational significance of other predisposing, 'within-child' factors.

Charlton and George (1993) produce a comprehensive account of such factors, including a discussion of the effects which chromosomal abnormalities, genetic irregularities and brain damage can have upon learning and behaviour. However, while certain syndromes, such as 'Fragile-X', have been associated with severe and profound difficulties in learning it is also found in pupils with normal levels of intelligence. This underlines the need for caution in attributing the causes of learning and behaviour difficulties to single factors, without careful consideration of the full facts. Similarly, a consistent relationship between Fragile-X and autism has been reported in the literature, with males with Fragile-X having 5–46 per cent prevalence of autism or autistic-like behaviours. However, children with autism have Fragile-X in only 15 per cent of cases. These facts underline the need for teachers to gather reliable information about the impact of these 'potential' 'within-child' sources of learning and behaviour difficulties through careful observation and consultation 'labels' can be very misleading.

Other predisposing, 'within-child' factors such as *food intolerance*, which can contribute towards learning and behaviour problems, may pass unnoticed and undetected except for concern over abnormal behaviours which are often associated with them.

Charlton and George (1993) draw attention to the relationship between diet and hyperactivity. They refer to the work of Shreeve (1982) who suggests that hyperactive children have abnormally low levels of essential fatty acids, and are, in this respect, biologically different to non-hyperactive children. Such a defect in metabolism allows hyperactive children to become extremely susceptible to certain substances, the result of which is an observable deterioration in behaviour.

Recent research into *autism* includes an exploration of the role of essential fatty acids and the secretion of hormones in the creation of this condition which affects the ability to use senses to the full. Although no specific neurological or neurochemical abnormalities have been consistently identified in autism, its biological base is no longer in doubt and it is suggested by Aarons and Gittens (1991) that autism is linked to certain physical disorders, including viruses, and to some inherited conditions such as Fragile-X syndrome.

There is also some evidence to suggest that learning and behaviour problems can be traced (in part) to brief disruptions in the normal *electro-chemical activity* of the brain. For example, *epilepsy*, which is caused by this type of abnormal activity, can lead to a higher incidence of behaviour disorders (Stedman 1973). Additionally, epileptic children often have very uneven educational profiles, which appear to be due, in part, to a wide imbalance of linguistic and spatial sub-skills. This can be compounded by the fact that on some occasions epileptic children may be unteachable for days at a time owing to fluctuations in their ability to attend and respond to their environment. As in all the other examples cited above, teachers should consider the impact of the condition upon learning and behaviour. Pupils who *experience* the condition are best placed to discuss its effects upon *their* learning. They should therefore be consulted and help to plan appropriate educational responses (aided by their elected representative if necessary).

While the above factors are important and should be taken into account, not all learning and behaviour problems will have causes which are related to predispositions within the child. Although some pupils may be affected by predisposing factors within themselves, this might only be one part of a whole spectrum of causal factors which are related to the curriculum and the learning environment.

SOURCES OF LEARNING AND BEHAVIOUR DIFFICULTIES 'WITHIN THE CURRICULUM'

For some children the planned curriculum, without modification, moves too fast, is at too difficult a level and/or is lacking in purpose. Others become frustrated because they are constantly revising work which is already familiar to them and which moves at too slow a pace. A number of writers have cited an inappropriate curriculum as a major source of pupil disaffection (e.g. Charlton 1986, Reynolds 1988). As Charlton and George (1993: 41) state, 'it is difficult for (and unreasonable to expect!) pupils to engage in, and sustain, good behaviour when their school days are filled with material and presentations which fail to arouse their interest and industry'. Charlton (1986) comments that those:

> who are disinterested in, or disenchanted and dissatisfied with the educational programmes schools offer to them, may well direct their interest and energies away from school tasks towards a variety of maladaptive behaviours (e.g. non-involvement in academic work, truancy, abuse towards teachers) which facilitate an excitement and involvement unavailable elsewhere in school.
>
> (p. 56)

While teachers can, to some extent, evaluate whether the curriculum is at the correct level, well paced and relevant, without reference to anyone else, they will be well advised to make judgements in *partnership with their pupils* (and significant others), for it is they who experience the curriculum at first hand. This unique position gives pupils a different perspective on the curriculum, thus allowing them to make visible potential sources of learning and behaviour problems, which might otherwise be overlooked by their teachers.

Teachers are often alerted to problems in the curriculum through the '*products*' of pupil learning. Incorrect written responses to exercises, poor verbal responses and uncoordinated motor actions are, to teachers, some of the most visible signs that children are experiencing difficulties. Such responses can signal that the level, or pace, of the curriculum is inappropriate for a particular child. For example, it would be unreasonable to expect children to calculate the amount of time which had expired between two given points, if they have not yet grasped the basic concept of 'time'. If the gradient of learning is too steep, pupils are likely to experience learning and behaviour problems, as in the case of Rachel, described at the beginning of this chapter.

The process of 'task analysis' (see Smith 1994) can help teachers to examine whether the level and pace of the curriculum are matched to the needs of the child. This process sets out to provide a detailed description of the various sub-stages within a task, the child's current level of performance, under what conditions he/she can do it and the level of success achieved. Once a baseline of current performance is established, teachers can then plan an incremental sequence of learning objectives, each of which should build upon preceding stages and be manageable and achievable for the child. An example is provided by Haylock (1991:61):

3 calculate, by an informal adding-on process, the time interval from one digital time to another

2 tell the time, to the nearest five minutes from a dial clock, or watch, giving the answer in the form 3:40 a.m.

1 time activities or events, in seconds using the second counter of a digital watch, starting from zero, or a simple stop clock, or stop watch

Activities are then provided to help the child achieve each of the objectives and thus reach the pre-determined goal. This 'analytical approach' (Jones 1992) has been supported because it can lead to measurable gains in skills development, and Gickling and Thompson (1985) claim that without it many teachers fail to make necessary adjustments to the curriculum for pupils who encounter difficulties in learning.

While teachers might be alerted to the possible cause of learning and/or behaviour problems through an analysis of the 'products' of a child's learning, they might overlook difficulties which children encounter with the *processes* of learning. For many years there has been a tendency to task-analyse the curriculum on the basis of the products of learning, to the detriment of an accompanying analysis of the processes by which children learn.

Smith (1994), in discussing the analysis of tasks along process dimensions, draws attention to the fact that children are likely to experience learning difficulties if they are trying to cope with learning processes which are at too difficult a level, or for which they have been inadequately prepared. For example, children will:

- find it more difficult to reason abstractly than with the use of concrete materials; it will be harder for them to add abstract numerals than to perform similar calculations with blocks, or real coins
- sometimes be unable to respond through language, while they can do so through non-verbal means. For example, a child may be able to match the word 'cat' with another printed 'cat', note that it is different when presented among three 'bats', and copy the word 'cat'. However, applying language so as to read the visual symbol is more difficult. For most children, recalling both the language and the visual symbols, in order to write words, as in spelling 'cat', is the most difficult task of all
- encounter greater difficulties in expressing what they know, rather than dealing with the same material receptively. For example, communicating knowledge through essays is harder than recognising the correct information on a multiple-choice test format. Spelling a word is harder than recognising whether a word is correctly spelled.

Similarly, children might encounter difficulties in learning if they are not taught study skills such as 'skimming' to gain an overall impression of text, 'scanning' to find specific information, or how to use a table of contents, index or dictionary and how to take notes.

Pupils will also be likely to experience difficulties in learning if their teachers do not give them control over learning processes. In Chapter 14, Jones, Charlton and Whittern suggest that many teachers, with the best of intentions, prevent their children from gaining control over learning processes, by 'over-prompting' them. They cite the example of the LOOK, COVER, WRITE, CHECK process (Cripps 1983) which is often used in the teaching of spelling. If teachers and/or parents prompt children at each stage, spelling by spelling, they will soon learn that they don't have to remember the process for themselves. They don't have to remember HOW to look at words, for there is always someone there to tell them; nor do they have to remember the sequence of this process. These pupils are not learning 'how' to learn (they may, in fact, be learning how not to learn).

Although teachers can be alerted to problems in the 'product' area of the curriculum through an examination of children's work, an analysis of misunderstanding of learning processes will require a closer observation of children at work, supplemented with consultation. Through careful listening, teachers will be able to gauge the extent to which learning processes have been understood and applied.

While some of the above-mentioned procedures (e.g. task analysis) can help pupils to learn essential skills, they can result in activities which lack '*purpose*' for pupils. A number of writers have suggested that strict adherence to end point objectives can lead to the acquisition of skills that can only be performed in limited circumstances and a narrow curriculum where only the measurable is taught (Thomas and Feiler 1988). Thus, while the 'analytical' approach (Jones 1992) can help teachers to appraise whether the level and pace of the curriculum is appropriate to the learning needs of the child, it could also contribute a new source of learning and behaviour difficulties if it is too restricting or leads to activities which are lacking in 'purpose'. Rowland (1987) criticises educational practices for their lack of attention to 'purpose'. He contends that:

if our concern leads us to concentrate primarily upon devising a machinery for diagnosing children and preparing detailed packages for learning according to clearly defined objectives, I fear we shall be missing out on the heart of what these children, and indeed all learners, need from their teachers.

The need is for teaching- and learning-relationships in which the children's interests, abilities and concerns are seen to be at the the centre of the curriculum, and in which their expressions, – whether in writing, painting, speech or other symbols – are taken as being serious endeavours to communicate something of significance.

The challenge with which children who experience learning difficulties present us is to listen more carefully, and take bolder steps towards understanding their world as reflected in the choices they make and the interpretations they form of their environment.

(pp. 57–8)

Learning difficulties and behaviour problems caused by a perceived lack of purpose have been highlighted by writers (UNESCO 1993) who claim that 'children who are not getting on with their work in class almost always seem to lack understanding as to the purpose of what they have been asked to do'. When children are asked why they are doing something, many will say that they are doing it because their teacher told them to. Very rarely do they relate it to any purpose which is personal to them. This is unfortunate because, as writers of a UNESCO study pack (1993) suggest,

Learning is about finding personal meanings from experience. It requires us to understand what we are about and relate this to our existing knowledge and previous experience. Consequently, if we are unclear about the purpose of an activity, learning is less likely. Effective teachers stress meaning in their work. They find ways of helping their pupils understand the purposes of particular tasks, the reasons they have been set, how they are to be carried out and by when.

(p. 4)

Additionally, if pupils do not understand why they are doing a particular task, they will not have any control over it. They will need to refer back constantly to the teacher for help, rather than building up skills with which they can manage their own learning (see Chapter 14). Teachers will only really know if their pupils understand the purpose of an activity by observing and listening to them as they set about the task.

Finally, it is important that teachers realise that 'apparent' difficulties in some areas of the curriculum may be partially, if not wholly, attributable to the cumulative effect of their total learning experiences. Difficulties experienced in one or two areas can have a marked effect upon learning and behaviour in otherwise unproblematic areas. The case of Gavin, referred to earlier, shows that undesirable conditions for learning in some settings can have a pervasive effect and intrude upon the child's total attitude to schooling; in effect spoiling what might be otherwise fruitful learning experiences. For this reason the total learning experiences of pupils should be reviewed. The process of ecological mapping can help teachers to carry out this task with their pupils (see Jones 1992).

SOURCES OF LEARNING AND BEHAVIOUR DIFFICULTIES 'WITHIN THE LEARNING ENVIRONMENT'

The experiences of pupils referred to earlier in this chapter drew attention to the significant impact which certain features of the learning environment (e.g. pupil–teacher relationships) can have upon pupil learning and behaviour. *Physical aspects of the learning environment*, such as the number and quality of books, computers, software, educational games and seating arrangements are probably the most visible, but not necessarily the most important, features of the environment which affect learning and behaviour. In the case of pupils who experience sensory difficulties, these (and other) aspects of the learning environment may have an even greater impact upon learning outcomes and social behaviours. Best's (1992) advice to teachers who have *visually impaired* children in their class helps them to examine the quality of the physical conditions and teaching behaviours which prevail. Some of Best's advice forms the foundation of the boxed checklist which is applicable to a wider range of pupils. As teachers works through the questions with a pupil, they will be alerted to conditions which could contribute to learning and behaviour problems.

Similarly, Martin (1988) offers advice to teachers who have children with *hearing impairments* in their classes. His listing, which summarises some of Martin's key points, also introduces teacher behaviours which are likely to affect pupil performance.

Checklist for visual impairment	
Item	*Comments*
Chair height enables the child to work with relaxed shoulders	. . .
For braille reader, wrists and elbows are comfortable when the finger pads are on braille	. . .
Desk angle/height enables child to work with straight back, comfortable lower back angle, unstrained neck muscles	. . .
Desk-top size allows for tidy arrangement of materials and books	. . .
Desk top has rim to prevent materials falling off	. . .
Surface is glare-free	. . .
Storage in desk is adequate for needed equipment	. . .
Distance for viewing teacher demonstrations is suitable	. . .
Sound levels are appropriate	. . .
Routes to door, storage areas, etc., are clear	. . .
Natural light from window is controlled	. . .
All light comes from behind, or the side of, the child	. . .
Task lamp, if needed, can be safely positioned to illuminate work surface	. . .

The absence of any of these conditions could have a detrimental effect upon learning. The majority of pupils will be able to help teachers to appraise the extent to which these conditions are present, or require amendment.

Other features of the learning environment which contribute to learning and behaviour problems are less visible to teachers and could easily be overlooked. A number of researchers (e.g. Mortimore *et al.* 1988, Bennet 1991, Cooper, Chapter 12) have drawn attention to certain factors which can precipitate and maintain difficulties in learning, some of which are noted below:

- a mismatch between the task and the pupil's current level of performance (one study indicated that 65 per cent of tasks were too difficult for low-attaining pupils)
- unstructured and poorly organised lessons
- poor specification of the learning tasks (pupils didn't know what they were expected to do)
- ineffective time management, thus reducing the amount of time available for teaching
- few opportunities to review, revise and reinforce learning

Checklist for hearing impairment

Item   *Comments*
Position the child and yourself carefully
Hearing-impaired children will need to supplement and
fill in information received by their defective hearing by
lip-reading. They should sit near the front, but not so
close that they have to look up at too steep an angle.
They will also encounter difficulties if the teacher
stands in front of a bright light or window. Hearing-
impaired children should also be allowed to move
to have clear sight of other children who are talking
during a lesson.   . . .

Point clearly and deliberately
When pointing out features on a blackboard, drawing
or illustration, move your hand or pointer somewhat
more deliberately and steadily than perhaps seems
natural.   . . .

Speak naturally
It is important to maintain the natural rhythm and
emphasis of speech, but sometimes it may be helpful
to slow down a little. Observe carefully and decide the
optimum speed of speaking to individual children.   . . .

Attract the child's attention
It will help if the teacher attracts the child's attention,
before speaking the main 'message'. Clues to the
nature of the topic can be given visually by writing key
words on the blackboard or by using a picture with a
brief caption.   . . .

Allow time for looking
Hearing-impaired children may need to be given more
time to examine and absorb pictorial or written
information, and the use of video and computer
programs where frames can be held and replayed
is particularly helpful.   . . .

- lack of choice
- the work having an image inappropriate to the pupil's chronological age
- a lack of 'purpose' in learning activities
- inappropriate grouping strategies
- an absence of teaching approaches which encourage independent learning

- poor social skills, thus leading to inappropriate behaviours in certain situations
- inconsistency among teachers
- a lack of focus in lessons
- poor record keeping
- lack of peer support.

Charlton (1992) claims that, although success and failure in learning will be affected by a range of factors, the beliefs which pupils hold regarding the influence of their own behaviour upon academic achievement are crucial. He describes these *affective factors* as follows:

> Internal locus of control beliefs characterise pupils who believe that academic outcomes are dependent upon their personal behaviour; where they desire success they believe it is attainable through their own efforts. Conversely, those who espouse external locus of control beliefs perceive academic outcomes being independent of their expenditure of time and energy and controlled by extrinsic forces such as fate, luck or chance. On occasions when they desire success they remain unconvinced that they are 'masters' of their own destiny. Beliefs of this type often preclude achievement-striving and serve only to help to guarantee failure.
>
> (p. 35)

Charlton (1992) also draws attention to research which supports the reasoning that an internal locus of control belief is a personality characteristic conducive to achievement-striving and high academic grades and test scores, while externality is linked with inferior grades/scores (Bar-Tal *et al.* 1980, Walden and Ramey 1983). Teachers, and associated professionals, in partnership with pupils, will need to appraise whether conditions within the learning environment are boosting, rather than deflating, self-concepts and also evaluate the extent to which teaching methods are helping pupils to take personal control for their own learning.

The feature of the learning environment which is probably of most importance to the majority of pupils is the *quality of teacher–pupil relationships*. The case of Gavin, referred to earlier, emphasises the impact which this factor can have upon the climate of the school, which in turn appears to affect learning and behaviour (DES and Welsh Office 1989). Similarly, in Chapter 12,

Cooper discusses how transfer to another school, or class (and in most instances a change to a more congenial teacher), was followed by a complete and apparently permanent disappearance of very overt signs of maladjustment. Reynolds (1984), in attempting to explain the genesis of a high-vandalism and high-disaffection school, refers to the following as probable causal factors, many of which are concerned with human relationships within schools:

- a highly coercive regime where control was more concerned with physically punishing, rather than seeking the root cause of, deviant behaviour, where many rules prevailed and were inflexibly enforced
- relationships between teachers being marked by friction
- the headteacher and staff apportioning the blame for school problems upon each other
- a high turnover of staff
- a paucity of pupil involvement in running the school
- classroom management practices which included public ridicule of miscreants and the administration of class punishment for individual rule breaking
- an unwillingness to welcome parents into the school
- an iniquitous investment of staff expertise, time, energy and other resources into 'A' streams, and a consequent low, or inferior, investment into other classes
- negative staff perceptions of pupils who were seen as 'irredeemable' and as having irremediable problems, stemming from apparent deficiencies in primary socialisation.

Patterns of academic and social behaviour will also be influenced by the *peer group*. In some cases the peer group will exert a strong influence on a pupil, while for others it will be mediated by other influences (e.g. family/teachers). As Charlton and George (1993) point out, peer groups often have their own sets of values and norms and where these conflict with, or are radically different from, those of the individual's family or the wider society, the individual has to determine which of the conflicting or differing expectations to adhere to. The behaviour of children who come from home backgrounds where little concern, or interest, is expressed about their 'out of home' activities, and who find satisfaction from becoming involved with high-status delinquent groups, is likely to be more strongly influenced by the peer group than the home.

Other pupils are emotionally upset by the fact that they do not feel accepted by their peers. In some cases this can lead to withdrawn behaviour which will mitigate against learning. Tisdall and Dawson's (1994) investigation into pupils' perceptions of learning support in a large comprehensive school reveals some of the feelings which pupils experience: 'It's sort of like an outsider coming in (to the group) and, like, it's quite hard to get accepted ... it's certainly still a problem in some (groups)' (p. 180). In extreme cases (e.g. bullying) the pressures which are inflicted upon a particular child create a total block to learning. In Chapter 6, Charlton and Jones explain how other pupils can help the victims of bullying to voice their feelings and concerns through the establishment of 'bully-lines'. In the same chapter, they describe the positive effects which other peer-support initiatives can have upon learning and behaviour. The influence of some of these initiatives appears to be so strong that one could argue that their absence could cause the occurrence of otherwise avoidable problems.

While the existence and quality of certain forms of peer support (e.g. buddy reading) will be fairly easy to appraise, other peer group influences will be hidden from the teacher's view. The nuances of human relationships (e.g. pressures not to 'inform' on others) may mean that teachers and other professionals will have to strive hard to reveal their impact upon the learning and behaviour of particular pupils.

Certain *conditions within the family* can also expose children to experiences which may render them more vulnerable to the onset of learning and behaviour problems. Wedge and Essen (1982) talk of *socially disadvantaged* children, who grow up in large, or single-parent families, are poorly housed and have low family income. These children, at the time of birth, already face substantially diminished prospects of normal development and progress through childhood experiences (compared with their non-disadvantaged peers), more health problems, increased rates of accidents requiring medical treatment, weighing less and being shorter, behaving less acceptably – as well as performing academically less well – in school, leaving school earlier and holding lower aspirations for further education. Charlton and George (1993) also point out that research evidence supports the notion that children with more serious behaviour problems often come from homes characterised by parental conflict, psychiatric illness or family disturbance.

Traumatic events, such as *bereavement*, *divorce* or *violence* are also potentially harmful to educational performance. For example, children from *violent families* often manifest withdrawn or disruptive behaviour which retards their development and impedes their progress in school (NSPCC 1974). While some children become withdrawn 'to keep themselves inconspicuous in a situation of conflict' (Hart 1976), others model their parents' behaviours and become aggressive themselves. In the latter instance there is the distinct likelihood that, in time, abused children become abusers of their own children (Rutter and Madge 1976).

Parents, in otherwise healthy families, can also act in ways which generate emotional problems for their children. Teachers are often well aware of pupils whose *anxiety* has been caused by parents demanding perfection from their children. By holding unrealistic expectations about their offspring's performance in school and habitually telling them that they should do better, they may precipitate fears and anxieties within them which cause untold misery and unhappiness. Similarly, overpermissive parents can also generate anxieties in their children. Children require boundaries and guidelines within which they can act and feel secure. Homes which fail to provide reasonable structure and where 'environmental predictability is lessened and uncertainty heightened' (Clarizio and McCoy 1983) may leave children feeling insecure and anxious.

Many of the above mentioned sources of learning and behaviour problems, which originate within the family, will not be immediately apparent to teachers or associated professionals. Indeed, many families will go to some lengths to hide them from view. While pupils might reveal some of the problems which they are experiencing, teachers (and associated professionals) will need to establish good working relationships with parents and pupils before they can hope to uncover deep-seated causes of learning and behaviour problems which occur within the family. Jones and Lock (1993) offer practical advice which can help teachers to develop partnerships founded upon mutual respect, sharing and trust.

CONCLUSIONS

Lasting responses to learning and behaviour difficulties require that teachers, and associated professionals, consider and respond to the whole range of underlying causes. This requires a three-pronged analysis of factors 'within the child', the 'curriculum' and the 'learning environment', as referred to in the foregoing text. A failure to consider adequately any one of these groups of factors is to risk overlooking the very heart of what might affect learning for a particular child. Teachers, and associated professionals, are only likely to understand the spectrum of interacting causes if they add to their own pool of knowledge by eliciting information from those (e.g. pupils) who are best positioned to identify causes of problems within each of the above mentioned locations (e.g. the learning environment). Pupils are often well placed to make visible certain features of the curriculum and learning environment which are potential causes of learning and behaviour problems. Many of these features are often overlooked by their teachers. Chapters 3, 4 and 5 consider ways in which teachers can help pupils to voice their opinions on such matters. Teachers, and their colleagues, should also be aware of the fact that their own theoretical inclinations (e.g. behaviourism) will encourage them to seek out causes in a particular way, and thus be prepared to be receptive to other explanations.

REFERENCES

Aarons, M. and Gittens, T. (1991) 'Autism as a context', *Special Children* 50: 14–17.

Ainscow, M. (1993) 'Teacher development and special educational needs', in P. Mittler, R. Brouillette and D. Harris (eds) *Special Needs Education (World Yearbook of Education)*, London: Kogan Page.

Ainscow, M. and Muncey, J. (1981) *Small Steps: a Workshops Guide about Teaching Children with Learning Difficulties*, Coventry: LEA publications.

Bar-Tal, D., Kfir, D., Chen, M. and Somerville, D. E. (1980) 'The relationship between locus of control and academic achievement, anxiety and level of aspiration', *British Journal of Educational Psychology* 31: 482–90.

Batshwa, M. L., Perrett, Y. and Trachtenberg, S. W. (1992) 'Caring and coping: the family of a child with disabilities', in M. L. Batshwa and Y. Perret, *Children with Disabilities: A Medical Primer* (3rd edn), Baltimore, MD: Brookes.

Beirne-Smith, M., Patton, J. and Ittenbach, R. (1994) *Mental Retardation* (4th edn), New York: Merrill.

Bennet, N. (1991) 'The quality of classroom learning experiences for children with special educational needs', in M. Ainscow (ed.) *Effective Schools for All*, London: David Fulton.

Best, A. B. (1992) *Teaching Children with Visual Impairments*, Milton Keynes: Open University Press.

Charlton, T. (1986) 'A special need in the curriculum: Education for life', in T. Charlton, H. Lambley and K. Jones, *Educating Children with Learning and Behaviour Problems: Some Considerations*, Faculty of Education Monograph, no. 1, Cheltenham: College of St Paul and St Mary.

Charlton, T. (1992) 'Giving access to the National Curriculum', in K. Jones and T. Charlton (eds) *Learning Difficulties in Primary Classrooms: Delivering the Whole Curriculum*, London: Routledge.

Charlton, T. and George, J. (1993) 'The development of behaviour problems', in T. Charlton and K. David (eds) *Managing Misbehaviour in Schools* (2nd edn), London: Routledge.

Clarizio, H. F. and McCoy, G. F. (1983) *Behaviour Disorders in Children*, New York: Harper and Row.

Cripps, C. (1983) *The Teaching of Spelling*, NARE insets, Stafford: NARE.

Croll, P. and Moses, D. (1985) *One in Five*, London: Routledge and Kegan Paul.

DES and Welsh Office (1989) *Discipline in Schools*, Report of the Committee of Enquiry chaired by Lord Elton.

Gickling, E. E. and Thompson, V. P. (1985) 'A personal view of curriculum-based assessment', *Exceptional Children* 52(3): 205–18.

Hart, D. (1976) *Violence, Disruption and Vandalism in Schools: A Summary of Research*, London: HMSO.

Haylock, D. W. (1991) *Teaching Mathematics to Low Attainers, 8–12*, London: Paul Chapman.

Hetherington, E. M. and Parke, R. D. (1986) *Exceptional Children* (5th edn), New Jersey: Prentice Hall.

Jones, K. (1992) 'Recognising successes and difficulties in learning', in K. Jones and T. Charlton (eds) *Learning Difficulties in Primary Classrooms: Delivering the Whole Curriculum*, London: Routledge.

Jones, K. (1994) 'Responding to learning difficulties in primary classrooms', *React.* no. 2, Singapore: National Institute of Education.

Jones, K. and Lock, M. (1993) 'Working with parents', in T. Charlton and K. David (eds) *Managing Misbehaviour in Schools* (2nd edn), London: Routledge.

Jones, K. and Quah, M. L. (in press) 'How children learn', in K. David and T. Charlton (eds) *Pastoral Care Matters: In Primary and Middle Schools*, London: Routledge.

Martin, F. C. (1988) *Helping Hearing Impaired Children in Mainstream Classes*, Stafford: NARE publications.

Mortimore, P., Sammons, P., Stoll, L., Lewis, D. and Ecob, R. (1988) *School Matters: The Junior Years*, Shepton Mallett: Open Books.

NSPCC (1974) *Yo Yo Children: A study of 23 Violent Matrimonial Cases*, School of Social Work, London: NSPCC.

Patton, J. R., Payne, J. S. and Beirne-Smith, M. (1986) *Mental Retardation* (2nd edn), Columbus, OH: Charles-Merrill.

Reynolds, D. (1984) 'Creative conflict: the implications of recent educational research for those concerned with children', *Maladjustment and Therapeutic Education* 2 (1): 14–23.

Reynolds, D. (1988) 'Changing comprehensive schools', *Children and Society*, 2 (1): 68–77.

Rowland, S. (1987) 'Ian and the shoe factory', in T. Booth, P. Potts and W. Swann (eds) *Preventing Difficulties in Learning*, Oxford: Blackwell.

Rutter, M. and Madge, N. (1976) *Cycles of Disadvantage*, London: Heinemann.

Shreeve, C. M. (1982) 'A state of perpetual motion', *World Medicine* 17 (15): 417–21

Smith, C. R. (1994) *Learning Disabilities: The Interaction of Learner, Task and Setting* (3rd edn), Boston: Allyn & Bacon.

Stedman, J. (1973) 'Epilepsy: a barrier to learning', *Times Educational Supplement*, 3 March.

Thomas, A. and Chess, S. (1977) *Temperament and Development*, New York: Bruner/Mazel.

Thomas, G. and Feiler, A. (eds) (1988) *Planning for Special Needs: A Whole-School Approach*, Oxford: Basil Blackwell.

Tisdall, G. and Dawson, R. (1994) 'Listening to the children: interviews with children attending a mainstream supporting facility', *Support for Learning* 9 (4): 179–82.

Tyler, S. (1990) 'Subtypes of specific learning difficulties', a review, in P. D. Pumfrey and C. D. Elliott (eds) *Children's Difficulties in Reading, Spelling and Writing*, London: Falmer Press.

UNESCO (1993) *Special Needs in the Classroom*, Paris: UNESCO publications.

Wade, B. and Moore, M. (1993) *Experiencing Special Education*, Buckingham: Open University Press.

Walden, T. A. and Ramey, C. T. (1983) 'Locus of control and academic achievement: results from a pre-school programme', *Journal of Educational Psychology* 75 (3): 347–58.

Wedge, P. and Essen, J. (1982) *Children in Adversity*, London: Pan Books.

Part II

Control and empowerment

Part II discusses notions and practices of control and empowerment within the classroom. It provides a cursory consideration of ways in which teachers can meet better the needs of their pupils by establishing particular forms of partnership with them. Tony Charlton considers basic practices which underpin the development of greater pupil autonomy within classrooms and schools. Fundamental to those processes is the provision of opportunities for children to express their feelings and thoughts about their own education and the chance to feel, from the inside, that they can become more involved. Traditional sources of control in classrooms and schools are examined and examples provided of ways in which some schools have shifted the balance of power to enable their pupils to overcome learning and behaviour problems. Jeff Lewis and Alison Scott-Bauman give advice about ways in which teachers (and associated professionals) can develop their own listening skills in order to provide conditions under which pupils feel able to voice their opinions and participate in decision-making processes in schools.

Chapter 2

Where is control located?

Tony Charlton

TRADITIONAL SOURCES OF CONTROL!

Until recently, matters of control (including decision-making) in classrooms and schools had little to do with anyone other than teachers, who exercised control over a wide range of areas including the curriculum, classroom pedagogy and school policies. (In talking of school-based control, we refer to an individual's opportunities – and, perhaps, responsibilities – to determine, or help implement rules, regulations, practices and expectations for some aspect(s) of behaviour.)

In primary schools, for example, it was once the teacher's almost unchallenged prerogative, as an individual or in consultation with colleagues, to exercise autonomy over curriculum matters; about *what* would be taught, *how* it would be taught, *when* it would be taught and *to whom* it would be taught. While teachers in secondary schools were often subjected to constraints imposed upon them by external examination boards, they still enjoyed considerable freedom to exercise dominion over their classrooms and the wider school. In general, teachers seldom undertook consultations outside the staffroom about a wide range of affairs centred around shaping policies and implementing practices in school.

From a more pedagogical perspective, teachers also appear to practise extensive control in their domination of classroom discourse. Although talk is common in classrooms, teachers seem to monopolise nearly 70 per cent of it. Too often, it seems, teachers are preoccupied with their own talking rather than engaging in active listening with their pupils. Even when children *are* allowed to speak, their contributions tend to be 'in a context highly constrained by the teacher, such as in answers to closed questions' (Kyriacou 1986: 144).

Perhaps, it is unsurprising that teachers invest such scant time in listening, and therefore discourage others from talking. Along lines considered by David (1992), this predicament may prevail because teachers' pre- and in-service training have ill-equipped them to practise, with competence, the fundamental skills of listening. Furthermore, perhaps there is a tendency to underestimate not only the importance of listening, but also the complexity of it, so we forget that:

> Listening – like conversation – does not happen easily in today's frenzied world. Exacting demands linked to many of our work, family and social settings can leave little time for interpersonal exchanges. Perhaps, also, listening is taken for granted; underestimated, undervalued and oversimplified. Yet listening is a highly complicated skill. According to Mehrabian (1972) a communication is conveyed only partly by words; in fact he contends that only 7 per cent of a message is conveyed in this way. The remaining 93 per cent comprises voice tone (38 per cent) and body language (55 per cent).
>
> (Charlton 1996: 50)

It seems, therefore, that teachers have usually made unilateral decisions on a wide range of matters about, and on behalf of, those whom they teach. Regrettably, practices of this kind have too frequently sanctioned little time for considerations of pupils' voices. At worst, pupils have been regarded as passive recipients of the knowledge and skills disseminated by the teacher. Moreover, on such occasions 'there was less listening to children and more regulating of them' (Pollock 1996: 28). The 'system' seemed unwilling – or unable – to heed pupils' opinions, their feelings, their needs and revelations about their experiences. Arguing from a more general perspective, Warren (1993) claims that: 'In modern western societies, young children have little real power. Their lives and activities are governed by older and more powerful human beings' (p. 83). While censuring this paucity of power, she stresses that learning to take control over their lives is an important facet of children's development. Additionally, she reminds educators of their responsibilities to 'consider safe and appropriate ways of transferring power from adults to children' (p. 83). Clearly, these responsibilities are linked to children's rights.

A QUESTION OF RIGHTS

As the above comment has highlighted, in recent times there has been widespread recognition and concern that children's rights have been largely ignored. This neglect has not gone unnoticed among the judiciary and legislators. For example, Lord Justice Butler-Sloss's comment in the report on the Cleveland Inquiry (Butler-Sloss 1988) admitted that the voices of the children were often unheeded. The report – in the aftermath of the child sexual abuse cases in Cleveland – recommended that the views and wishes of the child should be put before whichever court deals with the case. However, it made clear there was no suggestion that those wishes should predominate. Others have similarly drawn attention to oversights and omissions of this type (Newell 1991, Franklin 1989, Gardner 1987), while some have argued cogently for changes so children can be appropriately equipped, and consequently more empowered, to exercise more control over their lives, including their time at school (Davie 1993, Davie and Galloway 1996). These initiatives have been unequivocal in calling for these rights to be heeded not only by parents, the police, social services, the judiciary and carers, but by teachers also. Along these lines Charlton (1996) notes:

> people often worry about the degree to which adults respect youngsters' rights to have their feelings, opinions and views heeded by them. This concern has been heightened by cases involving the police, social services and other child-care personnel, where these rights appear to have been disregarded or dishonoured. It is unsurprising, therefore, that children's rights have now become a focus for attention in education just as they have in social services, health, the judiciary and policing.
>
> (p. 49)

Earlier, Davie – making persuasive arguments on behalf of children's rights – talked about this thinking as 'currently pushing at the frontiers of good practice in education . . .' (1993).

Indeed, the Children Act (1989) had already marked a type of watershed in the sense that it had called for children's voices to be heeded. In a similar manner, the UN Convention on the Rights of the Child (Article 12), which was ratified by the UK in 1991, expressed the right for a child who is capable of forming his or her own views, to express those views freely in all matters affecting him or her. In a manner not dissimilar to the Cleveland Report (Butler-Sloss 1988), Article 12 stressed that the views of the child should be given due weight in accordance with the *age and maturity* of the individual.

Many regretted that the ensuing Education Act (1993) failed to advance children's rights in the same spirit as the Children Act and Article 12. However, when talking about the 1993 Education Act Davie and Galloway (1996) comment: 'The absence of any reference to having regard to children's views in the legislation on which the Code of Practice is based is both illogical and, frankly, baffling' (p. 6). Commenting on this failure, in the Education Bill (as it was at the time), Hodgkin (1993) talks disparagingly about the missed opportunity which she saw as further entrenching into the education system three Victorian principles:

> that children are the chattels of their parents, that children should be seen and not heard, and that education is a one-way process for the teacher to give and the pupil to take, never the other way round.
>
> (p. 9)

Elsewhere, Newell (1993) claimed that pupils were insufficiently consulted when schools engage in decision-making about matters affecting the school community. This thinking had already been voiced by the Elton Committee (DES and Welsh Office 1989) who recommended that:

> in every secondary school, fourth and fifth year pupils should be expected and encouraged to take on more adult and responsible roles. Similarly in primary schools, every opportunity should be given for older children to set good examples to younger ones and to look after new entrants.
>
> (p. 143)

The Report suggested ways in which these responsibilities could become applied. It mentions, for example, school councils and – while cautioning about the danger of 'token' councils – it talks about pupils becoming involved in discussions about matters such as school policies, an issue which Garner takes up in Chapter 13. It comments, also, about the need for a 'commitment by staff to listen to what pupils are saying and to take their views seriously' (p. 144).

Of course, these involvements by pupils are not about either handing over control to pupils or allowing their wishes to predominate; it is about recognition, about participation, about consultation and about fulfilling responsibilities associated with pupils' rights. It is as much about pupils having opportunities for their views to be expressed as it is about pupils becoming involved in decision-making, processes which provide recognition that pupils have rights and that, for good reasons, those rights are being respected, valued, heeded and exercised.

Arguably, these involvements and rights have some affinity with philosophies once embedded in the best of residential special education provisions. Rodway (1993), for example, talks of well-established practices in the Barnes, Hawkspur and Bodenham communities where 'children had the right to have some responsibility for their own community' (p. 379). The benefits of such community involvement are espoused by Cooper (Chapter 12) and Garner (Chapter 13). It is regrettable (though no fault of theirs) that these special education practices have taken some time to percolate even slowly into more widespread opinion, as well as into legislation.

In the context of the Act, Rodway (1993) construes children's rights as being embedded within three broad domains; namely the rights *of care*, *to take part* and *to make decisions*. From a developmental standpoint it would be perverse for anyone to challenge such rights. However, a more radical interpretation of such rights *outside* this context is clearly questionable. Development is gradual, and 'at different stages in the progress from dependent baby to autonomous adult' these rights have differential implications and obligations (Flekkoy 1988: 308). The law, for example, makes such distinctions (though at times, it is not easy to establish the logic underpinning them). As Franklin (1989) points out: 'A child reaches the age of criminal responsibility at ten, is sexually adult at 16, but not politically adult until 18' (p. 57). While Rodway was talking in particular about children's rights in terms of segregated special educational provisions, his three rights have relevance to all schools. No one disputes that pupils have a right *to be cared for*, although this caring provision is more wide-ranging than a preoccupation only with pupils' academic needs. It is concerned with the whole child and her/his emotional, physical and social needs, too. The rights *to take part* and *make decisions* are undeniable, also; assuming we are talking about pupils *increasingly* becoming involved in matters to do with their schooling, as they develop emotionally, socially and cognitively and accumulate experience and skills. However, there is a need for vigilance, for these involvements can be perfunctory, rather than meaningful. Regrettably, the appointment of class monitors, school councils and school prefects has often seemed to epitomise the superficial and, at times, demeaning manner in which some schools have made claims to 'empower' their pupils with responsibilities. Those calling for pupil empowerment in schools are asking for an authentic, effective and mutually profitable participation. Along such lines, White (1986) argued that decision-making within schools should be opened up to students, and ancillary staff and parents as well as staff, while Sheat and Beer (1994) called for a reassessment of pupils' roles in school and for pupils to be more involved in decision-making processes.

BARRIERS TO EMPOWERMENT?

Some schools have shown that pupils can become successfully involved in decision-making processes as well as in a range of other school-based undertakings. These undertakings can range from acting as peer tutors to making decisions about aspects of the school's recreational layout. Teachers have remarked that pupils achieve considerable success in these types of involvements, as long as schools have given them opportunities to become so involved *and* have prepared them with the skills to enable them to make these contributions. Referring to the Code of Practice in particular, Russell (1996) makes a similar point by stressing that: 'Careful attention, guidance and encouragement will be required to help pupils respond relevantly and fully' (pp. 121–2). Part of the school's obligations on these occasions is, as Garner confirms in Chapter 13, to arrange for 'children, like adults, to have the opportunity to learn from mistakes and grow in knowledge and experience as a consequence' (Franklin 1989).

Opposition to moves to attend more to pupils' voices in schools often focuses upon three contentions. First, some are quick to point out that pupils are not skilled to assume such responsibilities. Charlton (1996) is mindful of this dilemma. He talks of some staff who may be quick to point out that pupils are ill-equipped to undertake these type of contributions and suggests that:

Of the many reasons for listening to children it is perhaps initiatives to involve them in decision-making processes which
encounter most resistance. Staffroom die-hards may point out
that children lack the skills and experience to become involved
in this way. This may be the case. It may also be that this
unpreparedness exists because schools have been unable, or
unwilling, to provide opportunities for pupils to acquire the
skills and experience in question.

(p. 63)

Second, some contend that pupils have 'become very much accustomed to having the teacher in control of what they do in school'
(Cowie 1993: 160). The very reason for this state is that teachers,
and society, have done precious little to encourage pupil involvement. Cooper (1993) talks not only of children's rights for
their views to be heeded but also of teachers' (and others') 'moral
obligation to enable pupils to articulate their views as effectively
as possible' (p. 129). Rogers (1983) suggests the teaching of these
skills involves an unlearning process – rather than being a learning one – where pupils are encouraged to unlearn notions that
they are under the control of others. Third, there is an expectation
held by more than a few adults that pupils are too young to participate in such 'adult matters'. If pupils were given an appropriate forum to articulate a response to such comment, they could
retort that they know many adults who are 'too young', too.
Chapters 3 and 4 discuss some of the conditions which need to be
created in order to encourage children to voice their feelings,
interests and concerns.

PRACTISING EMPOWERMENT

Outcomes from school initiatives empowering pupils suggest
many gains can emanate from them. Indeed, David (1992), referring to young children, argues that research has demonstrated:
'that the child's wishes and feelings, aspects of their personal and
social education, must be attended to if one is to engage that child
in any meaningful learning' (p. 205). Where pupils' contributions
are sought, heeded, valued and responded to, pupils' self-image
is likely to be enhanced. When schools help equip pupils with the
competencies which enable them to take on these responsibilities,
their social skills can be extended and refined as well. Schools can

benefit too from these involvements. Much evidence is available showing that where pupils are included in these ways, they can experience enhanced feelings of ownership which can lead to improved behaviour as well as increased learning. While examples of involvement (and associated empowerment) are given more extensive coverage later in this book, it is worth glimpsing at some of them here, to demonstrate the impressive range of responsibilities pupils *can* assume.

Making decisions about the school environment

Cowie (1993) outlines an initiative where a small group of junior school pupils assumed responsibilities for effecting improvements in their school. The pupils met regularly in order to identify problems or concerns around the school. Once problems were identified, potential solutions were discussed within the group, and then presented to the teachers for their consideration.

In Cowie's study the group realised that playtimes tended to be unacceptably boisterous and raucous. They consulted others about devising ways in which they could improve their playground facilities. When improvement plans were completed, pupils recommended to the teachers that the physical design of the playground should be altered (e.g. new layouts, new markings). With the teachers' approval they contacted local businesses for help with their project. During this time, the group presented progress reports both to the teachers and to the school assembly.

Eventually, pupils were able to see their ideas translated into practice. The playground layout was changed in accordance with their ideas. Not content with their achievements, they produced booklets of playground games, complete with step-by-step instructions, and arranged for demonstrations of the games to take place during the break periods.

Involvement in a whole-school policy on bullying

In another study (Sharp *et al.* 1994), secondary school pupils were largely responsible for the successful development of a whole-school policy on bullying. They also participated in the formation and implementation of what the pupils termed a 'bully-line'. The objective behind this initiative was:

to offer a listening service for pupils in the school. The pupils negotiated clear ground rules to achieve their aim of providing a safe forum where pupils could talk freely and explore possible solutions. If necessary, they are eager to act as advocates for the bullied pupil by telling a member of staff what was happening to them, or perhaps by accompanying the bullied pupil while they themselves told a member of staff.

(Cowie 1993: 164)

Listening to pupils' experiences

Extensive consultations with pupils were incorporated into the Keys and Fernandes' (1993) study. Their enquiry involved asking over 2,000 pupils in Years 7 and 9 to comment on their experiences in, and attitudes towards, school.

Many of the pupils' responses were illuminating although, at times, they were disconcerting. For example, only about half of the pupils reported that all, or most, of their teachers praised them when they worked well. More worrying was the finding that nearly half of the pupils said they never, or hardly ever, talked to teachers on their own about their work. Furthermore, a quarter of the older pupils admitted truanting at some time, while a third of Year 9 pupils disclosed they had been bullied in the last year.

Clearly, these conferences with pupils can open up teachers' minds to pupils' admissions and perceptions about their encounters in school. In turn, this knowledge can facilitate an understanding from which teachers and pupils can hopefully derive benefit (see also Chapter 1). At least one of these benefits – in a cyclical manner – can highlight advantages of consulting pupils with a real desire to listen to them, and heed their views and experiences.

Determining classroom rules

Views of pupils are given high priority within the BATPACK training materials (Wheldall and Merrett 1982) where junior school children are required to devise four positive rules for classroom behaviour.

There are at least two reasons why this conferring has success potential. First, pupils are involved in a decision-making process which has direct implications for the regulation of their own behaviour; there is a sense of empowerment and autonomy here which is unlikely to go unnoticed by many pupils. Second, where pupils are meaningfully involved in the exercise then it is probable that subsequent rules are going to be understood, accepted and supported by them. However, while this process can be advantageous, pupils will only be in full control when they are empowered to monitor the application of such rules; a role which, as Jones, Charlton and Whittern (Chapter 14) suggest, is usually reserved for teachers.

Reminding teachers about transfer problems

Adults can become forgetful about (and insensitive to) ways in which particular school-related ordeals generate fears among children. Transferring from primary to secondary school is one event which is a stressful experience for many youngsters (and their parents). For children with special educational needs, particularly those with visual impairments, fears can become heightened. In their enquiry Wade and Moore (1994) showed how children can provide a salutary reminder of these problems; if we listen to them. They consulted over 150 children with a wide range of special needs about their views of changing schools. Responses showed that most expressed fears about being bullied or picked on, and about not coping with academic work or about harsh teachers. Children with visual impairments expressed fears about finding their way around in an unfamiliar environment.

From a more positive perspective, the same pupils suggested ways in which the transfer could be made less anxiety-provoking. Their comments demonstrate a sensibility which may shame some schools. Pupils suggested that before pupils move to a new school, teachers at the new school should:

- tell you what it is like
- have things ready
- show you around
- be aware that you're coming
- let you have a day there
- let you meet the teachers, and
- know what a difficult and painful experience it is.

This last comment is particularly sensitive and mature. It helps illustrate the value of heeding children's views. If we wish to plan better for children's needs, there is much to commend initiatives like this one. The researchers conclude their report by stating that:

> By taking notes of these views, those concerned could help facilitate the change for children with special needs . . . It is our view that the majority of their [*the children's*] responses indicate that they have a right to participate in any decision making concerning choice of school for them.
>
> (Wade and Moore 1994: 27)

Pupils as bereavement counsellors

Justification for this type of involvement is given by Quarmby (1993). Using young secondary school pupils to counsel success-fully peers with bereavement experiences he noted that although 'the skill of active listening is one that is normally considered difficult to acquire ... it seemed to come naturally to these young people' (p. 203).

Pupils as non-directive counsellors

James *et al.* (1992) showed this peer involvement facility has dis-tinct benefits in secondary schools where it is often difficult for teachers to find time to undertake one-to-one counselling.

Twelve senior pupils were recruited to act as peer-counsellors to twelve younger peers experiencing difficulties with their learning. Counsellors were selected because their teachers felt they had natural attributes which would assist them to help others. Attributes included being good listeners and having the ability to make good relationships. Counsellors were then trained in very simple non-directive counselling techniques. The training stressed that not only should they listen attentively, but also that they should show that they were listening by employing appropriate facial and body expressions (e.g. mirroring surprise, excitement, concern, interest). Once again the counselling intervention was successful in improving the counsellees' reading and spelling performances, while the senior pupils empowered with the counselling responsibilities reported that their experiences bol-stered their self-confidence and deepened their skills of empathy.

Further details of this project, including details of the training programme, are discussed in Chapter 6.

Considering pupils' preferences

Talking within the context of what he sees as a consumer-led society, Garner (1992) stresses the wisdom of consulting pupils in order to gain information about their school experiences. In his investigation, he asked pupils to list their preferred learning experiences and teaching styles. This consultation proved particularly useful with pupils considered to be disruptive. As Jones, Bill and Quah suggest in Chapter 8, listening to and, where practicable and desirable, acting upon these preferences increases teachers' (and pupils') opportunities to make the learning process 'a more meaningful and rewarding activity' (Garner 1992).

CONCLUSION

Until recently, teachers exercised considerable control over their pupils. In many ways this control was expected not only by the teaching profession and by parents, but by society and pupils also. Children were expected to learn, and this outcome was likely to be successful where pupils worked in structured and tightly controlled classrooms. By and large, pupils had little expectation of being involved in any real decision-making. Similarly, they were rarely encouraged to participate in discussions where their views were heeded.

More latterly, this climate has been changing. Clear calls have been made for pupils to become more actively involved in their schooling. Examples and exemplars of these involvements are legion. Other chapters in this book will consider, in more detail, ways in which pupils have assumed more control over matters relating to their schooling.

REFERENCES

Butler-Sloss, Rt Hon. Justice E. (1988) *Report of the Inquiry into Child Abuse in Cleveland 1987*, London: HMSO.
Charlton, T. (1996) 'Listening to pupils in classrooms and schools', in R. Davie and D. Galloway (eds) *Listening to Children in Education*, London: David Fulton.
Children Act (1989), London: HMSO.

Cooper, P. (1993) 'Learning from pupils' perspectives', *British Journal of Special Education* 20 (4): 129–33.

Cowie, H. (1993) 'Ways of involving children in decision making', in P. Blatchford and S. Sharp (eds) *Breaktime and the School*, London: Routledge.

David, T. (1992) 'Do we have to do this? The Children Act 1989 and obtaining children's views in early education', *Children and Society* 6 (3): 204–11.

Davie, R. (1993) 'Listen to the child: a time for change', *The Psychologist*, June 1993, 252–7.

Davie, R. and Galloway, D. (1996) *Listening to Children in Education*, London: David Fulton.

Department of Education and Science (1989) *Enquiry into Discipline in Schools* (The Elton Report), London: HMSO.

Flekkoy, M. (1988) 'Child advocacy in Norway', *Children and Society* 2 (4): 307–18.

Franklin, B. (1989) 'Children's rights, developments and prospects', *Children and Society* 3 (1): 50–66.

Gardner, R. (1987) *Who Says? Choice and Control in Care*, London: National Children's Bureau.

Garner, P. (1992) 'Involving "disruptive" students in school discipline structures', *Pastoral Care in Education* 10 (3): 13–19.

Hodgkin, R. (1993) 'Pupils' views and the education bill', *Concern*, Autumn.

James, J., Charlton, T., Leo, E. and Indoe, D. (1992) 'A peer to listen', *Support for Learning* 6 (4): 165–9.

Keys, W. and Fernandes, C. (1993) *What do Students Think about School?*, Slough: NFER.

Kyriacou, C. (1986) *Effective Teaching in Schools*, Oxford: Basil Blackwell Ltd.

Mehrabian, A. (1972) *Silent Messages*, Belmont, CA: Wadsworth.

Newell, P. (1991) *The UN Convention and Children's Rights in the UK*, London: NCB.

Newell, P. (1993) 'Too young to be kept in chains', *Times Educational Supplement*, 1 January 1993, p. 27.

Pollock, L. (1996) 'Teacher–pupil relations in eighteenth- and nineteenth-century Britain', in R. Davie and D. Galloway (eds) *Listening to Children in Education*, London: David Fulton.

Quarmby, D. (1993) 'Peer group counselling with bereaved adolescents', *British Journal of Guidance and Counselling* 21 (2): 196–211.

Rodway, S. (1993) 'Children's rights: children's needs. Is there a conflict?', *Therapeutic Care and Education*, 2 (3): 375–91.

Rogers, C. (1983) *Freedom to Learn for the 80s*, New York: Macmillan.

Russell, P. (1996) 'Listening to children with special educational needs', in R. Davie and D. Galloway (eds) *Listening to Children in Education*, London: David Fulton.

Sharp, S., Sellars, A. and Cowie, H. (1994) 'Time to listen: setting up a peer counselling service to tackle the problem of bullying in school', *Pastoral Care in Education*, 12 (2): 3–6.

Sharp, S. and Smith, P. K. (1991) 'Bullying in school: the DfE Sheffield bullying project', *Early Child Development and Care* 77: 47–55.

Sheat, L. G. and Beer, A. R. (1994) 'Giving pupils an effective voice in the design and use of their school grounds', in P. Blatchford and S. Sharp (eds) *Breaktime and the School*, London: Routledge.

Wade, B. and Moore, M. (1994) 'Good for a change? The views of students with special educational needs on changing school', *Pastoral Care in Education* 12 (2): 23–7.

Warren, K. (1993) 'Empowering children through drama', *Early Childhood Development and Care* 90: 83–97.

Wheldall, K. and Merrett, F. (1982) *Batpack Positive Products*, Birmingham: University of Birmingham.

White, R. (1986) Decision making in a democratic school, *World Studies Journal* 6 (2): 12–15.

Chapter 3

Helping children to find a voice

Jeff Lewis

This chapter is concerned with ways in which adults may help children find a voice. I maintain that the issues I deal with concern all children, indeed all members of society. However, those pupils encountering learning and behaviour difficulties present us with a particular challenge if we genuinely wish to live in a society wherein all members are able and free to make their needs known in a socially wholesome way.

The Children Act (1989) stipulates that young persons should have the opportunity to have their views heard on any matters that concern their lives. This involvement has important implications for education, both in that schools have a responsibility to improve the skill levels in speaking and listening which allow dialogue to take place, and also in that schools make many decisions which affect the lives of the children in their care, decisions that the child is not often party to (see also Jones, Bill and Quah, Chapter 8). This involvement comes into particular focus when we consider the case of children with special needs. It is likely that children experiencing learning and behaviour difficulties will have had more difficulty than many of their peers in learning incidentally the skills of effective communication. This is especially the case when an initial mild difficulty in communication has led to failures in learning that contribute to the cognitive and emotional blockages which characterise many children with special educational needs. Further, it is precisely those with special needs who have exceptional arrangements made on their behalf, through the process of having a statement issued, or by having decisions made about provision and placement which is different in some way to those pertaining to the majority of the school population. Since the implementation of the 1981 Act, there has been an imperative to include wider constituencies meaningfully in these decisions, although there is evidence that progress towards this aim has been patchy (Rogers 1986). If the stipulations of the Children Act are to be realised, much attention will need to be directed towards the project of helping children find an effective voice.

In order for children to become more meaningfully involved in matters that concern them I suggest that three conditions would need to be met:

1 Children must be aware of the situation as it pertains to them.
2 They must have the necessary communication skills to frame a response concerning their needs and wishes.
3 This must happen in a situation in which the audience is genuinely predisposed to listen to them (see also Scott-Bauman, Chapter 4).

It may seem that three different projects could be utilised in order to realise effective responses to these conditions; lessons in the substance of children's rights, a programme of communication skills, and a programme of in-service education aimed at making the professional audience better listeners. While it is true that the programme I will advocate contains elements of all these three, I will claim that they should not be carried out in isolation. Specifically I will claim that the way in which we organise programmes to meet the first two conditions should include strategies that help the third condition to be realised. That is, I see changes in the communication behaviour of both the children and their professional audience to stand in a dialectal relationship, the one facilitated by the other in a bootstrapping way. If it is true, as I believe, that the skill of listening may best be defined as the activity of helping others to speak, then by extension I would see the practice of listening and communication skills to include helping others to speak. This dynamic view of speaking and listening is derived partially from counselling psychology (Egan 1975), partly from group theory (Johnson and Johnson 1975) and partly from the practical applications devised by Pinney (1981).

One consequence of adopting a view based on this thinking is that one is forced into some rather uncomfortable realisations of how things actually are, of how the world seems to work. Another consequence can be an optimism stemming from an insight that we know enough to change things for the better. This means that we first need to explore what it is in our normal way of going about things that causes unintentioned effects to arise (a potentially painful enterprise) and then learning from that exploration what it is that we must do to improve matters. This, paradoxically, reveals itself to be an enterprise that is surprisingly straightforward in terms of knowing what should be done, yet punishingly difficult in terms of applying, in a consistent way, that which is facilitative to the enterprise. This is because many of our convenient assumptions and habits are shown to be less than helpful, and habits, formed in a non-reflective way, are very resistant to change, especially if the effort required cannot seem to guarantee an outcome that is clearly more productive. This resistance, perhaps, stems from the fact that we seem to be willing to go to extraordinary lengths to deny the possibility that we are ultimately responsible for our own actions. We are far more predisposed to accept that what stops things working out well are fate, human nature and social determinants beyond our control.

The realisation that, as professionals, we are committed to helping children find a voice, may challenge many of our assumptions and practices. This view is also shared by Charlton (Chapter 2) and Scott-Bauman (Chapter 4). That is, we must face the very straightforward, but difficult, challenge of exploring the way in which some of the givens upon which our belief systems and behaviour are based must be systematically reviewed and then modified.

The particular habits that we really need to review are the personal and professional habits that conspire to make us such bad listeners and therefore poor models of effective communicative behaviour. Pinney (1981) suggests that our particular society is marked by a failure to listen, and that this failure operates at all levels of society. She suggests that children are perhaps more likely to suffer from the experience of not being listened to than other groups in society, and I would extend this to suggest that pupils with learning and behaviour difficulties may find it harder still to engage another in a listening transaction.

Later, I will indicate the means by which most of us have become habitually poor listeners, but first I wish to demonstrate that this deficiency *is* precisely habitual and context-bound. Given the correct conditions, we can all listen very effectively. Given the space to reflect, we can also learn how to acquire our good listening behaviour, as the following exercise shows.

The exercise consists in pairing people with others whom they do not know intimately. One of the pair is given the task of talking for two minutes on the subject of their family tree. This can normally be done automatically, and most of us have enough data to last us for the duration of the exercise. It is sometimes helpful to cue people by suggesting they may wish to describe the members of their family, or that they can include neighbours or pets or fictitious characters as long as they sustain two minutes of delivering information. The task of the partners is to attend carefully, without interruption, and then repeat back what they have heard. It must be emphasised that this is not a test of memory. In the short term we can retain such information *if* we listen well enough. Given the restraints of not being allowed to interrupt, and needing to listen so we can repeat back what has been heard, people naturally adopt a set of listening behaviours that are identical to those listed in most manuals on listening skills. Having congratulated themselves on their performance on the task, the participants are then invited to reflect on how it was that they listened so well and, further, how their own (mainly non-verbal) behaviour helped their partner to speak easily and comfortably. Almost universally this behaviour includes appropriate eye contact, a posture of involvement, the use of minimal encouragers (nodding, 'mmmm', 'ooh', etc.) and a welcoming and interested look on the face, usually with the head slightly tilted.

In order to underline how important these behaviours are in a listening transaction, the roles are then reversed. This time the listener is not to listen, by minimally reversing the conditions of attention that were displayed earlier. It is not wise to allow this phase to run the full two minutes. Even though it is known to be only an exercise, people soon become exasperated when their partners don't look at them, yawn, look at their watch, listen to another conversation, look miserable and uninterested. All of these activities give the signal that we don't really want to listen. Those who have not already given up trying to be heard after half a minute or so, are ready to admit that they only persevered because it was in the context of a formal exercise. The awakening of the insight that these unhelpful behaviours actually inhibit one's motivation to continue talking provides a powerful explanatory structure for understanding the predicament that faces many of us in all walks of life. It is a predicament which often faces young children trying to find a voice in schools. It particularly affects those who, perhaps, need more help in order for them to express their thinking and feelings into speech or writing.

What we learn from reflecting upon this exercise is that we are all systematically exposed to unhelpful listening behaviour. So rarely do we experience being fully listened to that we count it as one of the great hallmarks of friendship and more intimate relationships that someone is prepared to listen to us. In adult life, the effects of not being listened to can be reflected in the number of altercations in a family situation where one or more parties accuse the other of not listening. It can be gauged also by the number of people coming forward to avail themselves of the services of counsellors whose core skill is simply the ability to listen and to get their clients talking.

In the school situation the experience of not being listened to can have potentially devastating effects on children's ability to learn, on their self-concept, as well as on their view of themselves as people who have a say in their own life. As Jackson (1968) showed us in his classic study, the child entering the school is not only faced with learning the official curriculum of the three 'Rs' but also with learning the hidden curriculum of the three 'rs' of rules, routines and regulations that govern classroom traffic and communication. These rules can inure the child to the probabilities of delay, interruption, being ignored or having one's own agenda ruled out of order so that the life of the classroom can be expedited. The result of this, so Jackson claims, is that the child learns to accept a fourth 'r', resignation. This is similar to the feeling experienced by the participants in the exercise described earlier, where those who are talking became resigned to the fact that they were not going to be listened to, and so stopped trying. If, however, the schoolchild is not a cognisant and voluntary player in the game, and the venting of authentic feelings is seen as inappropriate, or just plain risky, and the experience lasts not just thirty seconds but is repeated day after day, the pupil pragmatically learns to be resigned to the situation. The practical consequence of this effect is that those who do not quickly adopt the mood and behaviours relating to resignation are seen as troublesome and are described as being attention-seeking, hyperactive, having EBD, or seen as coming from deficient families who cannot control them. Children who learn quickly and effectively the utility of resignation, however, soon seem to act as if schooling is an irrelevance to their real lives. On returning home from school and being asked, 'What did you do in school today?' they answer, almost universally, 'Nothing'. Believe me, they are not being evasive or stubbornly opaque, they are behaving perfectly in accordance with the survival strategies learnt through the hidden curriculum and occasioned by the experience of not being listened to. As Alice Miller (1990) reminds us, for the vulnerable and alone child, which we all are in this situation, it is just too painful to live with the reality. It is just easier to get by pretending that this is the normal and natural order, by learning to comply, and ultimately by glorifying the instruments and personages of our oppression. In the long run the child easily slips into the ritualised verbal and non-verbal exchanges that social psychologists see as hidden curricular learning, and which seem peculiar to school life, and which help me to understand why so much of children's so-called imagination is so barren, impersonal, ritualised and conventional. The fact that an entire class can produce such similar, stylised accounts of 'what I did in the holidays', all being of acceptable length, neatness and grammatical accuracy, is not attributable to their lack of ability or imagination, nor to the success or failure of the teacher's stimulus lesson. Rather it is symptomatic of the fact that the child doesn't really believe that anything that issues genuinely from his own experience is likely to be of the slightest interest to the teacher, who, it is assumed, only wants him to be quiet and busy for a while, and then to produce 'correct' work. This point is brought home to me by the story of a child who drew a gravestone, and wrote underneath 'I wish I was dead'. The teacher returned his work to him with only one contribution. The word 'was' was crossed out and replaced with 'were'. Further musings on the subject may be had by reading Wade's (1982) poem 'News' concerning the exciting ideas running through the head of a young boy while he fills in his news book entry for the umpteenth successive week with an untrue, trivial, yet plausible and sufficient one-line account of visiting his grandma.

It may be that reflecting on these dynamics may lead one to despair, to give up on the possibilities of improvement and opt for the more pessimistic line taken by some 'de-schoolers'. This is not what I am advocating, as I believe that we do now know enough about how these dynamics operate to alter our ways of relating with pupils in school so that we can develop more nourishing environments in which people may engage in the enterprise of education. Rogers (1983), summing up a huge corpus of research on affective education, offers us two scenarios of a child's first day at school, one leading to the kind of alienation and resignation discussed above, the other leading to the possibilities of growth and integrity. One of the key points he makes is that the second example is full of messages that the child is seen as personally important. I believe the child received these messages primarily by being listened to and being helped to find a voice so that he can be known to those around him. Pinney (1981) developed, as her original contribution to the development of creative listening techniques, the notion of children's hours. In an hour, the child is provided with an attentive, non-directive adult who reflects back to the child what she sees and hears and, above all, listens in a non-directive way. The Children's Hour Trust claim that young children in regular receipt of an hour develop within themselves an inner quality largely unknown in the West. This may seem to be an extravagant claim, but similar interventions (Lawrence 1973) claim similar advantages. If the claim is only part-justified, then it is a claim that needs to be taken seriously, and considered for translation into classroom pedagogy.

In order to undertake this translation both adults and children will need to experience systematic instruction in listening skills and groupwork experiences (Feest 1992, Thacker et al. 1992). Teachers also need to be helped to overcome the socialised influences which lead them to be such bad listeners, especially that set of influences which defines children as unequal partners in listening transactions. This theme is taken up by Scott-Bauman in Chapter 4 and by Temple (Chapter 5) who discusses the role of listening in non-directive counselling.

The most obvious set of influences which we need to raise to our awareness and then proceed to eliminate from our listening transactions is that derived from the ways in which we have become accustomed to behaving in the social interaction called conversation. Conversation is, of course, socially necessary, and fulfils a whole set of social functions. It is not, however, to be confused with actually listening to one another. In fact, when we import some of our conversational habits into a listening transaction, the effects are inevitably deleterious. In order to make this point in a training session on listening I start with the following poem, the origins of which are unknown to me, except that its author is a Dr Ray Houghton.

PLEASE LISTEN
When I ask you to listen to me and you
Start giving advice, you have not
Done what I asked.
When I ask you to listen to me and you
Begin to tell my why I shouldn't feel
That way, you are trampling on my
Feelings.
When I ask you to listen to me and you
Feel you have to do something to solve
My problem, you have failed me,
Strange as that may seem.
Listen! All I asked was that you
Listen, not talk or do – just hear me,
Advice is cheap; twenty cents will get
You both 'Dear Abby' and Billy Graham
In the same newspaper.
And I can do for myself. I am not
Helpless, maybe discouraged and
Faltering, but not helpless.
When you do something for me that I can
And need to do for myself, you contribute
To my fear and inadequacy.

BUT WHEN YOU
Accept as a simple fact that I do
Feel what I feel, no matter how irra-
tional, then I can quit trying to con-
vince you and get about this business
Of understanding what's behind this irra-
tional feeling.
And when that's clear, the answers are
Obvious and I don't need advice. Ir-
rational feelings make sense when we
Understand what's behind them.
So please listen and just hear me. And,
If you want to talk, wait a minute
For your turn, and I'll listen to you.

This poem puts into sharp focus the unhelpful behaviour we
actually practise when we are supposed to be listening, and the

adverse effects that it may have. In order to allow the group to come to an experiential understanding of these points, the following exercise is useful. The group is arranged into pairs, who alternately speak and listen under four conditions. The speakers are given the following tasks: to tell someone about an interesting experience, to describe to someone an event or a set of instructions that necessitate attention to details, to tell someone of a choice one is having to make, and to tell someone of a situation in which one feels one has a justified grievance against another. The 'listeners' are instructed how to respond to these situations. When encountering the first situation they are told to hi-jack the conversation by talking about a similar situation that they have experienced, so that they end up talking and not listening. In the second, they are told to ask repeated questions aimed at clarifying the complexities of the detail offered. In the third instance they are told to offer a solution, instead of helping their partners to find their own solution, and then to argue the case for their own solution regardless of how many 'yes but's' their partners counter with. In the final situation they are asked to placate their partner, and try to make them drop the issue.

The interesting feature of this exercise is that those who were trying to be heard very rarely guess the instruction that their partner was given. What they notice is that they are frustrated, patronised, interrupted or made to feel stupid, guilty or inadequate. In conversation the usual expectation is that the partners will show involvement by talking about their own experiences, by asking questions (which are really ways of changing the direction of the conversation), by offering solutions that have worked for them and by trying to avoid difficult issues. As the purpose of such conversation is merely to pass time in an agreeable fashion, no harm arises. But if someone really wants to be listened to, not entertained, colluded with, or given ready-made solutions, these habits interfere with our ability to listen or to be heard.

While these habits can interfere with our ability to listen genuinely to anyone, the disparity in power between worldly adults and naïve children, especially those with special needs, makes it all the more likely that these habits will intrude into adult–child interactions. Children wishing to tell their story are more likely to be interrupted by adults wishing to share their own experience by providing a cautionary tale. Children wishing to give their version of an event are more likely to be hindered by adults asking questions aimed at giving them a structure rather than being given space to learn how to structure. Children presenting a dilemma are more likely to be given a ready-made solution and an injunction to follow good advice, and children with a grievance are more likely to have their feelings exposed as irrational rather than being led to see the full implications of the situation by being encouraged to ponder the consequences of any reaction that they might feel is appropriate.

The probability of the above listed intrusions appearing is more likely in the context of schooling. As Charlton and Jones comment in Chapter 6, the teacher cannot possibly listen to thirty or more children all at once, especially when teachers are constrained to deliver an evermore prescriptive curriculum and also attend to the management of classroom traffic. Teachers therefore become skilled at halting, delaying or deferring a child's volitional speech and returning the class to task. While these management practices may be very necessary, at times, if it is the only experience that the child receives, it will soon learn to abandon the project of finding a voice.

What is needed then, is for children and adults to be taught alongside each other about how to listen so that both parties become more aware not only of how to listen, but also of how to be sensitive of the listening needs of each other, as well as the habits that each party is likely to fall into. I have written elsewhere (Lewis 1996) of a session at an international conference where a group of schoolchildren were allowed to run a session in which they taught adult delegates why, and how, they should be listened to. I have experience of an INSET programme, aimed at teachers of disaffected pupils, where children who had been suspended from school were trained to help in a programme aimed at training teachers to listen to them more effectively. I am convinced that the way ahead lies in an honest dialogue encounter between adults and children aimed at improving communication in a dialectical way. This seems better than giving both populations higher skill levels which cannot be utilised because of the inequities in the social situation and concomitant power differentials that often inhibit real listening on the part of the teacher.

The work of Habermas (1990) suggests that ideal speech situations are possible between equal parties, when they are freed from conventional restraints and assumptions. It is clear that adult–child interactions fall short of such felicitous conditions. As Blake (1995) reminds us, there is no reason to expect that all educative transactions should take place in ideal speech situations. I maintain, however, that some of the child's experience needs to take place under such conditions, especially when it is learning to find a voice.

To become better listeners teachers need to enter into meaningful communicative transactions where our socially acquired inhibitors to listening are overcome, and where the situation is meaningful to both parties. While programmes of listening skills are important, the most pressing need is to provide meaningful contexts in which authentic transactions may take place, and where both parties have real power to participate in the communicative act. The child should experience not the feeling of being the subject of an arid exercise, but rather should experience feelings of being involved in a transaction that leads to the growth of its integrity as a person, and allows it to take responsibility for the outcomes of its action. Teachers must also realise that they alone are not responsible for the listening that will encourage children to find a voice. The whole class needs to become a listening culture, all responsible for listening to and empowering each other.

In other chapters of this book can be found discussions of ways in which children may be authentically involved in their education. Many innovations in teaching also make it possible that the learning situation can be more sensitive to the personal needs of children and give them both the ability to communicate and a context in which communication is meaningful. It would take another chapter to detail these, but a flavour may be had from consulting the literature on whole-language approaches (see Newman 1985). Further, approaches such as High/Scope, referred to by Beruetta-Clements *et al.* (1984) have shown the importance of involving children fully, allowing them to have a voice, from a very early age.

I finish by suggesting that a particularly fruitful avenue to explore is finding a wider variety of ways to share the teaching function with children. I have often witnessed lessons given by young children when they have been invited to talk about a hobby or interest. When they don the mantle of 'expert', children often truly find a voice, and also engage their peers in an atmosphere of interest and support. The watching teacher is often humbled by the experience, especially when the child, as is often the case, exhibits mastery of an area and displays abilities that it does not normally manifest in class; abilities which the teacher has worked hard to encourage, but which have been elusive, so that the teacher has mistakenly concluded that the child has special educational needs.

REFERENCES

Beruetta-Clement, J., Schweinhart, L., Barnett, W., Epstein, A. and Weikart, D. (1984) *Changed Lives*, Ypsilanti, MI: High Scope Press.

Blake, N. (1995) 'Ideal speech conditions, modern discourse and education', *Journal of Philosophy of Education* 29 (3): 355–68.

Children Act (1989), London: HMSO.

Egan, G. (1975) *The Skilled Helper*, Pacific Grove: Brooks/Cole.

Feest, G. (1992) *Listening Skills*, Crediton, Devon: Southgate Publishers.

Habermas, J. (1990) *Moral Consciousness and Communicative Action*, Cambridge: Polity Press.

Jackson, P. (1968) *Life in Classrooms*, New York: Holt, Reinhart & Winston.

Johnson, D. W. and Johnson, F. P. (1975) *Joining Together: Groupwork Theory and Group Skills*, Englewood Cliffs, NJ: Prentice Hall.

Johnson, P. W. and Johnson, R. T. (1987) *Learning Together and Alone*, Englewood Cliffs, NJ: Prentice Hall.

Lawrence, D. (1973) *Improved Reading through Counselling*, London: Ward Lock.

Lewis, J. P. (1996) 'Children teaching adults to listen to them', in M. John (ed.) *Children in Charge*, London: Jessica Kingsley Publishers.

Miller, A. (1990) *Thou Shalt Not Be Aware: Society's Betrayal of the Child*, London: Pluto Press.

Newman, J. (ed.) (1985) *Whole Language: Theory in Use*, Portsmouth, NH: Heinemann.

Pinney, R. (1981) *Creative Listening*, London: A to Z Printers and Publishers.

Rogers, C. (1983) *Freedom to Learn for the 80s*, Columbus, OH: Merrill.

Rogers, C. (1985) *Encounter Groups*, Harmondsworth: Penguin.

Rogers, C. (1986) *Caught in the Act*, London: Spastics Society for CSIE.

Thacker, J., Stoate, P. and Feest, G. (1992) *Groupwork Skills*, Crediton, Devon: Southgate Publishers.

Wade, B. (1982) *Special Children: Special Needs*, London: Robert Royce.

Chapter 4

Listen to the child

Alison Scott-Bauman

Legislative changes over the last ten years have had a dramatic effect on the classroom. The introduction of changes such as the National Curriculum, league tables, OFSTED inspections and local management of schools have all tended to increase the pressure on classroom teachers as well as head teachers. For the most part the teaching profession has weathered the storm wrought by these changes. Teachers have shown resilience in their endeavours to maintain and develop their effectiveness in the classroom. This chapter seeks to celebrate the strength of the bond between teacher and learner and the challenge of listening to children so that they can become more effective learners. The intentions of this chapter are rooted in the life of the school: research findings will be discussed in that context and practical advice will be offered for listening to the child at school.

As Lewis points out in Chapter 3, we could all listen more effectively, although we can focus in on each individual voice for only a short time in the school day. In order to develop better listening techniques, a framework is offered here for improving listening skills, which we *should* already possess. Second, we will focus on listening to the child whose behaviour is causing serious concern, using solution-focused brief therapy. A third area for consideration is that of the teacher as researcher, using small-scale case-study techniques for listening to the child on issues of mutual concern.

> The good listening teachers are the ones who are more concerned to know that you are understanding the work or keeping up. They don't talk over you. They really listen and talk to you on their level.
>
> (Katie, 14 years old)

Katie's analysis shares similarities with some of the major features of active listening such as:

* encouraging the expression of feelings by the child
* concentrating on the child and forgetting your own experiences, feelings and opinions
* giving the child time to formulate comments and questions, and time to speak
* conveying understanding (e.g. by smiling, nodding, making eye contact)
* reflecting back to the child what you think you have heard, not only to check for meaning, but also to act as a mirror for the child's thoughts.

Before we consider good listening techniques in more detail, let us consider the reality of the situation; how do we, as teachers, do what we are committed to (i.e. how do we structure the curriculum in an effective, accessible way?).

'Teacher talk' is the most powerful means we have at our disposal for developing shared understanding. As Edwards and Mercer (1987) point out, 'children do not just happen to reinvent the knowledge of centuries'. Teachers and pupils work together to establish a shared construction of reality. This act of sharing, as Charlton points out in Chapter 2, is often teacher-dominated. Flanders (1970) showed that two-thirds of the talk in the average classroom is teacher talk, and that two-thirds of that talk is teacher questioning. Wood (1991) established that teachers who modified their teaching, by adopting a technique of terminating utterances or allowing silences, found out much more about their pupils' experiences. This is a technique which has been well documented by developmental psychologists, of course, in characterising the beneficial support given by many parents to their young children (Schaffer 1989).

In the intervening decades, much has been published about group work and more interactionist approaches such as Active Learning (Baldwin and Wells 1983). Over twenty years after Flanders' material was published, Keys and Fernandes (1994) carried out research on a sample of 2,000 pupils from Year 7 and Year 9. Of these pupils, 40 per cent reported that they had not had an individual conversation with their teacher about their school work in that school year – they were deprived of the opportunity to listen and be listened to about their own work. This is often the reality of much of our teaching.

There are many reasons for talking less and listening more and two of them will be discussed here. One is to give children the opportunity to voice concerns about some aspect of school work which they find difficult or irrelevant. The other is to give pupils the opportunity to express and clear up emotional problems which may be preventing them from learning efficiently. These can then be addressed and resolved with the help of the teacher and other pupils (see, for example, Chapter 8). Of course, these two types of distraction may combine to dishearten and confuse a child, and Carl Rogers developed the concept of 'student-centred' learning, which is based on the belief that both the emotional and cognitive domains of our personalities need to be developed if effective learning is to take place. (Rogers' beliefs have been contextualised by teacher researchers such as Brandes and Ginnis (1986) in their TVEI-funded project on student-centred learning where they give many practical examples of how to listen better in the classroom.) Rogers' humanistic concepts represent a daring challenge to us as teachers just to listen, not teach, and to offer a secure yet challenging environment in which we, and our pupils, can grow and change. In this vein Rogers comments, 'I know I cannot teach anyone anything, I can only provide an environment in which we can learn'. In Chapter 1, Jones and Charlton discuss the important role which pupils can play in the identification of features which enhance or diminish the effectiveness of learning environments.

Given the demands of the National Curriculum, it seems unlikely that we will be able to hand over all the learning decisions to the pupils in that way, yet it is vital to make some time in the hectic school day to take the subjective experiences and perceptions of the learner seriously (Boekaerts 1992, 1993). If we do not listen to the pupils' understandings of, and feelings about, their learning experiences, then there may be a fundamental mismatch between the tasks which we set them and the tasks which the pupils carry out.

Case study 1

Take Sam, a 5-year-old cited by Desforges and Cockburn (1987). He worked very hard at drawing objects to make up sets and then he coloured the objects in the sets. He called his work 'colouring' and he called his maths workbook his 'colouring book'. By listening to him it became clear that the next step might be to give him the language to talk about things that fell into groups or sets and why they did so.

We need to listen carefully to pupils' views about work, if we wish to monitor rigorously our own classroom practice. This will enable us to decide whether the tasks we set really serve to increase the pupils' understanding of that subject, or whether, although fitting well into the classroom routine, the tasks do not actually contribute much to the pupils' educational development (Clayden et al. 1994, Sharpe, Chapter 9). Similarly, we need to consider whether we listen with an open mind to children who appear to lack motivation, and who challenge our very existence as teachers by not doing their work. One way of approaching this is to get children talking about how they work or don't work (see also Jones and Charlton, Chapter 1).

We can learn a lot about how children learn, and whether the material is being presented appropriately, by listening to their views on their own metacognitive processes. As Wood (1991) suggests, we need to consider how children think about thinking. Many children, from junior age upwards, can tell us a lot about their learning habits. Those who cannot, can be helped to do so (Fisher 1990). The focus in this chapter is on how to listen better.

ACTIVE LISTENING

'Active listening' is a term which has developed from the counselling movement (Gordon 1974). Langham and Parker (1988) set these listening skills into the context of counselling in a form that is good for INSET work. There are many different levels of control which are possible when discussing a problem with a child: the chart shows the sequence, top to bottom, of least to most controlling. In its pure form, of course, listening represents the least intrusive and the most 'child centred' of these approaches. As teachers we have to know what we expect of the child, so our work usually needs to include components from further down the chart. In order to help the child achieve realistic goals, we may often end up working somewhere near the middle (for a discussion of the outcomes of different ways of working with pupils, see Jones, Charlton and Whittern, Chapter 14).

Different degrees of support

Child's viewpoint

	Active listening: teacher hopes to help child to be open.
A	*Mirroring*: teacher repeats back to child what the teacher thinks has been said, a) to check meaning, b) to help child to reflect.
C	
O	*Questioning*: teacher asks questions to find out more about the problem.
N	*Joint problem solving*: teacher and pupil use information shared, as above, for seeking a realistic solution.
T	
I	*Deciding what the problem is*: teacher may describe the problem.
N	*Looking at choices*: teacher offers different solutions.
U	*Recommending*: teacher makes one solution more 'right' than the others.
U	
M	*Telling*: teacher tells pupil what to do.
	Teacher solves the problem: by taking action on the pupil's behalf.

Teacher's viewpoint

Listening requires self-control; intellectual, emotional and be-havioural control. We need to set aside many of the techniques which we would normally use for initiating and sustaining a con-versation. As good listeners we will be subordinating certain parts of our personality in order to enable children to focus on topics which are of interest to them. Our body language is an important factor here, and one which we need to be aware of (Argyle 1975). This technique must, at all times, however, be balanced by our awareness of ourselves as professionals with specialist knowledge of our subjects and of the child. We need to work within the context of our role as teachers, not objectively as a counsellor would. Nelson-Jones (1988) provides excellent guid-ance on these aspects of the teacher's role.

Thus, these 'active listening' approaches are being offered as a means of enhancing our expertise as teachers, not as a means of turning us into counsellors. Nor will improved listening skills make it possible for a teacher to develop individual learning programmes for each pupil. It may, nevertheless, be possible to manage a whole class better if we can pay more attention to how individual pupils are perceiving the process of teaching that class.

In Chapter 6, Charlton and Jones discuss the valuable role which pupils can play in listening to their peers. They describe how the setting-up of a bully-line helped worried victims to voice their concerns and get help. Through the establishment of such practices the 'befrienders' should also gain the opportunity to develop their own listening skills.

OBJECTIVES IN LISTENING

1 We want the child to talk freely and openly. This may reveal gaps in knowledge or a state of mind which would not emerge by questioning because our questions may be the wrong ones. Teachers on INSET courses about 'working with children' often state that they fear an intimate disclosure that would enter realms of child protection legislation. This is, in fact, extremely rare and there are clear procedures to follow under the Children Act (1989).

2 We want to hear about matters and problems which are of concern to the child. Even though we are always short of time, a ten-minute session with the 'agenda' set by the child may make it possible for the teacher to see where support is needed and how to provide it.

3 We want the child to gain greater insight into the problem as a result of talking about it. Sometimes no further intervention is necessary – talking it through may be enough.

4 We want the child to give us as much information as possible about the problem, so that we can help with a solution.

5 We want the child to talk towards a solution, with support if necessary.

Carl Rogers believes that most people, including children, know the answer to most of their problems; what we all need is the opportunity to formulate the problem and work towards a solution. Temple gives more advice on this approach in Chapter 5.

Listening techniques

Types	Purpose	Examples
Supporting	1 To show that you are listening and that you are interested 2 To encourage child to continue talking	1 I see 2 Mm-mm 3 That's interesting 4 Please go on
Clarifying	1 To check meaning 2 To encourage clear thinking	1 Do you mean . . .? 2 Is this the problem . . .?
Restatement	1 To check child's viewpoint and show understanding 2 To encourage looking at another part of the problem	1 I understand that you are saying . . . 2 I can see this – have you thought of looking at . . .?
Reflective	1 To show that you understand the child's feelings 2 To help the child to evaluate its feelings, by mirroring them back	1 You feel that . . .? 2 You thought that was unfair
Summarising	1 To bring main themes together 2 To prepare to go on to a new aspect or problem	1 These are the things you have told me 2 I understand your feelings about . . .

In essence, listening techniques are techniques that we may use already in our daily lives. In working with children who have problems it is useful for us to become conscious of how powerful such techniques can be in giving the child a voice at school. It is similar to Rogers' 'unconditional positive regard' (i.e., showing respect for the child and thereby transmitting a sense of self-respect to that child).

These ways of listening can be supplemented by practical discussions about the curriculum or about the desired behavioural goals. Teacher and child will be working at joint problem solving which will have been made more effective by listening to the child's viewpoint first. This can be seen in Gordon's (1974) 'Teacher Effectiveness Training'. Sometimes this viewpoint needs to be reformulated or reframed if we feel that the child has developed a false, counter-productive, or simply inaccurate picture of events.

> To re-frame ... means to change the conceptual and/or emotional setting or viewpoint in relation to which a situation is experienced and to place it in another frame which fits the 'facts' of the same concrete situation equally well or even better, and thereby changes its entire meaning.
>
> (Cooper and Upton 1991: 23)

What can we do if we have listened carefully to the child for days or weeks (or however long it takes for us to become seriously concerned about this particular child) without having had any effect?

Solution-focused brief therapy

At this point you may wish to take more radical action as the child may well seem to have become locked into a personal script for failure: 'I think it is particularly helpful to think of problems as stories that people have agreed to tell themselves.' (George, Iveson and Ratner 1990: 95). Solution-focused brief therapy is based on one simple idea which, however, is difficult to put into practice: listen to the child, find out what it is that the child wants and work with the child towards achieving it. The prerequisite from the child must be a desire to change and the prerequisite from the teacher must be a willingness to look at all sorts of issues with the child. The teacher's goal is to help the child to learn, yet, in order to achieve this, issues may need to be covered that may seem to be wholly unrelated to work. Several meetings will probably be needed and could be as short as ten minutes or as long as an hour. Rhodes (1993) describes the implementation of brief therapy techniques within schools.

Brief therapy was originally developed by Steve De Shazer (1988) and his family therapy colleagues in the USA. The teacher who wishes to work in this way will need support, possibly in the form of training, or setting up a support network within the school. Cooper and Upton (1991) provide a framework for implementing an 'ecosystemic' approach to problem behaviour in a school. It is wholly consistent with brief therapy and would facilitate collaborative work among colleagues. Their framework offers ideas which go beyond the Elton Report (DES and Welsh Office 1989).

At a very early stage a goal needs to be established. It is not sufficient in this particular therapeutic framework to assume that the answer to the problem is always known to the child (Rogers 1993), although the child has the power to resolve the problem, if given help. Rather it is necessary to help the child decide upon a realistic and achievable goal and – even more important – to decide how to get there and predict what it will feel like and look like to be there. The teacher clearly must have views about the directions which the child can take.

Some examples of goal setting:

- What do you want to come out of this meeting that will help you?
- What do you want to happen in the school day that will be better?
- How can I help you to make French lessons better?

One technique in brief therapy, for highlighting change and building on it, is called 'exception finding'. Even children who never do any work must nevertheless experience some occasions during the school week when they do achieve something. Instead of the child (and the teacher?) perceiving these temporary lapses into school work as aberrations, exceptions which prove the rule, these events can be described, analysed and praised as exceptions to the rule and worthy of repetition. Brief therapy does *not* endorse the notion that children stand to gain by the futilities in which they can become entrenched.

To this end, discussion of the problem is minimised and solution-focused talk is emphasised: the teacher must cultivate and express a genuine and dispassionate belief that the child will achieve change and will concentrate on finding solutions. On the other hand, the child, particularly if at secondary level, may feel hopeless and may wish to concentrate on the problem. The teacher should use this tendency as a means of establishing rapport but must not be deflected from pursuing the search for a solution. Moreover, the therapist needs to avoid getting dragged down, as the following shows.

While using brief therapy technique in working with a group of adolescents I found myself entertained by their denunciations of terrible teachers: change seemed impossible in the face of their cutting analyses of caricatured teachers. Only after they had unburdened themselves of their bitterness was it possible to move forward and help them to be constructive. But even then it was a struggle. I had to get them to think about their future exams and hopes for adulthood, as well as specific classroom behaviours, while still listening to the bitterness. My brief therapy framework helped me to stay off my moralising high horse and to see some patterns emerging in the sessions.

(John, head of Year 9)

A sequence of constructive problem-solving techniques will include the following four major areas:

- identifying the goal which is appropriate and achievable
- identifying exceptions to the usual pattern of problems
- measuring the child's progress towards achieving the goal
- giving useful and positive feedback.

Clearly, at this point, teachers may experience considerable difficulties: if the child has been causing problems in terms of classroom management or poor work or both, teachers will naturally experience some mental and emotional exhaustion when dealing with that child . . . but it is worth a try, especially if all else has failed, even if at this point teachers themselves feel like clients in need of a therapist and seek out the educational psychologist in despair!

A major difference therefore between counselling and brief therapy is embodied in the degree to which the teacher is prepared to be directive; unlike counselling (particularly non-directive), brief therapy is based upon the need to be quite dominant in highlighting events which are good for the child. There are a number of ways of doing this:

1 Problem-free talk needs to be used at the start, to give the child a positive focus (e.g. a hobby).
2 Small steps of change can be traced – 'What have you done that is good for you since last time?'
3 Scaling can be used. 'On a scale of 0 (worst) to 10 (best) – a step-ladder image can be used for primary children – where do you

think you are in terms of your schoolwork (behaviour) friend-
ships, etc.?' Most children are surprisingly realistic. If a child
places himself on '4', discussion can focus on what he will need
to do to reach '5' or even '4.5'! Small realistic steps of progress
are powerful agents for change. De Shazer reverses the scale
values – i.e. 10 (worst) to 0 (best) – 'to create a rolling down
rather than a climbing up-hill feeling' (George *et al*. 1990).

4 The miracle question can be used: ' In the night a miracle takes
place; you don't know that it has happened. When you wake
up, what is the first thing that will happen which will tell you
that everything is better again?' This can be upsetting for both
child and teacher if the child describes an event which the
teacher knows to be impossible – e.g. father, who has left
home, is miraculously there again at breakfast. Nevertheless, it
can be used if we remember that children are better able to slip
in and out of unreality than adults are. This example could be
discussed and then replaced with a more realistic hope.

5 Near the end of a session a list of compliments emphasising
strengths and successes (which has been compiled during discussion) can be read out to the child. This may seem artificial,
but it represents a sincere and powerful device for making failing children feel better about themselves, and for emphasising
the good changes which are already taking place.

The sequence of a session would characteristically follow this
pattern:

1 Problem-free talk;
2 Problem definition;
3 Exception finding;
4 Goal setting;
5 Small steps of change;
6 Short breaks for teacher to think;
7 Compliments – which should in fact be used throughout the
session;
8 The intervention: set the child a task which seems appropriate,
realistic and likely to make things better.

Case study 2

Fiona, Year 6, has started running out of school. She says she is
being teased by the others about the fact that she is an adopted

child. Class teacher and head teacher have tried to help her talk about this but she seems to have reacted rather aggressively. The adoptive parents are contacted and agree to keep an eye on the situation. Listening carefully to Fiona's general, unfocused chat leads the teacher to believe that she is worried about secondary transfer and, more specifically, about her reading level. The task set to her is to make particular efforts with her reading using the scaling technique. School systems are used to support her (although her reading level is not low enough to merit such support). Four weeks later, her reading is improving. Four short sessions have sufficed since the teacher changed her focus towards looking for a solution, and reframing it into an achievable target.

The issue about being adopted seems to have become less important. She no longer runs out of school. This pattern of success is consistent of De Shazer's belief that increased confidence at school can be produced by success in one specific area. The class teacher reported that he found 'scaling' and 'exception finding' particularly useful. He found himself using 'active listening' techniques to look for a practical goal.

In conclusion, there are many aspects of solution-focused brief therapy which provide opportunity for useful listening. Brief therapy has some features in common with cognitive therapy techniques (Spence 1994) such as problem-solving skills training (see the Think Aloud programme: Camp and Bash 1981). Future developments in this area may see combinations of such therapeutic inputs.

THE TEACHER AS PRACTITIONER / RESEARCHER

There are many ways of listening to the child. The third method to be considered here, and one for which there is increasingly a demand within the teaching profession, is that of the teacher as practitioner/researcher. This makes it possible to listen to the views of groups. In initial teacher training courses, for example, the Office for Standards in Education and the Teacher Training Agency are looking towards the development of school-based courses which include a significant component of classroom research. This is intended to sharpen the critical faculties of the trainee teacher in reference to the processes and product of the teaching and the learning experience which one can provide. It will inevitably also have implications for the many experienced teachers in training schools, in their capacity as supervisors of the trainee teachers. Initial Teacher Training is not the only area in which this approach is effective. The Open University Diploma and Masters courses have incorporated these techniques for a number of years to cater for the desire which experienced teachers express to become practitioners who are more reflective 'in action' and 'about action' (Schon 1987). This is therefore a rich and complex model of ways of looking at learning which will benefit the whole school and, in the process, will enable us to use different ways of listening to the child (Cohen and Manion 1994). Questionnaires, interviews (unstructured, semi-structured, structured and/or group), classroom and playground observations of children and teachers, all these techniques and more can be used (Bell 1987).

In conclusion, a case study is offered which combines elements of the three approaches looked at in this chapter. Nina, a special educational needs co-ordinator in an inner city secondary school, used a combination of classroom observation, active listening techniques, sociograms, interviews, curriculum analysis and the scaling and goal-setting techniques in order to support a colleague and her class.

Case study 3

Nina. It was science group . . . a difficult Year 8. Thirty pupils, mixed ability and causing problems for the teacher. Lots of detentions, probably more than any other group in the school, for other subjects as well. The teacher got stressed and came to me asking for help. I wanted to support in class, both pupils and teacher. First of all, I wanted to observe. I found the teacher was using some assertive discipline techniques; name on the board for off-task behaviour and detentions. The pupils were getting angry about this. The teacher chose the groups for them to work in. Some in the groups had behaviour difficulties. Off-task a lot of the time. Rebellious.

My second strategy was to contact some of the parents, e.g. twins who had many problems. Some detentions were for both twins. I dealt with each twin as an individual, and it turned out that the parents had wanted them to be in different groups. I wanted the parents' support and told them that I wanted to find ways of getting positive encouragement. This went down well with the parents. I met each twin individually and a couple more children. I listened to their views. I also worked with each twin on spelling, using the brief therapy scaling and goal-setting techniques. They knew what was needed, what was causing detentions . . . one twin said that he should sit away from his brother, not call out, do his work, etc. These were achievable targets because he'd identified them himself. We agreed on positive feedback.

Next I wanted to work on the rest of the class; I tried to turn round their rebellious attitude by getting them to choose two people they thought they could work with. This was done in confidence to reduce animosity. I arranged groups of four, using a sociogram of results, sketching out choices and using two-way arrows. This method showed me who are the popular children and who are the social isolates. It worked very well and the teacher was surprised. She was also surprised that most of the groups were very similar to the groups they had been in before . . . the difference was that they felt they had made the decisions about who to work with and that helped. They had been listened to.

I also gave each group a name and I used a Thesaurus when I ran out of ideas; the names were all superlatives . . . Top, Ace, Excellent, Brilliant . . ., etc. And now the atmosphere has changed to being much more positive. The teacher is smiling again.

There was another area which we looked at. It seemed to me that the teacher was trying to impart much, possibly too much, of her information orally. The kids couldn't concentrate. It seemed that she needed to give information in different ways. Now she uses an OHP to give the aims and objectives of the lesson, plus a checklist to give theory and information and to list the material to be recorded. Also the equipment is now on areas round the sides of the lab, instead of on the pupils' work-benches. At the moment they are doing electro-magnetism, which seems to me to be quite hard, yet they are concentrating well and learning a lot.

In our commitment to improving the effectiveness of pupils as learners, we may need to stand back and listen. Nina was able to listen to a colleague. This chapter has presented ways in which we can improve on good practice: we can listen more effectively to a child and we can help children to become better at problem solving, using techniques such as brief therapy. It is also possible to use methods of classroom-based enquiry as a teacher-researcher. These are often commonsense ways of listening more systematically, as Shirley found out. In her capacity as a reception class teacher she asked her class of five-year-olds (individually) to comment on their mathematics tasks. She was amazed at the vehemence with which they responded, on a rating of 'I hate it, I like it, I love it', and decided to investigate their reasons. She also began to ask herself whether this might have implications for their motivation, and understanding of a task. By listening to the children in this way, Shirley was able to illuminate her own professional practice in an area which interested her.

Clearly there is a tension here between meeting the needs of the individual learner, and providing an appropriate environment for the whole class. Yet the teacher who develops these techniques will experience a twofold benefit. It becomes possible to listen very closely to each individual, from time to time, which benefits each child. It also becomes possible to use the insights gained in this way, for improving the teaching of all.

REFERENCES

Argyle, M. (1975) *Bodily Communication*, London: Methuen.

Baldwin, J. and Wells, H. (1979–81) *Active Tutorial Work: Books 1–5*, Oxford: Blackwell.

Baldwin, J. and Wells, H. (1983) *Active Tutorial Work: Books 16–19*, Oxford: Blackwell.

Bell, J. (1987) *Doing your Research Project: A Guide for First-Time Researchers in Education and Social Science*, Milton Keynes: Open University Press.

Bell, J. *et al.* (eds) (1984) *Conducting Small-Scale Investigations in Education Management*, London: Harper Row/Open University.

Bliss, T. and Tetley, J. (1993) *In Circle Time*, Bristol: Lame Duck Publications, 10 South Terrace, Redland, Bristol.

Boekaerts, M. (1992) 'The adaptable learning process: initiating and maintaining behavioural change', *Applied Psychology: An International Review* 41: 377–97.

Boekaerts, M. (1993) 'Being concerned with well being and with learning', *Educational Psychologist* 28 (2): 149–67.

Brandes, D. and Ginnis, P. (1986) *A Guide to Student-Centred Learning*, London: Basil Blackwell.

Camp, B. and Bash, M. A. S. (1981) *Think Aloud: Increasing Social and Cognitive Skills – a Problem Solving Approach*, Champaign, IL: Research Press.

Children Act (1989), London: HMSO.

Clayden, E., Desforges, C., Mills, C. and Rawson, W. (1994) 'Authentic activity and learning', *British Journal of Educational Studies* 42: 2.

Cohen, L. and Manion, L. (1994) *Research Methods in Education* (4th edn), London: Routledge.

Cook-Gumperz, J. (1977) 'Situated instructions', in J. Erin-Tripp and C. Mitchell-Kernan (eds) *Child Discourse*, New York: Academic Press.

Cooper, P. and Upton, G. (1991) 'Controlling the urge to control: an ecosystemic approach to problem behaviour in schools', *Support for Learning* 6 (1): 22–6.

De Shazer, S. (1988) *Clues: Investigating Solutions in Brief Therapy*, New York: Norton.

DES and Welsh Office (1989) *Discipline in Schools*, Report of the Committee of Enquiry chaired by Lord Elton, London: HMSO.

Desforges, C. and Cockburn, A. (1987) *Understanding the Mathematics Teacher*, London: Falmer Press.

Edwards, N. and Mercer, D. (1987) *Common Knowledge: The Development of Understanding in the Classroom*, London: Methuen.

Fisher, R. (1990) *Teaching Children to Think*, London: Blackwell.

Flanders, N. (1970) *Analyzing Teaching Behaviour*, New York: Addison-Wesley.

George, I., Iveson, C. and Ratner, H. (1990) *Problem to Solution: Brief Therapy with Individuals and Families*, London: BT Press, 17 Avenue Mansions, Finchley Rd, London.

Gordon, T. (1974) *Teacher Effectiveness Training*, New York: Peter Wyden.

Halmos, P. (1965) *The Faith of the Counsellors*, London: Constable.

Hopkins, D. (1993) *A Teacher's Guide to Classroom Research* (2nd edn), Milton Keynes: Open University.

Keys, W. and Fernandes, C. (1994) 'What DO students think about school?', in B. Moon and A. Shelton Mayes (eds) *Teaching and Learning in the Secondary School*, London: Routledge.

Langham, M. and Parker, V. (1988) *Counselling Skills for Teachers*, Lancaster: Framework Press.

Nelson-Jones, R. (1988) *Practical Counselling and Helping Skills*, London: Cassell.

Rhodes, J. (1993) 'The use of solution-focused brief therapy in schools', *Educational Psychology in Practice* 9: 1.

Rogers, J. (1993) *Client-Centred Therapy*, Boston: Houghton Mifflin.

Schaffer, R. (1989) 'Early social development', in M. Woodhead, J. Carr and P. Light (eds) *Becoming a Person*, London: Routledge.

Schon, D. (1987) *Educating the Reflective Practitioner*, San Francisco: Jossey Bass.

Spence, S. H. (1994) 'Cognitive therapy with children and adolescents: from theory to practice', *Journal of Child Psychology and Psychiatry* 35 (7): 1191–228.

Wood, D. (1991) *How Children Think and Learn*, London: Blackwell.

Part III

Working with individual pupils and small groups

Part III looks at particular ways in which teachers can work in partnership with individual pupils and small groups. Susannah Temple discusses the value of non-directive counselling techniques which offer pupils opportunities to explore, and make personal responses to, their own perceptions of the problems and concerns they encounter. Case-study materials help to relate counselling theory to practice. This is followed by Tony Charlton and Kevin Jones' examination of ways in which pupils can help each other to overcome the difficulties they encounter through the use of various peer support strategies. They examine research which shows that pupils can help each other to learn and overcome anxieties through activities such as peer tutoring, non-directive counselling, collaborative group work and the establishment of bully-lines. In Chapter 7, Julian Brown emphasises the value of involving pupils in drawing up and administering behavioural contracts. The quality of different types of contracts are discussed, together with an examination of the benefits of negotiation.

Chapter 5

Non-directive counselling in schools

Susannah Temple

If children are to grow up into adults believing in their own positive capacities, and acting in positive and productive ways in life, they need enough experiences of positive affirming messages throughout childhood about who they are and how to do things.

Many children grow up in families where this is the norm, and they duly learn to cope very well with life's ups and downs. School experience, on the whole, reinforces the positive beliefs already in place. When particular difficulties are encountered by such children, they usually seek out and receive some form of help which they use to good effect.

Some children's family and life experience, however, offers them few positive messages to affirm their unique qualities and talents. As Jones and Charlton explain in Chapter 1, the messages available may indeed be negative and destructive, and make it hard for a child to build a set of beliefs which supports and encourages positive and flexible attitudes and behaviour. These children often expect and invite further negative experiences in school. They may find it hard to be helped, and adults attempting to assist them may find themselves and their efforts rejected.

I think it is important to be specific about defining different ways of helping children in difficulties. Adults normally want to help, the question is, how to do so. There are important factors to take into account:

- developmental issues – the age of the child and its developmental needs
- the context of the difficulty displayed – home, school, community, family, peers

• the roots and extent of the difficulty – how long term is it and what are the manifestations.

Non-directive counselling is a particular form of 'helping'. Essentially it is no more and no less than the nurturing of attention which is so natural and so vital for children's healthy psychological development. The adult is offering availability, time, tuned-in attention, empathy and acceptance of the child as a person. The adult listens. This listening, specially to the child's feelings, has priority over any focus on modification of the child's actual behaviour. (That comes afterwards, as part of the problem-solving stage, which needs to be fuelled by the child's new understanding and confidence.) As Inskipp and Johns (1983) explain, in their training materials for counsellors:

> In this model, (and it is only one of several possible approaches), counselling is defined as a way of relating and responding to another person, so that person is helped to explore his thoughts, feelings and behaviour; to reach clearer self-understanding; and then is helped to find and use his strengths so that he copes more effectively with his life by making appropriate decisions, or by taking relevant action. Essentially then, counselling is a purposeful relationship in which one person helps another to help himself.

Depending on their developmental stage, children may of course need to express their thoughts and feelings in various forms of play. It may or may not be necessary for the younger child to become consciously aware of its process of communication. For example, 7-year-old Nicky used clay-play to overcome his obsessional desire to make things in perfect detail. In school this desire caused problems, as it actually meant he either never started a task, or started it and became violently enraged because he made a mistake of some sort. After several sessions with the clay in which he tried to inveigle me into setting him a task (which would have given him the opportunity to frustrate himself all over again) he finally succumbed to the delights of just playing with the clay, gradually relaxing and enjoying pretend games. He started initiating ideas and instructing *me* what to do. The day he told me not to worry how I did something ('any old way would do'), I knew he had begun to internalise the notion that 'Good enough is quite good enough'. In class his tantrums lessened, and he allowed himself to have a go at tasks without getting in a stew about imperfections. This way he let himself learn more, and began to achieve appropriately.

Non-directive counselling is but one of many ways of helping children. However, its principles of offering empathic understanding, non-judgemental acceptance of the person, and sincerity in the relationship are crucially important. They also enhance any other helping strategy which might be used.

I personally consider empathic understanding, non-judgemental acceptance of the person and sincerity to be more accurately *qualities* of a way of relating, rather than a set of skills. Techniques, or skills, of listening and responding, such as those discussed in Chapters 3 and 4, may be necessary to put these vital qualities to use. However, such skills of themselves, and without the above qualities, are of little use in terms of empowering others, and can even become tools for manipulation.

Pupils need a variety of forms of help at different times. Sometimes they need *information* – 'what are the library opening times?' Sometimes they need *advice* – 'what sort of calculator would it be sensible to buy for this particular maths course?' Sometimes they need *guidance* in planning a course of action (e.g. 'which subjects should I study next for the career I want?').

Other times they need *friendship* or *companionship* for support and having fun, or someone to *lend them a hand* physically. They may want to learn how to do something and need *teaching*. But what they may actually need, more than anything, is a *change of context* for living or learning such as a change of class, a change of group or teacher, or even a change of family to belong to (Inskipp and Johns 1985).

Any of these offerings may be helpful in particular situations. But suppose it's not clear what help is needed. Children cry for help in many ways and the most needy children may give confused, ambivalent or masked cries for help. Behaviour is a language. 'Watch the child', said Froebel, 'he will tell you what to do.' But it's often not as easy as that, especially when the children are creating havoc in lessons, and 'inviting' negative attention from their teachers, which can only reinforce the problems in the long run. When it is difficult to know how to help a particular child, *non-directive counselling* may be the most appropriate strategy initially.

What non-directive counselling can offer in the school context is a time, a place and a person, with clear and secure boundaries, for the creation of a relationship between child and adult, which will enable the child to make sense of its experience, thoughts, feelings, fantasies, wants and wishes, in a way which rekindles its feelings of self-worth and confidence and enables it to work out what to do in the circumstances. The adult cannot know in advance precisely how this will happen, nor what the outcome will be. Non-directive counselling practice rests on the humanistic assumption that when their needs are met, human beings tend to grow and flourish in their own best way (Maslow 1970). Most children, given enough ordinary support, inspiration and encouragement, do just that. Those that don't, are experiencing a degree of inner *confusion*, inner *conflict* or inner *deficit* with respect to their developmental needs which blocks, inhibits, restricts or distorts their natural tendency to grow and flourish (Gilbert and Clarkson 1990).

Take James, in his first year at secondary school. By the end of the first term he was in a state of generalised anxiety which was interfering with his sleep, his digestion, his learning and his relationships, both at home and at school. The doctor said there was 'nothing wrong', but James's state was getting steadily worse. Counselling started in January. He liked lessons and the teachers, but various aspects of the ordinary hurly burly of school seemed to frighten him out of all proportion. If another pupil misbehaved he was in an agony of suspense that the whole class would get 'told off'. If someone pushed him, he imagined it might be the start of being severely victimised. When a test approached, he was in a frenzy about how to get good enough marks. He defined himself as vulnerable and helpless, and felt nervous about what would happen to him.

Many children, like James, have learned a fundamental confusion. They don't know how to distinguish their sense of themselves as a person, from their awareness of their behaviour (this takes many forms – Simon acts the clown and thinks of himself as silly, Mary is unsure about how to do the task, but isn't surprised because she calls herself stupid). In the case of James, he frightened himself, by imagining scary scenarios. That felt 'normal' because he 'knew' he was nervous. He was 'the nervous one' in the family. His parents and sister too said he was nervous. He was not aware of the differences between feeling nervous, frightening himself, and believing that he was a 'nervous person'. To begin with, in counselling sessions, James related all the scary happenings and described how he felt. It was clear that the roots of his difficulties were established very early. The clues for that were in the irrational (magical) thought processes he demonstrated when talking about his scary ideas, together with immature egocentric assumptions (Piaget 1973, Piaget and Inhelder 1969): 'Kevin might think I'd taken his rubber when he lost it, then all the boys might chase me and the teachers would think it was all my fault and I'd get into terrible trouble . . .' James also viewed these external events as actively frightening him and felt powerless to cope. He badly needed someone to take him seriously, and not discount or explain away his experience (thus belittling it). Equally he needed the security of an adult who could understand his internal psychological processes, and how he managed to finish up in such a state, and, not only understand them, but help *him* to understand them.

Simply having someone listen calmly and take note of his story, in an ordinary matter of fact way, helped James a lot. Comfort and reassurance hadn't helped at all, especially accompanied, as they had been, by advice and admonitions from parents who were themselves feeling understandably anxious and irritated.

Non-directive counselling is not so much about believing what children say, as believing in their experience as they communicate it, in order to understand, and then enable the child's understanding. Children say they feel better when they can understand what is going on inside them.

By visibly separating 'James as a person' on the page from his 'behaviour', James came to differentiate between himself and his actions, and to realise, by separating out all the 'jigsaw' pieces, how he was actually frightening himself with his own imaginings. In fact, nothing much untoward ever really happened, there wasn't 'a real problem'. Other people couldn't understand what all the fuss was about. His mother explained it away by saying, 'He's just a terrible worrier'. The other kids teased him, which made it all worse, and thus his health deteriorated.

The counsellor helped James to work out how come he kept finishing up scared. She provided a structure for doing this. First James identified the *facts* – 'I put my book on the wrong pile' – and the *trigger thought* to do with the event or situation – 'That's naughty'. Then he related what he *imagined* would therefore happen ('I imagine the teacher will get upset and cross'). Finally he said how he *felt* – 'Cross with myself, disappointed (that I

James & the counsellor wrote & drew.

What James does   James

Worry about the French test

Imagine getting told off

Wonder what the big kids will do

Think of the most awful thing

S.F Temple

won't have a "perfect week") and very scared, that I might get into terrible trouble'.

The value of non-directive counselling in this case was the security and freedom it offered James, along with structures and ideas, to make sense of his own processes and gradually to take responsibility for his own attitudes, feelings and behaviour. He learned the difference between thinking something through rationally, and therefore creating the possibility of a problem solution, and the confusion of endless imagining of fanciful possibilities. At a certain point he said spontaneously, about the book in the wrong pile incident, 'Actually, the teacher's quite nice really, I suppose I could have just asked to fish out my book and put it in the right pile'! However, this sort of assertiveness which so easily resolves the problem is not possible when a child is paralysing itself with fear – even though the fear is about imaginary happenings. _It is James who needs to know, and understand this, and James who needs to 'discover' the solutions._ This is what empowerment is all about.

In this case, information, advice, doing things for him, even sympathy, had been of no use. Persuasion to forget it, and the adults' alternate sympathy and irritation were harmful for James. He felt less and less able to cope. This is because blame, criticism and finding fault by people who think they 'know better', convey a hidden message saying 'You're not good enough' or 'You're inferior in some way'. These messages are destructive of self-esteem and may produce passivity and anxiety, or on the other hand, rebellion and aggression as a form of defence. Children with problems, the same as anyone else, are more likely to respond positively to acceptance and encouragement, to respect and affection along with clear firm boundaries coming from someone who is clearly 'on their side', rather than in opposition (Illsley Clarke 1978).

After some months of counselling, during which James regained his physical health and his sense of humour, he instigated a special plan for protecting himself from anxiety through the summer holidays with respect to starting in a new Year Group in September. He had already identified the *trigger thought* for 'scaring himself'. 'I won't know what to do or who to ask.' He drew:

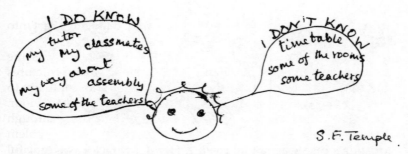

He acknowledged that, ' I might choose to frighten myself by imagining scary teachers', but concluded, 'but I can comfort myself now, I know I don't have to do that. I can organise myself'. James knew he was thinking about himself differently. He was well on the way to grasping that he was in charge of his own experience, and behaving in an assertive and competent way.

Confusion is not always the problem. For Amanda, at 14, her inner turmoil was a matter of *conflict*. She had suffered severe neglect and emotional trauma from her very immature mother. Amanda was extremely bright, but she was underachieving at school, and getting herself increasingly into trouble, because her energies were bound up in the endless psychological fights with her mother, which she found extremely disturbing. It wasn't clear who was in charge of what, or which of the two carried the authority. Amanda described vividly the warring in her head between her impulses (to be naughty and irresponsible) and her irrational punitive attitudes to herself (learned from her mother). She lacked calm, caring attention and someone with whom to think through the issues in a reasonable way.

Amanda learned in counselling to give these parts of herself names. Screeching Parent, Grumbling Child and Clever Adult. She drew these cartoon pictures to illustrate her counselling process. First she was blowing up her Adult balloon with new learning, then her Adult helped the other two balloons to get along together. Finally when she had really grasped the whole process, she saw herself holding all the balloons, and said, 'This is me, being "with it".'

Amanda's case was not all *conflict*. Her *deficit* factor was lack of experience of being consistently cared for, and kept safe. Similarly Carol's upbringing lacked an important element – that of having carefree fun as a little girl. This was an important *deficit* for her. It was as though she'd always been 'grown-up and responsible'. This meant that she got on fine with adults, but found it hard to enjoy the company of her peers, whom she thought of as silly. Soon she was feeling left out and miserable in her new school and desperately wanted some friends. In counselling, she told of the scary times as a little girl, seeing her drunken father threaten and hit her mother, who put up with it for many years. She was mother's best friend and shared much of the family responsibility. She held very pious and prejudiced views and was excessively well behaved which was not very appealing to her peers.

Counselling was a gradual process of settling into being her own age, learning how to have fun and be looked after sometimes. Mother came to counselling sessions every so often, and the two of them sorted out their respective roles. Mother took on more responsibility for family issues, and expanded her own social life, and also provided more opportunities for Carol to play with her own friends, instead of keeping mum company.

At school Carol involved herself with a new project to develop the garden area to make it more attractive and usable for pupils. It appealed to her sense of responsibility, *and* also provided lots of opportunities to co-operate with a group of youngsters working and playing together and having a good time. The finale was a barbecue and disco, and Carol came back saying she'd had a fine old time with her friends. She had even got told off in a minor way, which she thought was a bit of a lark (not a dreaded disaster!). She looked a whole generation younger, just ready on time for her thirteenth birthday and becoming a teenager!

Carol was not fully aware of her counselling process, and didn't need to be. She needed to catch up on missed childhood experience and let go of some of her anxious defences so that she didn't miss out on yet *more* crucial developmental stages. It might be that further counselling would be needed later to deal with residual effects of childhood trauma, or she might well complete her own recovery. As far as Carol was concerned, she had made lots of new friends and settled down well in school.

Counselling is no soft option. It is not cosy chat time. Success requires effort and commitment from both parties in a working relationship of mutual trust. Sometimes this takes a while to build up. Some children have learned *not* to trust grown-ups. Why should they trust the counsellor? What indeed *can* they rely on in the relationship? 'Confidentiality'? Children want to know if you'll tell anyone. I think it's vital to make it clear and explicit that I'm not into 'keeping secrets', that 'confidentiality' means I will do my best not to betray their trust. In other words, they can have confidence that I won't do things behind their backs. I'll say what I will do, and I will do what I say, so that they will be in the know about the whole undertaking, whatever that may entail.

Often we discuss whom to involve, whom they want me to have a word with, and what for. Jeremy, for instance, wanted his teacher to know about the efforts he intended to make to change his behaviour. He didn't think he was up to broaching the subject out of the blue by himself, but he knew he needed support, and trusted me to engage his teacher on his behalf.

I make it clear to children that they can choose what to tell me, and I say at the outset that I'm not sure how I can be of any help (to begin with), which is the truth. I invite them to put me in the picture, so that together we can work out what they want and need, and how I might be useful. This is 'respect for the child' in action.

Just telling troubled children what they should do in a situation does not necessarily have an enabling effect. At best it provides an answer for that occasion, at worst it implies criticism, and adds another level of anxiety, that of having to try to 'get it right' for someone else as well as having to solve the problem. Anyway, because each human situation is always slightly different, what might work in one, won't necessarily work in the next. There is a more serious aspect to the totally directive approach too. To assume that children should solve their problems by doing as they are told is to assume that obedience is preferable to responsibility (Crary 1990).

Such undermining of self-confidence and individual initiative-taking would be the antithesis of working in partnership, the antithesis of empowering children. This issue is taken up in Chapter 14, which discusses the extent to which various forms of adult–child partnership empower, or disempower, pupils.

An important factor about non-directive counselling is that the learning that children do through the process becomes a part of them, and they can generalise and use it in many ways, both for themselves and sometimes for others too. Anna learned how to say to other kids who called her names, 'I'm not going to let that get to me'. She taught this to a new girl in her class, whom she was befriending, and then they both came to consult with the counsellor about other tactics.

This sort of growing confidence and taking of initiative is encouraged by the nature of the non-directive counselling relationship. Self-esteem and self-confidence are the goals. Children develop their self-esteem and self-confidence through being accepted, valued, respected and challenged. This is how the listening counsellor inspires and encourages children to overcome their difficulties.

REFERENCES

Crary, E. (1990) *Pick up Your Socks*, Seattle: Parenting Press Inc.

Gilbert, M. and Clarkson, P. (1990) 'Transactional analysis', in W. Dryden (ed.) *Individual Therapy: A Handbook*, Buckingham: Open University Press.

Illsley Clarke, J. (1978) *Self Esteem: A Family Affair*, London: Harper & Row.

Inskipp, F. and Johns, H. (1983) *Principles of Counselling*, St Leonards: Alexia Publications.

Inskipp, F. and Johns, H. (1985) *A Manual for Trainers*, St Leonards: Alexia Publications.

Maslow, A. (1970) *Motivation and Personality* (2nd edn), London: Harper & Row.

Piaget, J. (1973) *The Child's Conception of the World*, London: Paladin.

Piaget, J. and Inhelder, B. (1969) *The Psychology of the Child*, London: Routledge & Kegan Paul.

Terr, L. (1990) *Too Scared to Cry*, New York: Basic Books.

Chapter 6

Peer support practices in classrooms and schools

Tony Charlton and Kevin Jones

INTRODUCTION

This chapter is concerned with peer support practices in classrooms and the wider school. By 'peer support' we refer to those instances (usually planned and under the supervision or guidance of a teacher) where pupils are directly involved in organising and delivering experiences to help maximise some aspect of their peers' functioning (i.e. their affective, social, physical and cognitive performance). This support, for example, may require pupils to listen to others read, to attend to them while they talk about their personal problems, to 'teach' some aspect of a curriculum area (e.g. chemistry, arithmetical computations), or to provide sympathetic support to someone who is encountering difficulty in adjusting to the demands of school. Whichever practice is employed, it usually includes a type and degree of interaction which is uncommon in classrooms which omit this support.

While peer support is usually offered to pupils of the same age, it can be offered also to younger ones (cross-age support). It can be delivered by high-achieving children to their less successful counterparts, though there are times when children encountering learning difficulties provide invaluable support to others who are encountering similar difficulties. No matter who administers, or is in receipt of this support, the object of the exercise is normally to help pupils overcome difficulties they are experiencing in aspects of their school life.

Finally, the chapter stresses that it is not only the recipients (sometimes referred to as tutees and counsellees) of this support who benefit. Peer providers of this support can also derive gains, as can their schools and their teachers.

CLASSROOMS ARE BUSY PLACES

Classrooms are commonly busy places for pupils as well as teachers. On occasions, thirty youngsters (or more) may vie for one adult's attention and demands upon the teacher's time may become so burgeoning that pupils are left to compete for – and often waste time awaiting – the teacher's attention. In these situations, it is not difficult for pupils' individual needs to be forsaken. Where this happens, pupils may have few – if any – options open to them. Collaboration with their peers about work-related matters is usually impracticable since differential work is often assigned to them (talk of this type is not always sanctioned, anyway). In such climates, Atkin and Goode (1982) caution us that too often 'the emphasis in school is very much on individual work and the adult is almost never a participant in the activity' (p. 9). Furthermore, it is estimated that the meagre adult attention a pupil receives in a month at school is equivalent to only half-an-hour of a parent's time (Atkin and Goode 1982). While the 'appropriateness of the speech that is directed towards the child is more crucial than the sheer amount of it' (Howe 1990: 19) classrooms do not seem always to encourage the amount (or type) of interactional dialogue that helps enrich pupils' all-round development.

If pupils have so few opportunities to interact with their teacher or their peers, what does happen (and who does it) in classrooms? Well, despite the comment made earlier, a lot of talk does take place in classrooms, although as Scott-Bauman points out in Chapter 4, teachers appear to monopolise nearly 70 per cent of it (and much of their talk is instructional). Even when children *are* allowed to speak, their contributions tend to be 'in a context highly constrained by the teacher, such as in answers to closed questions' (Kyriacou 1986: 144). Indeed, some have noted that with the dominance of teacher talk in classrooms, children rarely have chances to make any meaningful contributions, or even:

> ask them [*the teachers*] questions except to request permission. The only context in which children can reverse interactional roles with the same intellectual content, giving directions as well as following them, and asking questions as well as answering them, is with their peers.

> (Cazden 1988: 138)

Critical of these predicaments, Jackson chides that if young pupils wish to be successful they need 'to learn how to be alone in a crowd' (1968: 10).

While particular teaching styles (e.g. whole-class teaching) can encourage and sustain this imbalance, many teachers still manage to foster a more interactive discourse. Sometimes (hopefully), traditional roles become reversed; pupils assume the dynamic role while their teachers listen and learn. By attending to their pupils in this way, teachers can deepen their knowledge and understanding of them, and so become better equipped to help them (Charlton 1996).

There are times (as Cazden suggests) when pupils are helped not only by their teachers, but also – incidentally or otherwise – by their peers. While a variety of names exists for this help, the title 'peer support' is a fairly general and meaningful one.

PEER SUPPORT PRACTICES: PEERS HELPING PUPILS

Peer support – of one type or another – has not been an uncommon practice in our educational history. The Bell-Lancaster monitorial system was widespread in Britain at the turn of the early nineteenth century while the 'Youth Tutoring Youth' programme became popular in the USA in the late 1960s. Clearly, the idea that pupils can be used to benefit other pupils' learning had obvious appeals to both teachers and pupils.

Through peer support, peers can provide a sympathetic ear for fellow pupils to share – and help resolve – their concerns and feelings (e.g. James *et al.* 1991); at other times it can help them to voice their views and opinions about school-related matters (Blatchford and Sharpe 1994), it can aid pupils with disabilities to function more fully in school life (e.g. Forest and Lusthaus 1989) and, more frequently, it can be used to help pupils to improve their academic learning (e.g. Greenwood *et al.* 1989). Interestingly, peer support can effect 'gains' which are equally apparent for those *giving* the help (the tutors) as those *receiving* it (tutees). It has been suggested, also, that occasions arise when the peer tutor's contributions appear more effective than those given by the teacher (Goode and Brophy 1987). This effectiveness seems to stem from youngsters' use of: 'more age-appropriate and meaningful vocabulary and examples; as recent learners of material being taught, they are familiar with the tutee's potential frustrations and problems; and they tend to be more directive than adults' (Thousand and Villa 1988: 166). In more enlightened and adventurous schools and classrooms, all of these peer support facilities are practicable. As Jones and colleagues suggest (Chapter 8), if they are administered appropriately and carefully, peer support practices can offer opportunities for pupils to experience individualised classroom support of a degree – and type – which is not always as readily available as they should, and could be.

Given the impressive documentation of the positive effects emanating from peer support provisions, it is surprising that this type of learning facility is so frequently underrated and underused. Fortunately, there are times when teachers do note the potential value of children helping children. This support has been shown consistently to be of value in terms of producing social, personal and instructional gains, as well as improving cost effectiveness (Gartner and Lipsky 1990, Greenwood *et al.* 1989).

In the context of this chapter, peer support is defined as those planned practices when children are designated with, and are often equipped to assume, a defined responsibility to offer a learning experience to one or more of their peers. In reality it is often the case that they (the tutors) are required to listen to – and sometimes instruct – one, or more, of their peers (the tutees). This chapter now examines some of these practices.

TRAINING PEERS TO COUNSEL PUPILS

In a novel investigation undertaken by James *et al.* (1991), 12-year-old secondary school pupils (N = 12) were provided with a counselling facility by older students (N = 12) in the same school. All of the youngsters were encountering learning difficulties; some were also experiencing difficulties with their social behaviour. The counsellors (aged 16–17) had been selected for this work by their teachers because they were thought to possess the fundamental qualities necessary to undertake basic counselling; personal qualities such as:

• being genuine persons
• being real in their own right
• knowing their own feelings
• being capable of communicating feelings to others

- being able to care for, and accept, the other person in a non-judgemental way
- possessing an empathic understanding of the other's point of view.

As there is evidence that youngsters who are helped to become familiar with the tutoring or counselling aims become better equipped to undertake the task (Barron and Foot 1991), those selected to become peer counsellors received three one-hour training programmes intended to enhance their counselling skills by helping them to become:

- more sympathetic, non-judgemental listeners
- more able to attend with interest to what their pupils have to say
- more able to encourage their pupils to express their feelings and opinions
- more able to show that those feelings and opinions were valued in an uncritical way.

Counselling then took place on a one-to-one basis for an hour a week over a twenty-week period. The sessions were designed, primarily, to offer a sounding board for the 'clients' so they could talk about matters/concerns of their choice. In particular:

> Counsellors were requested not to ask personal questions, but if the pupils wanted to talk about personal problems as they would to a friend, then the counsellors should listen but should treat the information as highly confidential.
>
> (James *et al.* 1991: 167)

Whenever practicable, counsellors were encouraged to try to inculcate within the youngsters, feelings of responsibility for future outcomes (i.e. help them develop a more internal locus of control). When the counsellees commented, for example, that they were poor at reading, attempts were to be made to relate success to effort, and failure to lack of effort. If pupils commented they weren't very good at reading, they could be encouraged to accept responsibility for future progress by counsellor comment such a 'I know, it must be difficult for you, it means that you have to work twice as hard to catch up' (James *et al.* 1991).

The outcomes of these (cross-age) peer counselling practices showed benefits for both counsellors and counsellees. Compared to a comparison group who received only the normal classroom support, the counsellees evidenced greater gains in both reading and spelling over a six-month period. Additional gains were also reported in an unexpected quarter; teachers (many of whom were unaware of the experiment) remarked on improvements in the counselled group in terms of their: 'motivation and effort, hand-writing, oral English, self-confidence, attitudes to study, personal cleanliness and social interaction' (James *et al.* 1991: 168). From a different perspective, positive outcomes were also noted with the counsellors who showed improved confidence in their inter-actions with teachers and admitted that the experience had deep-ened their understanding of – and enhanced their regard for – others.

Interestingly, four of the counsellors (from Year 5) had them-selves experienced learning difficulties throughout their school career. They appeared to have that extra dimension of under-standing (i.e. first-hand experience of the condition they were trying to ameliorate) which seemed to make an important contri-bution to their overall effectiveness as a counsellor.

KIDS TEACHING KIDS

An earlier inquiry (Hill and Tanveer 1981) had already reported similar successful outcomes (though over a shorter period of time). Seventy-six sixth-graders were selected to tutor the same number of second- and third-graders in mathematics. The tutors received three 30-minute training sessions from their teachers before delivering six 30-minute tutoring sessions over a two-week period. At the conclusion of the experiment 88 per cent of the tutees evidenced considerable improvements. The tutees also 'showed greater confidence, more motivation to work and an im-proved attitude to mathematics' (p. 431). Equally important, the tutors were found to have gained in their own self-assurance as well as their willingness to assume responsibility.

Pagett (1994) reported on a similar experiment with junior school children where 8-year-olds all took on dual roles of tutors and tutees during reading lessons. Pupils were paired according to both their own preferences and the teacher's 'professional judgement' (e.g. less and more able readers were often paired). For half an hour each day they read together; they listened to and, where difficulties were encountered, they helped each other.

Pagett claims that collaborative work of this type not only empowered children with additional control over (and enhanced
responsibilities for) their own learning but also helped to make
reading interesting and enjoyable. Evaluations of this kind are
supported by pupils' comments upon the work such as:

> We like it because it's fun
> You can ask your partner questions
> Because it's fun and you both learn what's going on
> I like it because the teacher and I hear readers and they love to
> read.

(Pagett 1994: 34)

In an earlier experiment, peer tutoring was used as part of collaborative teaching in chemistry (Bland and Harris 1989). Pupils
in a chemistry class were ranked in order of ability in chemistry.
More able pupils were paired with less able peers. The teacher
gave a taught lesson which led into collaborative work in pairs.
Bland and Harris (1988) outline a number of successes stemming
from the work. They suggest that peer tutoring of this type
encouraged more on-task work (including discussion) among
pupils, encouraged a non-threatening atmosphere for pupils to
experiment within. More importantly, perhaps, pupils were
given opportunities to assume more responsibility for their learning outcomes. Some of the success of this experiment appeared to
derive from pupils (particularly the low achievers) having three
opportunities to succeed; first through teacher instruction, then
from their more able partner and, third, by working independently on the task.

Similar results were reported in Atherley's (1989) inquiry
where, compared to a comparison group, significant reading
gains were found for a group of senior primary school pupils
engaged in a twelve-week peer tutoring programme. Additionally, along the lines suggested by Winter (1986), social improvements were noted where 'Children who had formerly been
aggressive and argumentative in their behaviour towards their
peers showed remarkable patience and commitment when in
their "teaching" role' (p. 151). Furthermore Atherley suggested
gains for the teacher where s/he was: 'released from the instructional and authoritarian role which she so much disliked . . .
and was able to spend her time more positively and profit-
ably becoming involved with all the children' (p. 151). While

rudimentary training was provided for peers in the studies already discussed, other enquiries have invested more time and structure in this preparation (e.g. Wheldall and Mettem 1985, Bourgault 1991, Greenwood *et al.* 1989, Whitney and Smith 1993). It is now worth while considering some of the sophisticated training administered to those giving the peer support.

TRAINING PEERS TO TEACH PUPILS

Wheldall and Mettem's (1985) research involved eight 16-year-old pupils (all of whom were low achieving) tutoring eight 12-year-old pupils who were experiencing difficulties with their reading. In contrast to many other practices making use of peer support, their study incorporated a refined and structured peer-tutoring training package. During two 30-minute training sessions the 16-year-old tutors were instructed how to use the 'Pause, Prompt and Praise' method of behavioural tutoring (McNaughton *et al.* 1981). Tutors then met with the tutees from this experimental group for twenty-four sessions spread over a period of eight weeks.

A second group (control group 1) received no intervention but was provided with opportunities to read silently, without a tutor. To help control for possible Hawthorne effects, a third group (control group 2) of eight similarly aged youngsters received help from another eight 'untrained' tutors who received only a general talk on reading tuition.

At the conclusion of the treatment period the experimental group was found to have made significantly greater gains in reading (mean gain of six months) than either control group 1 (1.8 months) or control group 2 (2.4 months). Wheldall and Mettem (1985) argue that at least some of the trained tutors' success derived from their employment of praise for tutee self-correction of reading errors. In support of this contention they noted that 'the tutor who used the highest number of praise statements for self-correction had the tutee with the highest rate of self-corrections' (p. 42). Earlier, in noting that the untrained tutors had used praise far less frequently than the trained peers, they reasoned that this paucity may be related to the 'view held by some teachers that appropriate behaviour is to be expected and hence deserves little recognition' (p. 42).

INTEGRATING PEER SUPPORT TRAINING INTO THE CURRICULUM

Bourgault (1991) described a novel form of peer support which is offered by senior pupils to younger pupils when transferring to the secondary school. Interestingly, peer support training has been integrated into the secondary school curriculum. Those interested in undertaking such work have opportunities to elect to study 'peer support training' as a semester-length study option during Year 10 (age 16). The course 'promotes self-concepts and confidence among the students and then trains them in the skills of active listening, assertiveness and leadership – to mention but a few' (p. 26). Prior to their transition to the secondary school, the newcomers were introduced to their 'peer leaders' so that when they moved school they would have a familiar face to turn to for help. After transfer, the Year 8 newcomers met regularly with the peer leaders (now in Year 11) during a weekly 45-minute session. The content for these sessions was based around a structured programme of activities arranged by the co-ordinating teacher, which provided opportunities for a number of concerns to be raised about a number of matters including homework, peer group pressure and sexuality. Throughout the year the co-ordinating teacher maintained regular contact with the peer leaders in order to advise and support them. At these meetings the older students had opportunities to raise any matters of concern to do with their duties and to seek help from the teacher and other peer leaders.

Among the many benefits emanating from the programme, Bourgault (1991) maintains that the greatest observable impact was upon the 'personal growth of the peer leaders during their training and especially during their tutorship of the Year 8 pupils' (p. 27). With his own school's experiences of peer support in mind, he notes three essential ingredients to ensure peer support becomes successfully established within a school. The first is a desire by staff and administrators to establish a peer support programme. Second, a 'special' teacher is required to co-ordinate the programme and, third, a five-year implementation period is required so that young pupils can themselves graduate into the peer leader role.

PEER SUPPORT: LONG-TERM EVALUATION

While there is a consensus that peer support produces short-term academic – and other – gains, few enquiries have studied long-term effects of this type of support. One such study was undertaken by Greenwood *et al.* (1989) who investigated benefits of 'classwide peer tutoring' upon low-SES pupils over a three-year period. Classwide peer tutoring (CWPT) is a highly structured instructional programme based (like the Pause, Prompt and Praise method) upon principles derived from behavioural psychology. It also incorporates a competitive element where the class is divided into two separate teams competing for 'contingent individual tutee point earnings' (p. 372). According to Greenwood *et al.* (1989) it is designed to 'increase the proportion of instructional time that all students engage in academic behaviour and to provide pacing, feedback, immediate error correction, high mastery levels and content coverage' (p. 372). All class members were arranged in tutor–tutee pairs. While the pairing of partners was completed randomly for work in mathematics and spelling, in reading the pairing was undertaken between pupils of roughly similar performance levels. Pupils in each pair alternated between the role of tutor and tutee. Each week, the teachers organised the academic content to be tutored (i.e. in spelling, mathematics and reading) into daily units. At the beginning of each tutoring session, teachers distributed units to the day's tutors, releasing themselves from much of the instructional and authoritarian role which had characterised much of their earlier work in the classrooms. Consequently, teachers were free to monitor and – where necessary – offer additional support to tutors. When fully implemented the CWPT took place for ninety minutes a day.

Greenwood and colleagues' (1989) inquiry involved three groups of young pupils (N = 416) whose academic progress was monitored from first through to fourth grades. Two of the groups (experimental and control) were formed from low-SES pupils; the third group comprised high-SES pupils (a comparison group). While the experimental group received CWPT, a more normal instructional programme was administered to the other two groups. Results from their four-year study were supportive to earlier short-term evaluations of peer-tutoring effects. Compared to a control group, the CWPT group spent less time engaged in time-wasting activities such as raising hands to await teacher assistance, and achieved significantly greater gains in language, reading and mathematics. Equally important, the research revealed that the experimental group – many of whom were educationally at risk at the beginning of the CWPT – 'exceeded or approached the national norm in all three academic domains, whereas the control group remained consistently below this level' (Greenwood *et al*. 1989: 380)

PEER TUTORING AND SOCIAL DEVELOPMENT

In their school-based inquiry, Whitney and Smith (1993) found that bullying had been experienced by some 25 per cent of primary school pupils. Furthermore, among secondary school pupils, around 10 per cent had been bullied at some time during the term when the survey was conducted. Subsequently to these findings a DfE-funded project at the University of Sheffield explored ways in which the problem of bullying in school could best be resolved. One of the ways was to train pupils to offer a peer-counselling facility which those being bullied could turn to in their time of need (Sharp *et al*. 1994).

The counselling service involved recruiting and training peer counsellors, and providing associated teacher support. In the recruitment stage, pupils were invited to apply formally to become a peer counsellor giving written details of their reasons for applying, and listing what qualities they could contribute to such a role. Successful candidates attended a one-day training course at which they were taught rudimentary counselling skills. They 'learnt how to be good listeners – to refrain from interrupting, to paraphrase, to be comfortable with silence and emotion. They were taught about body language and social distancing' (Sharp *et al*. 1994: 4). Those pupils then deemed to be ready to assume responsibilities, as 'bully-line counsellors' to their clients, were provided with further training before they were allocated to teams of three or four pupils and placed under the supervision of a suitably experienced and trained member of staff. The member of staff met with the team during a weekly lunch time gathering when the progress of the peer-counselling service was assessed.

While the project outcomes have yet to be comprehensively evaluated, the researcher noted anecdotal evidence that the bully-line was valued both by staff and pupils. Like their more skilled counterparts in more advanced counselling networks, such as

Alcoholics Anonymous and Bereavement Counselling, the effectiveness of the peer counsellors in this study seemed to have
derived – in part-from their own recent experiences of, and hence
their empathic understanding of, the anxious experiences of their
clients. For the counsellors there were advantages too. Sharp *et al.*
(1994) showed that counsellors can:

> gain self-esteem and are able to contribute positively to the
> school community. They gain skills which will be of benefit to
> them throughout their school lives and learn early the sense of
> achievement which can be gained through helping others.
>
> (p. 6)

Within this project the pupils, in their role as counsellors, assumed not only a primary role of support for their peers, but also
assumed managerial responsibilities for 'fund raising, advertising, role planning and administration' (p. 5).

Another way in which pupils can be helped to help their peers
is through an active involvement in school decision-making matters (see also Cooper, Chapter 12, and Garner, Chapter 13). Cowie
(1994) describes one such involvement where primary school
pupils were involved in attempts to 'make their school a better
place'. They used the Quality Circle (QC) method. While such
methods are derived from industry, in the school context it
requires:

> groups of people – of around five or six pupils – who meet
> regularly to identify problems, evolve solutions and present
> these solutions to 'management' – in this case a panel of adults,
> such as the head teacher, school governors, parents.
>
> (p. 162)

The pupils were trained in QC skills relevant to decision-making,
data collection, developing strategies for solutions to identified
problems and communication.

In their attempts to improve their school environment, the
pupils turned their attention, and newly developed skills, to the
school playground which they identified as an area which was
causing concern both to pupils and teachers. Improvements were
eventually made after they had approached local shops for help,
and provided detailed plans (to the management group and then
to the shop proprietors) of how they thought the playground
should be changed. Another noteworthy product of their work

was the production of a book on playground games so that younger children could be introduced to them. Subsequent evaluations showed that both these initiatives were successful in improving the playground environment for their peers.

CONCLUSION

It seems that teachers often dominate classroom discourse. In doing so, it may be the case that they are less than successful in maximising opportunities for their pupils to benefit from their time in the classroom.

On occasions, this dominance may reflect an over-simplistic notion of teaching – and one that obscures the skills and under-standing required of the 'educator' – which suggests the teacher is a mere disseminator of facts and knowledge. Arguably, a more attractive, and effective, stance is to view the teacher as a learning facilitator; one who utilises every opportunity – and resource – to help orchestrate pupils' learning. The peer support resources out-lined in this chapter offer one opportunity which teachers can use to assist with this orchestration.

They have the potential to produce considerable dividends for both 'teachers' and learners (i.e. tutors and tutees) as well as the 'adult teachers'. It is worth summarising some of these now.

From the tutees' perspective

1 They are likely to have unprecedented opportunities for some-one to attend individually – for reasonably frequent and pro-tracted periods of time – to their work. They can be listened to by peers, they can consult them, they can seek help from them, they may relate to them, and their efforts and accomplishments can be reinforced by them. Collaboration of this type can help facilitate pupils' personal, social, as well as their academic, competencies. Along the lines suggested by Vygotsky (1978), it can be argued that social interaction of this type is essential for the healthy development of learning.

2 It can help boost their self-esteem. There is evidence that peer support helps pupils to show 'greater confidence, more motivation to work and an improved attitude' to academic work (Rogers 1983: 154). These gains help 'inoculate' children from the risk of future failure. Similarly, many of the studies discussed suggest that peer support can be used to reduce

affective concerns. These concerns are the very ones which may precipitate learning difficulties and, as many teachers will know, the advent of learning difficulties can encourage further affective concerns. If peer support can break into this damaging cycle of failure then it more than justifies itself.

3 On occasions, some studies have observed that tutees can be helped in ways which assist their learning to generalise to other situations. James and colleagues (1991), for example, arranged a form of peer support where positive outcomes were not confined only to the targeted behaviours. They commented:

> apart from gains in spelling and reading, even staff who were unaware of the research project remarked on improvements (within the counselled group) in motivation and effort, handwriting, oral English, self-confidence, attitudes to study, personal cleanliness, and social interactions.
>
> (p. 168)

4 Pupils with personal concerns may also gain from just being listened to by a peer. While this benefit may derive from nothing more than the availability of a 'sympathetic ear', the value of this facility should not be underestimated. The pace and complexity of life can make it difficult for adults, as well as children, to find someone who genuinely wants to – and is available to – listen and help. In this sense, peer support is an invaluable – and available – aid to learning.

From the teacher's perspective

1 It frees their time so they can become more watchful over, and more supportive to, individuals' learning tasks and outcomes. This type of role provides greater opportunities for teachers to orchestrate pupils' success. By making their classroom duties more manageable this freedom may also reduce teachers' stress levels.

2 Evidence shows that by harnessing peer support practices the teacher helps to improve pupils' all-round performances. Teaching becomes more individualised and, perhaps, more 'needs-orientated'.

3 Peer support practices can help redress the imbalance between teacher talk and pupil talk which currently seems to be 'weighted in favour of the teacher' (Kyriacou 1986: 145).

From the tutor's perspective

1 Tutors also gain from 'learning by teaching'. Their involvement helps to improve their own academic competence, a long-held belief which has now been established empirically (Goodlad 1979, Thomas, 1994).
2 Peer counselling can raise the counsellor's feelings of worth. It is suggested that as peer support practices become more widespread within a school they can contribute to a healthy ethos. Related to this, there is evidence that tutors can gain in self-assurance and willingness to assume responsibility (Hill and Tanveer 1981).
3 Without access to adequate instruction and good example, it is not difficult for children to grow up to become selfish and uncaring. The notion of helping others, and feeling that their help is valued, becomes a commendable practice. Peer support offers important classroom opportunities to promote the development of healthy prosocial attitudes.

A LAST THOUGHT

Those who have used some of the various peer support practices recognise the considerable gains which emanate from them (for schools, teachers, tutees and tutors). Others – unfortunately – appear less enthusiastic about them. Atherley (1989), for example, regrets that:

> Parents' and teachers' doubts about the acceptability of children 'doing the teachers' job for them', however, and the value of peer tutoring for the tutors who are considered to be 'wasting their time' has prevented the adoption of this valuable pedagogic strategy in all but a few schools in Britain in recent years.
>
> (p. 145)

Given the considerable evidence showing long- and short-term positive outcomes of peer support, it is regrettable that some schools and their teachers refrain from using these opportunities not only to help overcome their pupils' learning and behaviour difficulties, but also to make positive contributions to their school's ethos.

In conclusion, there is evidence showing that peer support

practices seem to produce 'benefits to both students giving and receiving instruction, include learning gains, the development of positive social interaction skills with another student, and heightened self-esteem' (Thousand and Villa 1988: 166). Hopefully this chapter may provide some fundamental directions for those interested in adopting some of the practices outlined.

REFERENCES

Atherley, C. A. (1989) 'Shared reading: an experiment in paired tutoring in the primary classroom', *Educational Studies* 15 (2): 145–54.

Atkin, J. and Goode, J. (1982) 'Learning at home and at school', *Education 3–13* 10 (1): 8–10.

Barron, A. and Foot, H. (1991) 'Peer tutoring and tutor training', *Educational Research* 33: 174–85.

Bennett, N. (1985) 'Interaction and achievement in classroom groups', in N. Bennett and C. Desforges (eds) *Recent Advances in Classroom Research*, British Journal of Educational Psychology Monograph Series no. 2, Edinburgh: Scottish Academic Press.

Bland, M. and Harris, G. (1989) 'Peer tutoring as part of collaborative teaching in chemistry' *Support for Learning* 3(4): 215–18.

Blatchford, P. and Sharpe, S. (1994) *Breaktime and the School*, London: Routledge.

Bourgault, G. (1991) 'Peer support in high schools: a programme to complement pastoral care strategies', *Pastoral Care* 9 (3): 25–7.

Cazden, C. B. (1988) *Classroom Discourse: The Language of Teaching and Learning*, London: Heinemann Educational.

Charlton, T. (1996) 'Listening to children in classrooms', in R. Davie and D. Galloway (eds) *Listening to Children*, London: David Fulton.

Cowie, H. (1994) 'Ways of involving children in decision making', in P. Blatchford and S. Sharp, *Breaktime and the School*, London: Routledge.

Forest, M. and Lusthaus, E. (1989) 'Promoting educational equality for all students: circles and maps', in S. Stainsback, W. Stainsback and M. Forest (eds) *Educating All Students in the Mainstream of Regular Education*, Baltimore, MD: Paul H. Brookes Publishing.

Gartner, A. and Lipsky, D. (1990) 'Students as instructional agents', in S. Stainsback and W. Stainsback (eds) *Support Networks for Inclusive Schooling: Interdependent Integrated Education*, Baltimore, MD: Paul H. Brookes Publishing.

Goode, T. L. and Brophy, J. E. (1987) *Looking into Classrooms* (4th edn), New York: Harper & Row.

Goodlad, S. (1979) *Learning by Teaching: An introduction to Tutoring*, London: Community Service Volunteers.

Greenwood, C. R., Dequadri, J. C. and Vance Hall, R. (1989) 'Longitudinal effects of classwide peer tutoring', *Journal of Educational Psychology* 81: 371–83.

Hardman, F. and Beverton, S. (1993) 'Co-operative group work and the development of metadiscoursal skills', *Support for Learning* 8 (4): 146–50.

Hart, S. (1992) 'Collaborative classrooms', in T. Booth (ed.) *Curricula for Diversity in Education*, London: Routledge.

Hill, J. C. and Tanveer, S. A. (1981) 'Kids teaching kids: it works', *Educational Forum* 45: 425–532.

Howe, M. J. A. (1990) *Encouraging the Development of Exceptional Skills and Talents*, Leicester: British Psychological Society.

Jackson, P. (1968) *Life in Classrooms*, London: Holt-Rinehart.

James, J., Charlton, T., Leo, E. and Indoe, D. (1991) 'A peer to listen', *Support for Learning* 6 (4): 165–9.

Kyriacou (1986) *Effective Teaching in Schools*, Oxford: Basil Blackwell.

Lawrence, D. (1971) 'The effects of counselling upon retarded readers', *Educational Research* 13 (2): 119–24.

McNaughton, S., Glynn, T. and Robinson, V. M. (1981) *Parents as Remedial Reading Tutors: Issues for Home and School*, Wellington: New Zealand Council for Educational Research.

Pagett, L. (1994) 'No fears with peers: a personal reflection on peer group tutoring in the context of reading development', *Reading*, 31–5.

Rogers, C. (1983) *Freedom to Learn for the 80s*, New York: Macmillan.

Sharp, S., Sellars, A. and Cowie, H. (1994) 'Time to listen: setting up a peer-counselling service to help tackle the problem of bullying in schools', *Pastoral Care* 12 (2): 3–6.

Thomas, A. (1994) 'Conversational learning', *Oxford Review of Education* 20 (1): 131–42.

Thousand, J. S. and Villa, R. A. (1988) 'Accommodating for greater student variance', in M. Ainscow (ed.) *Effective Schools for All*, London: David Fulton.

Tizard, B., Blatchford, P., Burke, J., Farquar, C. and P. Lewis, I. (1988) *Young Children at School in the Inner City*, London: Erlbaum.

Vygotsky, L. (1978) *Mind in Society: The Development of Higher Psychological Processes*, Cambridge, MA: Harvard University Press.

Wheldall, K. and Mettem, P. (1985) 'Behavioural peer tutoring; training 16-year-old tutors to employ the "pause, prompt and praise" method with 12-year-old remedial readers', *Educational Psychology* 5 (1): 27–44.

Whitney, I and Smith, P. K. (1993) 'A survey of the nature and extent of bullying in junior/secondary schools', *Educational Research* 35(1): 3–25.

Winter, S. (1986) 'Peers as paired reading tutors', *British Journal of Special Education* 13: 103–6.

Chapter 7

Contracting

Julian M. Brown

INTRODUCTION

The term 'contract' is one that is familiar to most of us yet it does not often inspire positive emotions or enthusiastic applause. To some the term is associated with signing away one's life savings and possibly future earnings to obtain a house or car; to others the dread and uncertainty of putting one's faith in the hands of the legal profession, or perhaps an equally doubtful arrangement with a Mafia hit man. Few would immediately associate the idea of a contract with education, yet in recent years contracting has received positive reviews for use in both life skills training (e.g. Nelson-Jones 1983) and behaviour monitoring and management (e.g. Fletcher and Presland 1990) within primary and secondary education.

THE EDUCATIONAL CONTRACT

In its most simplistic form the educational contract is little different to any other in as much as it represents an agreement between two parties, typically the teacher and pupil. In practice the educational setting is awash with contracts which have not been formally agreed or negotiated. Most teachers have expectations of pupil behaviour in the classroom, and most pupils have an understanding of these expectations and the consequences of adhering to them, or not as the case may be. Such informal contracts take the form of being unstated or verbal. In the case of developing a behavioural contract with an individual or small group, essential additional features become necessary if the outcome is to benefit those involved. Typically such contracts are written and either unsigned, or signed by all parties. Some of the issues that might be covered by such formalised contracts might include desired behaviours, reward schedules and constraints regarding times and frequencies. Nelson-Jones (1983) offers guidelines for such contracting in group-counselling settings. One of the key factors in determining the likely success of any behavioural contract would seem to be negotiation leading to agreement before the contract is implemented. In Chapter 14, Jones, Charlton and Whittern suggest that when pupils are consulted they are more likely to understand, and have more control over, their own behaviour. Without such agreements it is unlikely that a contract will be adhered to successfully (Houseman and Mitchell 1989). Additionally focusing upon positive, rather than negative behaviour would seem to be crucial in determining contract outcomes (Arnold *et al.* 1992, McNamara 1987).

The following two case studies are typical of contracts used in the school setting and serve to illustrate the importance of taking into account the essential features in determining the eventual success or failure of such behavioural contracts.

Sean

Mrs Peace had been experiencing difficulties with a new arrival to her class, Sean. He had moved from another school recently because his father's work was relocated. Previous records seemed only to confirm the conclusions that Mrs Peace had come to, namely he was frequently late for classes, rarely returned homework and, during lessons, failed to complete tasks. None of these difficulties in their own right were serious, although the frequency of them was a source of considerable worry to Mrs Peace. She decided to draw up a contract and have Sean and his parents sign. His parents were willing to co-operate as they had previously had unpleasant dealings with his former school for similar reasons.

Conduct contract

Sean will agree to the following conduct:

1 Arrive at lessons on time
2 Bring homework to school on time
3 Pay attention during class and complete work set.

If Sean fails to follow these conduct regulations, the following will result:

First violation	Loss of break time
Second violation	30-minute detention
Third violation	One-hour detention
Fourth violation	Parent conference

Pupil's signature   .... S. Jones ....

Parent's signature   .... R.T. Jones ....

After a short period the contract appeared to be breaking down, in addition Sean had begun to truant regularly and was reported to have been seen in the company of other truants suspected of abusing solvents.

Very clearly this contract has not only failed to reach its goal of changing Sean's behaviour favourably, but seems to have compounded the concerns with considerably more serious ones. Why? On first inspection the contract Mrs Peace had drawn up seems to be clear and reasonable, yet there are evidently some serious flaws for it to have failed so badly. Let us ask some pertinent questions that may explain the disastrous outcome in this instance.

Are goals identified in the contract objective?

In other words, is it possible to say that Sean is fulfilling his contract or not? The answer would seem to be yes, although in the third goal, '*Pay attention* during class and complete work set', the term 'pay attention' may mean something different to Sean compared with Mrs Peace's understanding of what this means. Even so, it is unlikely that this can be the cause of the contract failing.

Are the identified goals realistic?

Possibly not. Since we know from previous records that this behaviour has been around for some time, it is likely that the goals
are too distant and unachievable for Sean to be able reasonably to
attain them. The consequence of setting such unrealistic goals is
merely to guarantee failure. Additionally, it is not clear whether
or not Sean was actively involved in setting these objectives, I
suspect not. By consulting with a child when identifying goals, it
is more likely that achievable goals can be identified and thus
incorporated into a contract.

What is in the contract for Sean?

Certainly no evidence of praise, rewards or other potential incen-
tives, somewhat the reverse, a list of four potential punishments
would seem to be all he has to look forward to.

Why did Mrs Peace not sign the contract?

Something of an oversight, and one which merely reinforces the
idea that Sean's own destiny was not a concern of his teachers.

Are there any other reasons for the contract failing?

Quite possibly yes, the most likely being peer pressure, a factor
which, although largely beyond our control, can be extremely
powerful in resisting change, especially when we consider that
there does not seem to be much in the contract for Sean as he
might see it.

Shirley

Shirley was a little older than Sean, being a first year pupil at
Springvale Secondary School. The problems that she presented
were not dissimilar, although they occurred in varying degrees
depending on which subject teacher she was with. Records
from Shirley's Primary School gave little help, but did contain
the view that she was substantially underachieving: that is to
say, her attainments fell far short of her ability. Mr Davies, her

first year tutor, had received numerous verbal and written complaints regarding Shirley's behaviour in class and had frequently endorsed detention periods, which, after the first term, had become more frequent. Clearly such action was not changing Shirley's behaviour, and so it was decided that an interview with Shirley and her parents be requested in order to establish a contract. This had been discussed with the various subject teachers, who gave their full support together with recommendations regarding the priority behaviours which they felt needed addressing. These priority behaviours were:

1 Bringing equipment such as books, pens, sports attire to lessons.
2 Remaining in her seat where appropriate.
3 Not to talk when others were doing so, especially not to the class teacher.

Subsequently an interview was arranged with Shirley, both her parents and Mr Davies. The initial phase of the interview was essentially concerned with attempting to establish that the priority behaviours, which had been identified by teachers, were also ones which Shirley accepted as being a problem for herself, and further that she wanted to overcome these problems. This having been established verbally, the idea of what a contract meant and the implications of signing a contract were discussed so that the parents and Shirley had a clear idea of what was involved, the purpose and the processes. Only then could Mr Davies begin to draw up the contract. One that has been drawn up prior to the interview can be construed as having been imposed, the child may feel persecuted and controlled and consequently such a contract is doomed to failure. In drawing up the contract each part was clearly explained to both parents and Shirley. Each part of the contract had to be fully understood and agreed upon by Shirley and her parents. Upon the conclusion of the interview everybody left with a feeling of relief that perhaps a solution to a lot of unhappiness may, at last, have been found. This is the contract that was finally agreed upon:

Behaviour contract

Shirley agrees to:

1 Bring the equipment to each lesson according to the subject teacher's request.
2 To remain in her seat during lessons.
3 To remain quiet when the teacher is giving instructions.

The school agrees to:

1 Sign Shirley's contract report at the end of each lesson.
2 Write positive comments about Shirley's behaviour and work when appropriate.
3 Communicate with home at the end of each week giving a detailed report of breaches of contract and *all* of the positive comments received from individual teachers.
4 To review the contract after 5 weeks, or earlier, at the request of Shirley's parents, or Shirley herself.

The parents agree to:

1 Add an extra 25p pocket money for each day that the contract has been successful.

Signed   *S. Godsell* .... Pupil
         A.R. Godsell .... Parents
         M. Davies .... Springvale School

Date   *24/6/96*

It is most important to note that, because a number of people were being represented in the above contract, all involved were asked if they felt the contract was acceptable; this being the case the contract was initiated. A progress chart was retained by Shirley and given at the conclusion of each lesson to the respective subject teacher, and at the end of each day sent home. A weekly report was sent by Mr Davies to Shirley's parents.

A sample progress report for week 1 is shown below. This was attached to a copy of the contract in order to ensure teachers and Shirley remained clear about what had been agreed.

Day	Lesson	Contract kept	Teacher comment	Parent comment
Monday				
Tuesday				
Wednesday				
Thursday				
Friday				

At the end of the five-week period Shirley had achieved 100 per cent success for the final two weeks, and both parents and teachers had noted significant improvement in other areas – she seemed more relaxed, happier and her work had improved. Subsequently the contract was modified to include weekly instead of daily progress reporting. At the end of a further five-week period, the contract was discarded as all parties, including Shirley, felt it was no longer needed. She continued to receive the additional pocket money.

In contrast to the first case study, the above demonstrates a desirable and successful outcome. What are the features in Shirley's case that enabled such a positive outcome? Let us ask the same questions that were asked about Sean's contract.

Are goals identified in the contract objective?

The answer in this instance is yes, all of the goals are discrete, that is, it is possible to observe whether they happen, or not; either Shirley *is* or *is not* in her seat, for example. Additionally, it is important to note that the three items Shirley has agreed to are positive behaviours which are to replace the negative behaviours. Rather than merely stating what Shirley should not do, it tells her what she should be doing instead. This focus on positive behaviour is one which has been reported to be a crucial factor in determining whether or not a contract is likely to succeed or fail (Santa-Rita 1993). However, Harrop and McCann (1983) draw attention to the idea that in replacing negative behaviours with positive ones, an improvement in academic performance does not always follow. As an alternative they suggest that the contract might be directed at improving academic performance, say in test results or grades at end of term, and that good behaviour will result. Such a contract, however, is likely to require considerably more administration and may be problematic for that reason alone.

Are the identified goals realistic?

It is not truly possible to answer this question until the contract has proven effective or not. However, by involving Shirley in drawing up the contract, the likelihood of success should be significantly increased.

What is in the contract for Shirley?

Precisely £1.25 a week, and time to go out and spend it! Furthermore, it has been noted at the conclusion of the contract period that she is happier and more relaxed. While it is necessary to specify more tangible rewards initially in a written contract, it may be possible to talk about the less obvious intrinsic satisfactions during the contract negotiation phase.

Are there any other reasons for the contract's succeeding?

Almost certainly, and by debriefing the respective parties at the conclusion of the contract these reasons may become clear. It is important to focus on the contract as the medium of change, rather than dwelling upon factors beyond our control.

CONTRACTS AND BEHAVIOUR TYPES

It is undoubtedly true to say that there is no specific approach to changing behaviour that can successfully traverse the spectrum of age, ability, educational setting and behaviour or learning type. Contracting has been successfully applied to both behaviour and learning difficulties in primary schools (Smith 1994) and secondary schools (Houseman and Mitchell 1989). I do not, however, wish to give the impression that contracting is a solution to all types of learning or behaviour problems, this is not so. Without specifying particular behaviour types, or resorting to complex and usually unhelpful behavioural descriptors, the following model may be of help in determining whether or not contracting is a suitable intervention strategy.

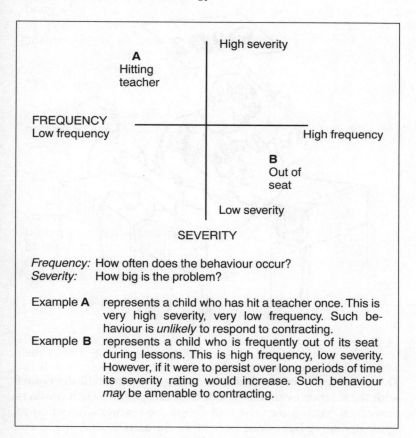

Frequency: How often does the behaviour occur?
Severity: How big is the problem?

Example **A**   represents a child who has hit a teacher once. This is very high severity, very low frequency. Such behaviour is *unlikely* to respond to contracting.

Example **B**   represents a child who is frequently out of its seat during lessons. This is high frequency, low severity. However, if it were to persist over long periods of time its severity rating would increase. Such behaviour *may* be amenable to contracting.

As a general guide, behaviours which are low to medium in severity and medium to high in frequency are those which respond best to contracting as an intervention strategy. The following examples, which most teachers will be familiar with, if not frustrated by, are given to illustrate the point.

The terrorist

This child revels in the drama of seeing another child in conflict with the teacher, even if s/he does not escape from such conflicts unscathed. Such a terrorist will defeat the teacher's intention to ignore irritating behaviour from other children by drawing attention to it.

Such behaviour is not uncommon and usually represents a child who is seeking attention. As the frequency is high and severity low/medium, contracting may well be helpful. Such a contract could provide rewards which give the child attention through class responsibility, time on a desired activity with the teachers' or friends' assistance, as well as time with parents (e.g. a special weekend trip). It is important to remember that there is no generalised formula which will always work, but it is always essential to negotiate the contract with those involved in it.

The underachiever

The underachieving child is one who is unable to attempt or complete work and as such is likely to engage in alternative behaviours which will undoubtedly be those the teacher least wants in the classroom.

Children underachieve for a number of reasons. It will be important to try and answer the question 'why is this child underachieving?' before deciding on contract intervention. If the reasons are complex, such as abuse, then contracting may be harmful, but if the reasons are attention-seeking, then go ahead and try contracting. It is important in setting objectives in such an instance to ensure that target goals can be easily achieved in the early stages of the contract so as to ensure success and break the pattern of underachievement.

The tormentor

This child is perpetually bullied and teased, or so it believes. Such children see themselves as innocent, although they are the tormentor, to whom others respond negatively.

Such children do not know how to gain social approval from their peers by appropriate means. Possible contracts should include, in the objectives section, the need for pupils to judge their own actions. One possible reward may be to set a relatively straightforward assignment over a few lessons with the ultimate reward being that their work would be displayed, and thus the child might gain approval for appropriate behaviour.

The class clown

In most classes there can be identified the class wit or clown who seeks to try the teacher's patience beyond reasonable bounds. He or she is not a terrorist, but is unsure of how to gain attention by appropriate means, is the ultimate attention-seeker, and probably the most responsive to contract intervention. During the contract period, which should emphasise and reward achievable behaviours, it is also important to ignore, as far as one can, the undesirable behaviours.

All of these characteristic behaviour problems are common, high in frequency, of relatively low severity and, moreover, have been shown to respond to contracting. Those interested in a more detailed description of behaviour characteristics and contract types may refer to the work of Smith (1994).

DEVELOPING YOUR OWN CONTRACT

As with other approaches to behavioural intervention, contracting, if it is to be successful, needs to follow a sequence of development and implementation. The following is merely a guide, which includes the essential features needed in any context, although it is likely that modification may be required.

Stage 1 *Identifying the problem, and describing it in observable and objective ways*
As in other intervention programmes it is important at the outset that both teacher and pupil are clear about what behaviour is causing concern and what alternative, desirable behaviours should take its place; it is not possible to replace negative behaviours within a vacuum. It is not necessary to use formal tests at this or any other stage, although accurate observation can help in clarifying the type, frequency and severity of the problem.

Stage 2 *Seeking co-operation and agreement for the need to develop a contract*
It is essential to obtain not only consent, but agreement actively to take a role in a contract from, at the very least, the teacher/s and child, and preferably the parent/s or guardian. It is possible to include other parties (e.g. social workers, psychologist), although this may complicate matters, especially concerning communication. Of particular importance at this stage is getting the child to agree to take a responsible role in a contract.

Stage 3 *Drawing up a contract*
The actual content of a particular contract will vary considerably from child to child. There is no standard format, but all contracts should:

- specify realistic, objective and understandable goals with the child
- focus on positive rather than negative behaviour
- specify what *all* parties involved will do in precise terms
- be negotiated with all parties present, and signed by all parties
- have a positive outcome for the child written into the contract

- provide all parties with a copy of the contract
- specify how the contract will be monitored
- have the full understanding and agreement of the child.

Stage 4 *Monitoring the contract*

The contract needs to be monitored in order that all parties can see and respond to changes in the child's behaviour. If progress is not evident then perhaps the contract needs to be revised or an alternative approach used. In Chapter 11, Hanson describes how pupils in one school learn to manage their own behaviour through self-monitoring.

Stage 5 *Concluding the contract*

Once the child has met all of the goals stated, the contract can be withdrawn, modified or replaced with an alternative less formalised reward strategy to ensure progress does not stop or, worse, negative behaviours return.

Stage 6 If all the above work, don't forget to reward yourself! If not, keep trying!

CONCLUSION

It has already been said that contracts are used widely across a range of human activities including varied educational settings. Often their use is highly successful, but, as has been mentioned, this is not always the case. McNamara (1987) found, in a comparative study evaluating the effectiveness of such intervention amongst secondary pupils, an improvement in 61.9 per cent of cases, with no change in 33.4 per cent of cases and a deterioration in 4.7 per cent of cases. Other studies have found similar ranges of success. While these figures suggest that we must proceed with caution, it is reassuring to note that Fletcher and Presland (1990) indicate that objectives-based approaches to changing behaviour, including learning behaviour, are the only ones which have been consistently successful.

While there is ample evidence of contracting having been successfully applied in both primary and secondary settings, Fletcher and Presland (1990) suggest that it is most effective in the primary school. They postulate that this may arise from the fact that primary children usually spend most of their time with one teacher, but also note that the most effective behavioural procedure in use in the secondary setting is the contract, as this can travel between a number of teachers. Santa-Rita (1993) provides evidence of contracts being successfully applied to social problems. Houseman and Mitchell (1989) demonstrate its effectiveness in reducing truancy levels.

While this approach may have limitations in some settings, there is clearly a need for more research into this effective and valuable aid to education. In a nutshell, there are three key benefits to contracting in education:

1 happier children;
2 children who learn more effectively;
3 happier and less stressed teachers.

REFERENCES

Arnold, C. B. *et al.* (1992) 'Positive classroom management', *The Mathematics Teacher* 85 (9): 720–1.

Fletcher, P. and Presland, J. (1990) 'Contracting to overcome adjustment problems', *Support for Learning* 5 (3): 153–8.

Harrop, A. and McCann, C. (1983) 'Behaviour modification and reading attainment in the comprehensive school', *Educational Research* 25 (3): 191–5.

Houseman, J. and Mitchell, M. (1989) 'Our two-pronged plan means keeping fewer kids after school', *Executive-Educator* 11 (5): 30–1.

Jones, K. and Charlton, T. (eds) (1992) *Learning Difficulties in Primary Classrooms: Delivering the Whole Curriculum*, London, UK: Routledge.

McNamara, E. (1987) 'Behavioural contracting with secondary aged pupils', *Educational Psychology in Practice* 2 (4): 21–6.

Nelson-Jones, R. (1983) *Practical Counselling Skills*, London: Holt, Rinehart & Wilson.

Santa-Rita, E. (1993) *Classroom Management for Student Retention*, Bronx Community College, NY: Department of Student Development (ERIC Accession Number ED 360021).

Smith, S. E. (1994) 'Parent-initiated contracts: an intervention for school-related behaviours', *Elementary School Guidance and Counselling* 28 (3): 182–7.

Part IV

Classroom-based support

Part IV shifts attention towards partnership at classroom level. Kevin Jones, Graham Bill and Mayling Quah examine ways in which teachers, pupils, parents and other professionals may work together to support learning within the classroom. They discuss responses which can be made to the range of factors which cause pupils to experience learning and/or behaviour difficulties, thus building upon Chapter 1. It is recommended that some of the most potent forms of 'support' are achieved when teachers help pupils to 'help themselves' and their peers. In Chapter 9, Pamela Sharpe suggests that 'personal problem solving' helps young children assume greater control for their own learning. She questions the value of adult-imposed programmed approaches and refers to research which shows that children's thinking develops in individualistic ways which should be respected by their teachers. Finally, Ian Leech describes how information technology has helped one pupil to communicate his educational and life needs to his parents and teachers. Through an individual case study he provides a convincing argument that modern technology can enhance the quality of learning relationships.

Chapter 8

Supporting learning within the classroom

Kevin Jones, Graham Bill and Mayling Quah

'Support' for pupils who experience difficulties in learning can be provided in many different ways. Pupils are placed in special units or a special school, withdrawn from their classrooms for specialist teaching, and presented with different or modified curricula, on the grounds that their special educational needs call for the provision of something 'extraordinary'. For others, 'support for learning' is interpreted as the development of optimum learning conditions within their regular classrooms. Many practices make up the kaleidoscope of educational provisions which are made for pupils who encounter learning and/or behaviour problems. This diversity of practice is reflected in the fact that there is 'often no clear definition of the function, role and development of personnel who undertake to support the learning of pupils' (Lacey and Lomas 1993: 11).

Potentially, a multitude of practices are available to those who strive to help pupils overcome, or circumvent, the difficulties they encounter. However, the *actual* support which a child receives will be determined, amongst other things, by the teachers' confidence and ability in providing appropriate teaching and learning experiences, their relationship with the child, their willingness to reflect upon and make changes to teaching practices, the help received from colleagues, the resource constraints within which they have to work and the 'process' by which special educational needs are determined. It is against this backdrop that we consider the appropriateness of different kinds of support which can be provided for pupils within their own classrooms.

DETERMINING SPECIAL EDUCATIONAL NEEDS

Children who experience learning and/or behaviour difficulties will only receive appropriate support if it takes account of, and responds to, the range of factors which contribute to their successes and difficulties, as described by Jones and Charlton, in Chapter 1. This requires a three-pronged analysis of factors *within the child*, the *curriculum* and the *learning environment* which help or hinder learning. Any attempt to build support from a consideration of just one of these domains might miss the heart of what a particular child actually requires.

An examination of the various fashions of learning support which have emerged over the past thirty years reveals that each style focused, in the main, on just one of the above mentioned sets of factors. For example, at one time it was fashionable to provide remedial activities which were designed to correct certain weaknesses 'within the child' (e.g. poor auditory discrimination), upon the assumption that this would facilitate learning. This particular style of support was outmoded by an approach which focused upon an examination of the extent to which 'the curriculum' was matched to the needs of the learner. Proponents of this 'analytical approach' (see Jones 1992: 17) persuaded teachers to write precise behavioural objectives, from which teaching programmes were developed, and against which progress was evaluated. More recently it has been fashionable to encourage teachers to evaluate and amend certain features of the 'learning environment' (e.g. pupil grouping strategies) in order to optimise learning conditions for all pupils. Inevitably, as fashions change, important elements of earlier styles are left behind and virtually forgotten. While it might be claimed that each of the above styles of support can facilitate some form(s) of learning, we maintain that the most appropriate and effective type of assistance will only emerge from careful considerations of, and responses to, the *range* of factors (within the child, the curriculum and the learning environment) which cause pupils to experience learning and behaviour difficulties.

WHOSE RESPONSIBILITY ?

Who, then, is best placed to reflect upon, and plan responses to, the *range* of factors which causes pupils to experience successes and difficulties in learning? The class/subject teacher is in regular contact with the child, has in-depth knowledge of the planned curriculum and can make changes to the learning environment. Theoretically, they are in the best position to co-ordinate the planning process. However, while some teachers have the necessary training and experience to carry out this task, others lack the knowledge, experience, or the appropriate attitudes to plan suitable support for pupils who encounter learning and/or behaviour difficulties. The SEN Code of Practice (DfE 1994) sensibly recognises that while the majority of class/subject teachers should be able to determine and provide for the teaching/learning needs of pupils who encounter mild difficulties, many will need to work closely with colleagues and other professionals when assessing and providing for the needs of pupils who encounter more serious difficulties.

The responsibility for 'supporting' pupils can be shared in many different ways. Traditionally, learning support professionals have dominated this process, while others have actively encouraged teamwork. Given the fact that *all* professionals have a potentially valuable contribution to make, each of them must be given the opportunity to describe a pupil's special educational needs as they perceive them, and to debate the most appropriate form of provision for that child in the light of their collective contributions. The important roles which pupils should play in the planning of 'support' will be discussed, at some length, later. Given the realities of current levels of training, prior experience and the constraints of time, we consider ways in which teachers and other learning support professionals might best work together in order to respond to the *range* of factors (i.e. within the child, the curriculum and the learning environment) which causes pupils to experience learning and/or behaviour difficulties.

When an in-depth analysis of '*within-child*' factors (e.g. auditory discrimination, visual memory) has been carried out (see Chapter 1), the class/subject teacher should be given the responsibility (with the help of a learning support professional) for translating the resultant information into practical action in the classroom. This subtle shift in the locus of professional responsibility, away from the learning support professional, will help class/subject teachers to build up their own skills in assessing and responding to the needs of pupils who experience difficulties in learning.

When teachers try to help children to overcome learning difficulties which are partly caused by sensory-processing difficulties (e.g. poor auditory discrimination), they have two choices. They can either plan activities to (a) remediate those areas of weakness, or (b) make use of the child's strong channels (e.g. visual and kinaesthetic). Children are likely to learn much more effectively if their strengths are utilised. For example, those with strengths in the visual and kinaesthetic areas are likely to experience more success in learning to spell if they are given activities which help them to remember the visual characteristics and the feel of the words through the fingertips (Cripps and Cox 1989). Conversely, other research (Thomson 1991) suggests that approaches to the teaching of spelling which contain a more significant listening element – such as 'Simultaneous Oral Spelling' (Bradley 1985) – will lead to better progress with children whose 'auditory' channel is stronger than the visual one.

However, it will not be necessary, or even possible, to conduct an in-depth assessment of 'within child' factors for *all* children who require special consideration. Fortunately, a class/subject teacher can circumvent some difficulties (e.g. those caused by poor auditory discrimination and/or poor auditory memory) without the need for detailed assessment. The following statement, written by a student teacher during initial training, demonstrates the way in which all teachers can respond to such difficulties by adopting a multi-media approach to teaching and learning:

> the more media available to the teacher the more chances students have to fully comprehend the subject. The teacher employs a variety of media such as verbal symbols (textbooks), visual symbols (charts), photos, recordings, films, exhibits, field trips, demonstrations, drama, contrived and direct purposeful experiences, *to differentially cater to the stronger senses of the students.*

While a learning support co-ordinator or educational psychologist might play a key role in assessing, and planning responses to, 'within child' factors, the prime responsibility for the analysis of factors within the 'curriculum' and the 'learning environment' should, wherever possible, rest with class/subject teachers in their own classroom, for it is they who are ideally placed to carry out this task. However, we are mindful, in the short term (and possibly the long term), that many teachers will be unable to do this without the support of experienced colleagues (see Quah and Jones in press). Thus, learning support co-ordinators and/or other professionals will need to help class teachers to develop the necessary observational and reflective skills so that they can 'recognise' (Jones 1992) factors within the curriculum and the learning environment which might cause their pupils to encounter learning and/or behaviour problems. A number of researchers (see Chapter 1) have drawn attention to key factors which can precipitate and maintain such difficulties, some of which are repeated below:

- a mismatch between the task and the pupil's current level of performance (one study indicated that 65 per cent of tasks were too difficult for low-attaining pupils)
- poor specification of the learning task
- ineffective time management, thus reducing the amount of time available for teaching
- lack of appropriate pacing
- few opportunities to review, revise and reinforce learning
- the work having an image inappropriate to the pupils' chronological age
- a lack of 'purpose' in learning activities
- inappropriate grouping strategies
- an absence of teaching approaches which encourage independent thinking.

If class teachers can be helped to recognise those factors which appear to be 'blocking' a particular child's learning, they will then be in a position to make changes to the curriculum or learning environment so that these obstacles can be removed. For example, when there is a mismatch between the task and the pupil's current levels of performance, teachers can adjust the size of learning steps, the pace with which they are introduced, as well as introducing more opportunities for revision. The 'behavioural objectives' approach (Ainscow and Tweddle 1978) can help teachers to amend the curriculum in order to make it more compatible with pupils' current levels of performance.

However, a number of studies have shown that strict adherence to end point objectives can lead to the acquisition of skills that can only be performed in limited circumstances and a narrow curriculum where only the measurable is taught. For this reason Thomas and Feiler (1988) recommend that when precise individual learning targets are developed the resultant activities should be purposeful and of intrinsic value to pupils, rather than a means to a predetermined end. The following strategies (UNESCO 1993) are offered to teachers who strive to make the curriculum more meaningful for their pupils:

1 Build new learning from the previous knowledge and experience of students by:
   • brainstorming with the students on a specific topic and letting them relate what they know;
   • giving students a problem and encouraging them to use whatever they already know to 'get into the problem'. The teacher can then introduce new concepts and skills required to solve the problem.
2 Use a student's daily experience to clarify new concepts.
3 Make learning more functional by giving the students a chance to apply it to everyday life.
4 Use stories to raise interest in lesson content.
5 Plan field trips and projects.
6 Introduce games and simulations.

Quah (1994) describes how the language curriculum can be made more meaningful for pupils if teachers use a 'language experience' approach to the teaching of reading. This approach (see also Chapter 14) utilises the child's own interests to generate material for reading and writing, thus ensuring that the teacher works within the child's current level of language competence.

Teachers can also create learning environments which meet the diverse teaching and learning needs of pupils by heeding the following advice (see Jones and Quah, in press), which is based upon the recommendations of Ainscow and Muncey (1989) and Charlton (1992):

• emphasise the importance of meaning and purpose in learning activities
• set tasks that are both realistic and challenging
• ensure that there is progression in children's work

- provide a variety of learning experiences
- give pupils opportunities to choose
- have high expectations of success
- create a positive atmosphere for learning
- provide a consistent approach
- recognise and reward the efforts and achievements of pupils
- organise resources to facilitate learning
- encourage pupils to work co-operatively
- monitor progress and provide regular feedback
- help pupils to develop negotiating skills such as listening, managing conflict, assertiveness training, taking risks, accepting responsibility and dealing with feelings
- support the development of a positive self-concept as well as an internal locus of control.

Thus, class/subject teachers and other learning support professionals will only obtain a real understanding of a child's teaching and learning needs if they accept that learning and/or behaviour problems can be caused by a combination of factors 'within the child', 'the curriculum' and the 'learning environment' (see Chapter 1). By pooling their knowledge about the influence of these various factors upon a particular child's learning they will develop a solid foundation from which to build positive responses to that child's difficulties, which should involve:

- the utilisation of a child's strong learning channels (e.g. visual and kinaesthetic)
- the construction of purposeful learning objectives for that particular child
- the adaptation of the learning environment so that more effective teaching methods can be used and blocks to learning removed.

THE MISSING LINK

While the above mentioned assessment/planning procedure has much to commend it, there is one major flaw; it *fails to involve pupils* in the determination of their own 'support' requirements.

A similar situation used to exist in the health service. Many people can remember occasions during which they were lying in a hospital bed, straining to listen to whispered conversations between consultants, doctors, nurses and other professionals who were discussing *their* fate, without having the decency to ask for their opinion on the matter! While acknowledging that this practice might persist in some places, real efforts have been made to improve levels of consultation and patient choice. The best services are now founded upon the belief that many patients (or their representatives) are able to describe accurately their symptoms and throw light upon their causes, and predict responses to certain forms of treatment. Additionally, their involvement helps to prepare them for a course of 'treatment' and heightens the chances of a good recovery.

The practice of involving pupils in the determination of their own support requirements has been far from widespread, but is now encouraged in Paragraph 6.7 of the Code of Practice. It is a pity that so few pupils have been consulted, because many of them could indicate the extent to which a particular form of provision is likely to help them. To ignore such potent sources of information would be both inefficient and, as Charlton states in Chapter 2, disrespectful of their 'rights' to be involved (Children Act 1989).

A simple example of the benefit of involving pupils in the assessment/planning process is illustrated in the following case, which is recalled by one of the authors:

During a visit to a small primary school, in a rural part of England, a teacher expressed some concern about a 10-year-old boy's progress in mathematics. The child seemed to be having considerable difficulty undertaking activities which involved 'measurement'.

Having been asked to investigate the reasons for this child's difficulties, several avenues were open to me. I could have used commercial tests, analysed past work and the child could have been observed over a period of time. Being short of time (a reality in this line of work) I chose to talk to the child and listen carefully to his responses. When asked about his 'measuring' activities, the child said that he 'hated it' and 'didn't like doing it'. When asked whether he had any idea why he found it so difficult the child replied 'it's these flipping things' (referring to a pair of callipers). It transpired that the child couldn't 'read' the complicated calibrations which were printed on the measuring device. The mathematics scheme required the child to measure the thickness of real objects (e.g. trees) using callipers. When I examined the callipers, I too had difficulty in 'reading' the calibrations. No wonder the child was encountering difficulties. Additionally, given the individualised nature of the teaching, the child had to wait a long time to get the teacher's help. When help did arrive it was so short and sharp that the child never really understood the explanation, nor the instruction.

When I asked the child how we might best help him to learn to measure the thickness of everyday things using callipers, he asked if he could do it with the easy ones first (the school possessed another set of large callipers, with simpler calibrations). He went on to suggest that if he could get the exercises 'right' using the easier ones, he could then try to learn how to use more complicated ones with the help of a friend – 'not', as he said, 'to get them to do it for me, but so I could ask them to explain the marks on the ruler'.

These suggestions were taken up by the classteacher. The child learnt to measure with callipers and the teacher was able to use a similar strategy to help other children.

Wade and Moore (1993) provide several examples of insightful comments made by pupils, which further support the argument that if they were considered to be 'partners' in the assessment and planning process, their responses would provide a good foundation from which simple changes could be made to overcome, or circumvent, the difficulties which they were experiencing. A very simple, but powerful example concerns two partially sighted boys of secondary school age, who revealed the same worry about arriving late for their next lesson. If they had been encouraged to voice their anxiety, their teachers would have been able to adopt the simple policy of dismissing them first to give them adequate time to change rooms. In this case the teachers were simply unaware of the problem, yet the information was easily available.

In the same study (Wade and Moore 1993: 5) twenty students gave 'lack of direction by the teacher' as the cause of their anxiety. Pupils said: 'I don't know what to do; the teachers don't explain things properly; I'm not sure what to do and I've annoyed my teacher enough about the problem.' If their teachers had been aware of these problems they could have encouraged these pupils to seek clarification (from themselves or other pupils), thus preventing the occurrence of unnecessary problems.

These simple, but very powerful, insights provide valuable information which could help teachers to make straightforward and effective changes which would alleviate the difficulties faced by pupils. In so doing, they would begin to create classrooms which are much more supportive to learning (see also Jones and Quah, in press).

To summarise thus far, while support for learning can be conceptualised in many ways, appropriate provision is most likely to occur if the particular knowledge, skills, insights and experience of teachers, pupils, parents and other professionals are brought together in the planning process. This should involve an appraisal of factors within the child, the curriculum and the learning environment which precipitate and maintain learning difficulties and problem behaviours. To omit one of these factors, or to ignore a key informant/decision maker, might be to overlook significant needs, be they something extraordinary, or simply the implementation of a strategy which opens up learning for more children. Pupils should play a key role in the assessment/planning process and not be left on the fringes. They can often throw light upon the causes of problems and suggest appropriate solutions. The decisions which are being made will affect *their* present and future lives.

LIVING IN A CHANGING WORLD

Children who experience difficulties in learning, like all others, live in a rapidly changing world. The support which they receive will only be appropriate if it responds to their future as well as present learning needs. David (1992: 175) draws attention to some of the challenges which children face within a rapidly changing society:

> The changing nature of family life produces children whose lives are more complicated and whose attitudes are more sophisticated and demanding. The modern 'information explosion' is obliging teachers to realise that the knowledge they deal with is more transitory, the demands of learning are more complicated, and the human skills of communication and relationships are becoming more essential, for survival in the future.

These changes produce new challenges for *all* pupils. For those who encounter difficulties in learning, the challenges could be even more demanding. New emphases in curriculum content (e.g. the increasingly important status of science in the primary school curriculum) underline the need to reconsider the 'special' educational needs of pupils. Changing attitudes also lead to the passing of new laws which underline the rights of all children to share in a set of *common* curricular experiences. This requires 'that school staff are committed to the provision of a curriculum that is 'broad, balanced, relevant and differentiated' and will meet the full range of pupils' needs' (Beveridge 1993: 56).

Consistent with this theme is Ainscow and Tweedle's (1988) suggestion that the skills of thinking and learning might be more important to children's future lives than content knowledge. He states that teachers should encourage:

> pupils to learn more about themselves as learners and to become sensitive to their preferred methods of learning. In a sense nurturing self-confidence and independence is a means to an end. The ultimate goal is to *help pupils to take responsibility for their own learning*.
>
> (p. 5)

Ingram and Worrall (1993) are critical of the fact that thinking skills are not prompted in large numbers of classrooms, which are still run along traditional lines, where the teacher does most of the learning, in terms of hunting out information books, preparatory reading, thinking through and reflecting on how best to transmit and organise the children's experiences and knowledge; all skills that children are themselves capable of learning and applying (see Chapter 9). This raises questions about the extent to which current practices help or hinder the development of such skills, which are likely to be of increasing importance to pupils in future years.

Galton (1994) questions the appropriateness of traditional forms of 'individualised' special educational provision for another reason:

> Given the rapid changes in the global economy, promoting a need for greater inter-dependence between states, future generations of pupils will need to extend their social and intellectual skills so that they can solve complex problems, often as

members of multi-national teams. Children, therefore, from an early age need to learn and value the skills that come from working together in this way.

(p. 2)

Thus, appropriate support for learning must be based upon a clear appreciation of pupils' present and future needs. While it is likely that the development of basic skills in literacy and numeracy will continue to be important, pupils will also need to develop independence in thinking and learning across a number of different subject areas, some of which will feature more prominently in their lives than they did for previous generations. Additionally pupils will need to be self-confident and possess interpersonal skills which allow them to function as effective members of teams and enjoy social/leisure pursuits.

SUPPORTIVE CLASSROOMS

New priorities for learning, such as those mentioned above, call for a reappraisal of the kinds of support which are offered to pupils who encounter difficulties in learning. If the present and future needs of pupils are to be met, some elements of existing practices might have to be reshaped or replaced.

While positive responses to a child's learning difficulties should still include features such as multi-sensory teaching methods, to cater to different learning preferences, and the development of carefully designed purposeful learning activities for individuals and/or small groups of children (e.g. for the teaching of spelling), it is likely that other pressing needs will be best met through a greater emphasis on the development of 'classroom strategies' which facilitate learning for *all* pupils. Interestingly, and in keeping with the theme of this book, some of the most effective approaches are those in which teachers empower pupils to take control of their own learning and those which encourage them to offer support to, and learn with, their peers, examples of which are provided below.

Helping pupils to help themselves

When we encounter someone who is 'in difficulty', the natural inclination is to 'do things for them', rather than helping them to confront the problem for themselves. With similar sentiment, teachers can easily take over the task of learning *for* their pupils, rather than helping them to develop their own learning and problem-solving skills. Westwood (1993) is critical of teachers who encourage pupils to be dependent upon them, for another reason. He fears that relationships in which pupils are dependent upon teachers will reinforce children's beliefs that they will only learn by relying upon the support of others (e.g. teachers) rather than realising that their performance is also attributable to their own actions and efforts.

Westwood (1993: 21) claims that these students display ineffective self-management skills and need positive help to become independent learners. In particular they need to know:

- how to organise their own materials
- what to do when work is completed
- when to seek help of peer/teacher
- how to check their own work
- how to maintain attention to task
- how to observe rules and routines.

However, he cautions against attempts to force responsibility on pupils too quickly, suggesting that children who are markedly external respond best, at first, in a highly structured, predictable, teacher-directed setting, particularly for the learning of basic skills. He maintains that suddenly placing children in a very open, child-centred teaching environment may only increase the number of occasions when they fail and develop an even greater feeling of helplessness and lack of ability.

Pupils are likely gradually to shift their 'locus of control' beliefs towards internality if teachers use strategies such as those suggested by Charlton (1992) and Westwood (1993), some of which are listed below:

- develop simple contracts with pupils (see Chapter 7)
- use positive reinforcement judiciously, making it clear what behaviours are being rewarded
- use some self-instructing materials which provide immediate feedback to pupils
- use WAIT TIME when orally questioning pupils in order to give them ample opportunity to reply
- encourage pupils to practise analysing problem situations, in

order to make them aware of the influence of people's behaviour upon their outcomes and experiences.

As pupils develop more 'internal' control for their own learning
and actions, teachers can increasingly 'let go' of their own control,
thus further empowering pupils to utilise their new-found self-
management skills. The following example illustrates the delicate
balance which teachers and support professionals have to
achieve:

> Alan, a Year 5 pupil with a pronounced stammer and very poor
> self-image was supported by a well-meaning and kindly sup-
> port assistant who worked conscientiously and closely with
> the parents in trying to build up his confidence. She was
> always near to hand in the classroom and often took Alan to
> one side to explain problems with which he may be having
> difficulties. After much cajoling and encouragement he was
> persuaded to accompany his class on a residential week. His
> support assistant went too. Arriving at the hostel the support
> assistant's time was in demand from several pupils suffering
> from home sickness to sprained ankle. Alan, often left to his
> own devices, found a freedom he had never before experi-
> enced. Returning to school he began to reject the support
> and became far more of an independent learner. By the time
> he transferred to secondary school, his statement had been
> terminated and his speech problems were improving.

Support in the classroom is a very delicate matter. There is a very
fine line between creating dependence and independence.

Meaningful, negotiated support

Since the Code of Practice was published and authorities have
been implementing its recommendations, there has been an increase in the involvement of pupils in the planning and negotiating of learning programmes and teaching activities. This has
probably been in evidence most in the annual review of statements where schools and LEAs have encouraged pupils to be
present for all or part of the review meeting. The benefits of this
have been felt by staff and pupils.

At a recent annual review in a grant-maintained secondary
school, the teacher reported on the progress made by a second-

ary pupil in the curriculum areas in which he received support. These were English, Mathematics and Science. The teacher explained that progress was most satisfactory, particularly in Science. When the pupil was asked to comment on how he saw his performance he agreed that he had made some really positive progress but was not all that enthusiastic, in fact he appeared quite disconsolate about the whole affair. The LEA officer conducting the review, sensing that all was not well, pursued the question.

'You don't seem very happy with your achievement.'

'I am happy with my Science and Maths. What about my History? I'm always in trouble with that and I get no help at all. Mr Williams, in Science, makes it easy for me anyway. I don't think I need help in Science. I like Science. Can I have help in History?'

In this episode it became obvious that teachers and associated professionals had seen the problem in relation to the three core subjects, rather than with respect to the child's total learning experiences. Teachers who are able to differentiate their approach and work through the interest of the pupil will often not need in-class support and there is no better source of information to identify where support is needed than by consulting the consumer, the pupil.

Others (e.g. Ingram and Worrall 1993) have shown that pupils can take an active part in decision-making, about issues as far-ranging as curriculum, resources, organisation and classroom management. The process of negotiation can help to ensure that special educational provision is meaningful and purposeful to the pupils for whom it is designed. Rowland (1987: 58) suggested that if teachers really want to help pupils with special educational needs they should take bolder steps to understand their world as reflected in the choices they make and the interpretations they form of their environment.

Modular programmes, which allow a certain amount of choice and negotiation, can result in a curriculum which is more meaningful and appropriate to the special educational needs of particular pupils. Sayer (1987: 289) draws attention to the fact that these programmes can give pupils the opportunity to see and understand what they are committing themselves to, to set targets within reach, to have credit for achievement in the short term, the option for continuing if so motivated, or of striving for achievement in a different module if not.

Peer support

In Chapter 6, Charlton and Jones discuss a number of ways in which pupils can support each other's learning and the potential benefits which this can have. Others (e.g. UNESCO 1993) go so far as to suggest that support received from other pupils can be equally, if not more, effective than that provided by adults. They suggest that this may be due to pupils' tendency to be more directive; their familiarity with the material being taught; their understandings of the other child's frustrations; or because of their use of more meaningful and age-appropriate vocabulary and examples (UNESCO 1993). These attributes are particularly relevant to the needs of pupils who experience difficulties in learning, for whom the teacher's instructions often appear confusing (Bennet 1991).

In Singapore, for example, a number of primary schools have instigated a *peer buddies* approach to help pupils who experience difficulties in reading. Good readers volunteer to 'adopt' a peer who is experiencing difficulties in reading. They coach, read to and read with their 'buddy' with the aim of helping him/her to improve in reading and other school-related activities. These reading sessions are given at different times of the school day, whenever the two buddies have time to spare. This arrangement gives pupils many opportunities to learn to read through the very act of reading itself. The extra time, interest and encouragement which they receive from their peers is invaluable.

Pupils can also support each other's learning through '*collaborative group work*'. At its best this form of peer support enables children to share the resources of knowledge, experience, social relationships and their capacity to support and stimulate one another through shared interests. In order for all children to be given the opportunity to contribute, the tasks set for group work should have the widest possible base.

A teacher experiencing problems ensuring that a group of pupils with difficulties in reading were contributing to the class project divided her class into five mixed-ability groups. She gathered together a considerable collection of books, photographs, articles and artefacts connected with the topic. She distributed these among the groups making sure that each had a share of the different types of resource and urged each group to find out as much as they possibly could about the subject simply by examining the resources. She found that those pupils who could not read well managed to contribute considerably by simply looking at the pictures and talking. Each group found it necessary to appoint a scribe and the teacher realised that there are many aspects of learning, besides reading and writing, that are often ignored. Previous experience shared, deduction from pictures, assumptions discussed, shared knowledge and argument, all these and more were readily used by the pupils each at their own level. From this base she was then able to develop many avenues of study which had been opened by the pupils themselves.

It is important when planning collaborative learning activities to think carefully about the structure of the group. The temptation is often to use groups already formed through seating plans, house systems, ability grouping, etc. Each group should meet the demands of the task set. Slavin (1990) and Kagan (1992) describe a number of co-operative structures which teachers can use to encourage pupils to develop the skills of collaborative working, some of which are summarised below:

Pairs check
1 Put students into pairs, within subgroups of four.
2 Give pairs practice sheets.
3 Person 'number 1' in each pair does the first problem. Person 'number 2' acts as the coach and offers praise. If the answer is incorrect, the coach will help his/her partner to arrive at the right answer.
4 Partners then exchange roles.
5 When two problems have been completed the pair checks with the other pair in their subgroup.
6 If the two pairs disagree about the answer they can call on the teacher's help.

Team webbing
1 Give each student a different coloured marker.
2 Write the word/topic in the centre of a large piece of paper and enclose the word within a rectangle.

3 Each member (in round-robin fashion) contributes a core concept related to the word/topic.
4 Let the members, in a free-for-all, add other core concepts or supporting elements to the word/topic. Do not pass judgement on the quality of responses. Allow only minimal talking.
5 Give them time to discuss what patterns they see, or what conclusions can be drawn from the webbed data.
6 Tape the webs to the wall. Facilitate a whole-class discussion about them.

Jigsaw 2
1 The teacher introduces the topic and provides a broad overview of the main facts or concepts.
2 Each team member is assigned one section of the topic to read.
3 Those with the same section of the topics meet in new 'expert' groups to discuss the information which they read.
4 The students return to their 'home teams' and take turns teaching their team-mates about their sections.
5 Students may be given a test, which they take individually.
6 Team scores are added up; awards are given to the teams according to their performance.

Collaborative work with other pupils can help children to take risks. When they learn something new they often have to feel their way around the topic, grapple with partially formed ideas and try out half-formed solutions to problems without really knowing what the outcome might be. For many this can be a daunting, lonely and frightening task. It can be likened to travelling alone, down a long dark meandering tunnel, with only the flickering beam of an old torch as a guide. Many children gain greater confidence and feel more able to take risks which lead to learning when they undertake collaborative work in small groups.

However, a supportive atmosphere for learning, in which pupils help each other to clarify instructions, concepts and methods of learning, will not emerge without careful planning. A suitable sharing environment will need to be created and opportunities for collaboration sought. Hart (1992) states that teachers will have to reinforce the need for pupils to listen to one another, to show interest in what each of them has to say, to respect one another's views. Teachers, themselves, should act as models by demonstrating active listening, responding to new ideas, questioning, exploring and sharing with their pupils.

CONCLUSION

Appropriate support for learning is most likely to occur when the various perspectives of class/subject teachers, pupils and other professionals are brought together in the assessment/planning process. While all of these people might share some common views about special educational needs, the unique position which they are in will give them a different perspective from which they can analyse the causes of learning and/or behaviour problems and the appropriateness of any special provision which is made in response to them.

The best forms of support are most likely to emerge from an appraisal of the range of factors which cause pupils to encounter learning and/or behaviour problems. To omit one of these groups of factors, or to ignore a key informant/decision maker (e.g. the pupil), might be to overlook significant needs. While some traditional forms of provision might continue to play an important part in the education of children who encounter problems, other classroom strategies, which empower pupils to take more control for their own learning and support peers, might be more effective in meeting their present-day and future learning needs.

REFERENCES

Ainscow, M. and Muncey, J. (1989) *Meeting Individual Needs in the Primary School*, London: David Fulton.

Ainscow, M. and Tweddle, D. A. (1978) *Preventing Classroom Failure: An Objectives Approach*, Chichester: John Wiley.

Ainscow, M. and Twedle, D. A. (1988) *Encouraging Classroom Success*, London: David Fulton.

Bennet, N. (1991) 'The quality of classroom learning experiences for children with special educational needs', in M. Ainscow (ed.) *Effective Schools for all*, London: David Fulton.

Beveridge, S. (1993) *Special Educational Needs in Schools*, London: Routledge.

Bradley, L. (1985) *Poor Spellers, Poor Readers: Understanding the Problem*, University of Reading: Centre for the Teaching of Reading.

Charlton, T. (1992) 'Giving access to the National Curriculum', in K. Jones and T. Charlton (eds) *Learning Difficulties in Primary Classrooms*, London: Routledge.

Children Act (1989) London: HMSO.

Cripps, C. and Cox, R. (1989) *Joining the ABC*, Wisbech: LDA.

David, K. (1992) 'A classroom plan for personal and social education', in K. Jones and T. Charlton (eds) *Learning Difficulties in Primary Classrooms*, London: Routledge.

Department for Education (1994) *The Special Educational Needs Code of Practice*, London: HMSO.

Galton, M. (1994) *Meeting the Challenge of Diversity through Collaborative Learning*, Paper presented at the 8th Annual Conference of the Singapore Educational Research Association, Singapore: National Institute of Education.

Hart, S. (1992) 'Collaborative classrooms', in T. Booth, W. Swann, M. Masterton and P. Potts (eds) *Curricula for Diversity in Education*, London: Routledge.

Ingram, J. and Worrall, N. (1993) *Teacher–Child Partnership: The Negotiating Classroom*, London: David Fulton.

Jones, K. (1992) 'Recognising successes and difficulties in learning', in K. Jones and T. Charlton (eds) *Learning Difficulties in Primary Classrooms*, London: Routledge.

Jones, K. and Quah, M. L. (in press) 'How children learn', in K. David and T. Charlton (eds) *Pastoral Care Matters: in Primary and Middle Schools*, London: Routledge.

Kagan, S. (1992) 'The structured approach to co-operative learning', *Educational Leadership* 42, (4): 12–15.

Lacey, P. and Lomas, J. (1993) *Support Services and the Curriculum*, London: David Fulton.

Quah, M. L. (1994) 'A gentle push for reluctant readers', Singapore, *ASCD Review* 4 (2): 56–8.

Quah, M. L. and Jones, K. (in press) 'The professional development needs of learning support co-ordinators in Singapore primary schools', *European Journal of Special Needs Education*.

Rowland, S. (1987) 'Ian and the shoe factory', in T. Booth and W. Swann (eds) *Preventing Difficulties in Learning: Curricula for All*, Oxford: Blackwell.

Sayer, J. (1987) 'Secondary schools as a resource for everyone's learning', in T. Booth, P. Potts and W. Swann (eds) *Preventing Difficulties in Learning: Curricula for All*, Oxford: Blackwell.

Slavin, R. E. (1990) *Co-operative Learning: Theory, Research and Practice*, Hemel Hempstead: Prentice Hall.

Thomas, G. and Feiler, A. (eds) (1988) *Planning for Special Needs: A Whole-School Approach*, Oxford: Blackwell.

Thomson, M. (1991) 'The teaching of spelling using techniques of simultaneous oral spelling and visual inspection', in M. Snowling and M. Thomson (eds) *Dyslexia: Integrating Theory and Practice*, London: Whurr Publications.

UNESCO (1993) *Special Needs in the Classroom*, Paris: UNESCO.

Wade, B. and Moore, M. (1993) *Experiencing Special Education*, Buckingham: Open University Press.

Westwood, P. (1993) *Common Sense Methods for Children with Special Educational Needs*, London: Routledge.

Chapter 9

Children's personal problem solving

Pamela Sharpe

INTRODUCTION

> Each time one prematurely teaches a child something he could
> have discovered for himself, the child is kept from inventing it
> and consequently understanding it completely.
>
> (Piaget 1970: 715)

Just how do children solve problems and make sense of their
world? The pioneers of attempts to answer this kind of question,
Pestalozzi, Froebel and Montessori, arrived at their conclusions
after careful and systematic observations of young children. Subsequent authorities have attempted to find answers by seeking
relationships between selected characteristics of children's development, the teaching and learning materials children are exposed
to, and the teaching methods they experience. As a result, suggestions as to the best way to identify and exploit children's thinking,
learning and problem-solving strategies have emerged. One of
the outcomes has been a plethora of educational programmes,
especially for pre-school children and specifically for those who
have been labelled 'disadvantaged'. These programmes have
been designed to maximise, and in some cases equalise, the academic, social, emotional, physical and artistic potential of young
children. Not all authorities are comfortable with such outcomes,
however, especially if this involves interfering with children's
naturally developing spontaneity, which is regarded as being
vital for normal development.

In sharing his misgivings about the climate of the 'must have'
pre-school programmes, and programmes for disadvantaged
young children, be it the 'lasting effects' view, or the 'sooner the
better' view, Elkind (1988, 1989) warns of the dangers of adults

focusing their expectations on *what* young children think and learn, and neglecting to observe the process of *how* young children think and learn (see also Chapter 8).

In the race to maximise the potential of young children, adults are not only reminded of the value of such programmes of study but impressed, and frequently overwhelmed by the availability of the teaching aids and tools also designed to give children a head start. While acknowledging the usefulness of such technology in providing access to knowledge, skills and information, Elkind (1988) proposes that children are only able to extend their thinking and learning when given opportunities to talk and reflect. Merely exposing them to new skills, knowledge, information, and experiences *per se* is unlikely to have much effect. We often fail to appreciate that children's thoughts and abilities are childlike and spontaneous and that children cannot see the world in the same way as the adults who have conceptualised it for them and who take it for granted.

Different types of learning relationships are associated with these disparate responses to children's special learning needs. Some 'programmed' interventions are dominated by adults and require children to learn in a prescribed way, to give set responses to closed questions and to adopt a passive role. In contrast, those who seek to promote educational growth through natural and spontaneous learning acknowledge the need to provide experiences which are in tune with the child's way of thinking; in a sense a precursor to the kinds of negotiated learning referred to by Jones and colleagues in Chapter 8.

The account which follows in this chapter aims to illustrate the importance of understanding just *how* young children are thought to try to make sense of their world. Reference is made to research which has revealed some of the ways in which children solve problems, and the implications for teachers, parents and others involved in their care and education. We will only begin to understand the thought processes of individual children if we listen to them, with the intent to discover how they make sense of their world. One way in which this can be achieved is through, what Scott-Bauman (Chapter 4) refers to as, practitioner-research. The insights which are gained through such research can help pre-school educators to form learning partnerships with children which are less dominated by an adult view of the world, and more in tune with the learning needs of young children.

LANGUAGE AND EXPERIENCE

One study, conducted by the author (Sharpe 1979) attempted to discover the kinds of thinking and understanding involved in the problem-solving activities of young children. The study investigated children's responses to particular questioning techniques which had previously been found to be effective in assisting older children to arrive at solutions to selected Piagetian conservation tasks (Sinclair 1967, 1969). In Sinclair's 1967 study, the aim was to investigate the kinds of expressions used spontaneously by young children to describe and compare quantities and dimensions such as length, width, height and number, and then to establish whether training children to use such terms would facilitate the acquisition of 'conservation' (e.g. recognise that a fixed number of tightly grouped objects would still be of the same *quantity* when spread out). Sinclair's results indicated that training children to use certain qualitative terms such as 'more' and 'less' did not enable them to 'conserve', whereas training children to use differentiated terms such as 'long and thin', 'short and fat', helped to direct their attention to the relevant aspects of transformations. Such verbal training, of qualitative terms and four-part structures (long but thin; short but fat), was found to be useful in that it enabled conserving children to justify their answers.

The questions asked of the children in the author's study were extensions of those used by Sinclair. Children were trained to use qualitative descriptive terms spontaneously (more, less, same, fewer), and provoked to use qualitative relational terms (same as, fewer than, more than, and less than), and co-ordinated descriptions (four-part structures – shorter but fatter, longer but thinner, longer but fatter, the same).

Just as in Sinclair's study, after training the children's knowledge and functional use of qualitative descriptive terms and co-ordinated descriptions enabled them to demonstrate conservation of continuous quantity, liquid and solid in the two post tests. In the author's study, provision in the training of kinaesthetic experiences, where the children were able to demonstrate physically movement shapes in response to verbal stimuli, appeared to augment their conservation skills.

The results of this study indicated that verbal factors alone were insufficient to provide the necessary conceptual understanding associated with conservation concepts. Children also needed *experiences* which could provide opportunities for spontaneous, as well as provoked, expressions of understanding. These expressions include judgements, predictions and explanations as well as those which signal resistance to alternative (illogical) suggestions.

Examples of such experiences involved movement activities such as 'moving and stopping' and involving activities such as stepping, hopping, balancing and stillness, which the children would engage in. The spatial aspects involved in movement on the spot and travelling would be stressed at the same time as dimensional attributes and qualities such as size using qualitative terms (more/few) and differentiated terms (tall/short). Other movement ideas were developed where progressively more complex activities, spatial aspects, dimensional attributes and qualities were developed.

Brainerd (1973) believes that if children are to be enabled to think in a truly logical way they should be provided with appropriate experiences, such as those referred to above, which would allow them to develop this kind of conceptual understanding and language facility. Eventually, through such experiences and linguistics explorations, the logically thinking primary school child might well respond to questions in this way:

- *prediction:* 'if I spread the counters out like this, would this row have more?'
  logical response: 'no, they would still have the same number'
- *judgement:* 'does each row have the same number now?'
  logical response: 'you have not added any or taken any away, one row just looks to have more'
- *explanation:* 'how do you know that both rows have the same number of counters?'
  logical response: ' this row looks to be longer but it does not have any more or any less than the other row, the number in each is still the same'
- *generalisation to related problem:* 'if I rearrange the counters in this (another) way, are there still the same number of counters in each row?'
  logical response: 'this row looks shorter than this one, but there are still the same number of counters in each row because you have only moved them and not altered their number.'

In a more recent study (Sharpe 1994), the aim was to investigate the relationship between children's use and understanding of verbal expressions and their performance on tasks of:

- one-to-one correspondence
- seriation and one-to-one correspondence, and
- the conservation of number.

The tasks which were presented to the children were adapted from Inhelder *et al.*, (1974), Sinclair (1969), Piaget and Inhelder (1969), Sharpe (1979), and focused on the following:

- spontaneous use of qualitative terms: same, more/less, fewer
- provoked use of co-ordinated descriptions: shorter but thinner, longer but fatter, shorter but fatter, shorter but thinner, same
- provoked use of relational terms: same, fewer, more than, less than.

The tasks were selected because of their significance for the development of number operations. For example, one of the tasks, involving the provoked use of a co-ordinated description 'same', required children to select two dolls with identical attributes and then to justify the choice. A truly logical response would involve the child selecting correctly with a justification reflecting an awareness of the whole rather than significant parts, indicating that the child would 'decentre'.

Other tasks involved questions focused on the concept of 'equality' and the children were asked about sameness (e.g. 'Are they the same ?') and fairness (e.g. 'Is it fair ?'). In certain encounters, some children were uncertain of the meaning of 'fair' and the question was then rephrased to: 'Is it OK?' It was predicted that given these modifications the tasks would, as Dahlberg (1985) suggested, be more meaningful than the traditional conservation tasks. It was hypothesized that the children might benefit from opportunities to form judgements, and give explanations and, to use the necessary language structures both in everyday activities, and responding to questions about solving problems, e.g.: 'Why is it the same?' 'But isn't this pencil thinner as well as longer?' 'How are those triangles different from these triangles, can you say something about their size, their shape?'

As others have noted (Hughes 1986, Donaldson 1978, Wood 1988, Sharpe 1995), the children's responses appeared to reflect their own individual interpretations of the tasks presented. For example, in response to the question 'But isn't this pencil thinner as well as longer?', one child pointed out that it was much easier to write with. When pressed for a further explanation he commented 'because it's easier to hold'. Some children appear to give the correct solution to problems, and as such, give the impression that they are comfortable with certain problem-solving tasks, yet, without exception they were unable to produce judgements, predictions and explanations to support their statements.

The results of this study show that the children in this small study are able to give some logical judgements and explanations for pre-number tasks, but by far the majority, especially the younger children, are heavily dominated by perceptual cues and their inability to decentre, focusing on their immature interpretations of the tasks and questions. The results show that some of the children appear to provide the correct solutions to the tasks, but when pressed for generalisations of their strategies to similar problems and when asked to provide explanations for their responses, few children are able to demonstrate true logical thought. These results reveal the immaturity in young children's thought processes and may suggest to some, the importance of the provision of an appropriate learning environment for young children if they are to develop their thinking skills independently and successfully. For this to happen it is suggested that pre-school children need exposure to developmentally appropriate experiences which both tap their exhaustive repertoire of skills and knowledge and which challenge them to discover new problems and to invent new solutions for themselves.

OVERCOMING DIFFICULTIES WITH NUMBERS

Preferences for different types of teaching and learning activities also come to light when we examine the methods by which teachers try to help young children to overcome difficulties with numbers. Some (e.g. Boulton-Lewis and Tait (1994)) suggest that children only appear to make sense of number operations when using their *own* strategies, regardless of those introduced by teachers, while others recommend a teacher-dominated 'programmed' approach.

Carraher *et al.* (1990) came to a similar conclusion when observing the mathematical abilities of Brazilian street children. It appears that children respond with strategies they are comfortable and confident with and which have been previously successful. This was found to be no less so in the study conducted by Cowen and Foster (1993). By encouraging them to count, these researchers tried to convince the children in the study how helpful counting could be in solving number problems. They found the training to be ineffective and noticed that children developed successful problem-solving strategies of their own which they later generalised to new situations. Cowen and Foster (1993) concluded that merely *telling* children how to solve a problem is not effective. As a result, they suggest that teachers might best encourage learning if they support (and provide feedback about) the development of individualised personal problem-solving strategies.

Durkin (1993), in a review of research into different methods of helping children to overcome difficulties with numbers, also questions the effectiveness of traditional 'programmed' interventions, and cites some studies which refute assertions, such as those made by Gelman and Gallistel (1978), that young children who have been taught number words have a greater preference for counting and perform better on numerical tasks as a result. For example, Saxe *et al.* (1987) suggest that although children appear to relate number words to countables during teaching sessions, they make little attempt to do this in one-to-one correspondence, and are often unaware of the cardinal value of numbers, failing to realise that the last count word is equated with the total quantity.

In contrast, Fuson (1988) suggested that children learned more effectively when they were encouraged to make connections between number symbols, pictures, countables and hands-on experiences. In making such connections children could, for example, create a story for the mathematical statement '3 + 4' (e.g. Susan had three pence and her friend gave her four more pence), they could then dramatise the situation, using real coins, and finally draw a picture about it. Haylock (1991) also supports this view and suggests that the growth of understanding in mathematics can be conceptualised as the building-up of cognitive connections:

> When a child encounters some new experience I reckon that they understand it if they can connect it to previous experiences, or better, to a network of previously connected

experiences. The more strongly connected the experience the more they understand it. Learning without making connections is what I would regard as learning by rote. Such learning is easily confused or forgotten, particularly by many low attainers with poor memories, and is of little value to them in application to real-life situations.

(p. 62)

Durkin (1993) suggests that this development process thrives in the everyday diet of experiences with number activities, where children discover for themselves possibilities and inconsistencies in number knowledge and number use. They learn the functions and traditions associated with numbers from the practices of adults in a socio-cultural context. Durkin's review, however, goes on to illustrate that in spite of children's inevitable progress, this process can often intimidate, rather than facilitate, children's use and understanding of numbers in a problem-solving context. The types of experience which children are given will determine the extent to which learning difficulties are prevented or overcome.

Durkin (1993) also cites the work of Riem (1985) who noted that parents have misperceptions of their children's abilities with numbers. In asking questions such as 'What comes after?' or 'How many?', parents seemed to assume that because their child had a repertoire of number words, they would also know their cardinal value. In attempting to help their children, parents often used drill-like methods which didn't allow their children to build up connections between words and countables. Consistent with this theme are Donaldson's (1978) and Hughes' (1986) comments which emphasised how young children, with their disembodied thinking abilities, often have a different understanding of task requirements than adults. Solomon's study (quoted in Durkin 1993) showed that children followed the adult's instructions literally when asked to imagine how many buttons of the ten in the bag would be left if eight were sown on to a garment. The children could not follow this hypothetical situation and attempted to count and use all the buttons. The general conclusion appears to be that failure on such tasks may be due to factors other than lack of ability. Children often appeared to be unclear about what they were supposed to do, but, under certain circumstances they can succeed on similar tasks which are appropriately modified, as the following example illustrates.

McGarrigle and Donaldson (1974) proposed that for children having difficulty with certain number tasks, such as the conservation of number, a deliberate rearrangement of the problem might signal to the child that an important clue has been given, and the child may want to alter its response. Thus, in their study of number conservation involving the naughty teddy, who knocked the pieces about the table and spoiled the game, McGarrigle and Donaldson found that of the children who experienced this arrangement, more of this group solved the problem than the children from the group experiencing the conventional task arrangement.

In accounting for these results, Donaldson suggests that the child may not interpret the situation 'naturally' if it is confused, especially by the questions, the spatial arrangement of the task, and an inability to express in words what it sees and/or thinks. It appears then that successful problem solving involves a process whereby children have to learn to resolve the tensions inherent in discovering what adults mean and what adults expect in such situations.

THE ADULTS' ROLE IN FACILITATING THINKING AND PROBLEM SOLVING

Wood *et al.* (1976) emphasised the important role which empathising and supportive adults can play in children's problem-solving activities, and, in offering some suggestions as to how adults might maximise children's number skills more effectively, Haylock (1987) shows how games can help. His aim was to teach certain language structures such as 'less than' and 'more than' through card games, which he found assisted the necessary linkages and associations of language symbols to pictures and concrete experiences, such that their meanings made more sense to the children.

For example, Haylock shows how involving two children in a game where they have to say out aloud how many more or less unifix cubes they have than their partners when they turn over a card which indicates either 'more than' or 'less than', helps their functional use of 'more' or 'less' when making comparisons.

Evans (1992) showed how role-play activities facilitated young children's understanding of place value and written subtraction sums involving large numbers. In a game where children assumed the role of 'units', 'tens', 'hundreds', 'thousands', four children are involved. One child has a pretend house with 9 'units', one child sits next to her in a pretend house with 9 'tens', one child sits next to the 'tens' house and has 9 'hundreds', with the next child having a 'thousands' house. The children are told that even though they each represented a digit, they were given a specific number of pieces of apparatus which they each represented, which would represent what was to be the larger of two numbers in a subtraction sum. The children were told that these houses were in a terrace and that even though they lived separately they were part of a row of neighbours. They were shown that when their numbers were represented side by side, the whole row represented a 'whole' number. A fourth child acted as a robber who then stole a certain number. The teacher wrote a whole number on the board and the robber 'stole' from each of the 'units', 'tens', 'hundreds' and 'thousands'. If the number to steal is more than what is available, the 'units' for example have to 'borrow' from the 'tens', etc. The children, who remembered and understood how many of each they represented, were able to see relationships between the subtraction incidents acted out and similar written problems in cartoon strips.

Others have shown how adults and peers working collaboratively with children can be useful also in facilitating their problem solving. For example, Perry and Simmons (1987) have shown that involving parents in shared-maths experiences can be just as successful as shared reading, and Tudge and Caruso (1988) are amongst a number of researchers who have emphasised the success of co-operative learning approaches.

These researchers examined the notion of cognitive conflict in situations where neither partner was an expert, but where both could develop from collaboration on a problem. Using a balance-beam problem, the researchers paired children according to their levels of rule sophistication. The results with both American and Russian children suggested similar conclusions. Children whose partner used a higher rule were influenced by this partner and such reasoning prevailed. Higher partners were influenced by lower rule partners and did worse than children who had never been paired. Tudge and Caruso conclude that merely pairing an expert child with a novice child provided insufficient motivation for the children to succeed at the problem-solving tasks presented. They found that such collaborative learning needed to be supplemented with opportunities for independent decision-making.

Clearly, with some children it is necessary to provide a variety of activities and experiences to facilitate their use of certain verbal expressions and their use and understanding of number concepts. With other children, merely providing for the emergence of verbal expressions and number concepts may be sufficient. All this is in addition to adults needing a thorough understanding of how young children think and try to solve problems in their own time, in their own way, and at their own rate.

SOME CONCLUSIONS

This chapter has stressed that children do their own problem solving when trusted to do so. This is only possible once they have been given the opportunity to develop the necessary language proficiency; the ability to generalise their own previously successful strategies; and are confident in their judgements, predictions and explanations which are resistant to change and alternative suggestions. It is also important for adults to:

- understand that children think and learn like children and do not see the world in the same way as adults
- be able to emphasise and give cues according to children's developmental levels
- structure appropriate activities and experiences to match what children know
- be able to tease out and encourage successful solutions and provide for reflection and practice
- be able to make certain adjustments and modifications to tasks
- provide motivating games and role play to enable children to make connections between language terms and symbols, and hands-on activities related to the problem-solving situations.

In a classroom climate where emphasis is placed on effort, and where all children are undifferentiated according to ability, and where they are expected to perform at an optimal level, irrespective of any individual differences in ability, it has been found that for the most part, children falsely adapt to these adult expectations. They know they are expected to perform at a similar level to their peers even though they know they are not so capable, and such children often resort to alternative behaviours which they know will attract the attention of their teachers, when they know they can't succeed as expected (Stevenson *et al.* 1985). Clearly, in such situations, the implications would be for teachers and parents to rethink about the capabilities of young children, who bring their own experiences to bear on the problems posed, and, who often cannot fit their explanations or their manipulations to the expectations of adults. The real need is for the development of learning partnerships which are attuned to the child's way of making sense of the world.

REFERENCES

Boulton-Lewis, G. M. and Tait, K. (1994) 'Young children's representations and strategies for addition', *British Journal of Educational Psychology* 64 (2): 231–42.

Brainerd, C. J. (1973) 'Judgements and explanations as criteria for the presence of cognitive structures', *Psychological Bulletin* 79 (3): 172–9.

Carraher, T., Carraher, D. and Schliemann, A. (1990) 'Mathematics in the streets and in schools', in V. Lee (ed.), *Children's Learning in School*, London: Hodder & Stoughton.

Cowen, R. and Foster, C. M. (1993) 'Encouraging children to count', *British Journal of Developmental Psychology* 11: 411–20.

Dahlberg, G. (1985) 'Context and the child's orientation to meaning', *Studies in Curriculum Theory and Cultural Reproduction*, 12, Stockholm: Institute of Education, Department of Educational Research.

Donaldson, M. (1978) *Children's Minds*, London: Fontana.

Durkin, K. (1993) 'The representation of number in infancy and early childhood', in C. Pratt and A. F. Garton (eds) *Systems of Representation in Children: Development and Use*, New York: John Wiley & Sons Ltd.

Elkind, D. (1988) 'The "miseducation" of young children', *Education Week*, October: 11–14.

Elkind, D. (1989) 'Handle with care: educating young children', *USA Today*, March: 66–8.

Evans, L. (1992) 'Robbing Peter to pay Paul: teaching subtraction through role play', *Education 3–13*: 48–53.

Fuson, K. C. (1988) *Children's Counting and Concepts of Number*, New York: Springer Verlag.

Gelman, R. and Gallistel, C. R. (1978) *The Child's Understanding of Number*, London: Harvard University Press.

Haylock, D. W. (1987) 'Towards numeracy', *Support for Learning* 2 (2): 13–17.

Haylock, D. W. (1991) *Teaching Mathematics to Low-Attainers*, London: Paul Chapman Publishers.

Hughes, M. (1986) *Children and Number Difficulties in Learning Mathematics*, Oxford: Basil Blackwell.

Inhelder, B., Sinclair, H. and Bovet, M. (1974) *Learning and the Development of Cognition*, London: Routledge & Kegan Paul.

McGarrigle, J. and Donaldson, M. (1974) 'Conservation accidents', *Cognition* 3: 341–50.

McGarrigle, J., Grieve, R. and Hughes, M. (1978) 'Interpreting inclusion: a contribution to the study of the child's cognitive and linguistic development', *Journal of Educational Psychology* 26: 528–50.

Perry, J. and Simmons K. (1987) ' "Shared maths": a successful home-school project', *Support for Learning* 2 (2): 9–12.

Piaget, J. (1970) *Science of Education and the Psychology of the Child*, New York: Viking.

Piaget, J. and Inhelder, B. (1969) 'Intellectual operations and their development', in P. Fraisse and J. Piaget (eds) *Experimental Psychology: Its Scope and Method*, vol. VII, *Intelligence*, London: Routledge & Kegan Paul.

Riem, R. (1985) *Children Learning to Count: A Social Psychological Reappraisal of Cognitive Theory*, unpublished Ph.D. dissertation, Canterbury: University of Kent.

Saxe, G. B., Guberman, S. R. and Gearhart, M. (1987) 'Social and developmental processes in children's understanding of number', *Monographs of the Society for Research in Child Development* 52 (5): 57–159.

Sharpe, P. J. (1979) 'The contribution of aspects of movement education to the cognitive development of infant school children', *Journal of Human Movement Studies*, 5: 125–40.

Sharpe, P. J. (1994) 'Children's responses to questions about transformations and their relationship to strategies used in problem solving', *International Journal of Early Years Education* 2 (3): 37–47.

Sharpe, P. J. (1995) 'A study of selected mismatch problems encountered by young children in number games', unpublished paper presented at the 8th Asian Workshop on Child and Adolescent Development, Singapore, June 1995.

Sinclair de Zwart, H. (1967) *Acquisition de Langage et Development de la Pensée*, Paris: Dunod.

Sinclair de Zwart, H. (1969), 'Developmental psycholinguistics', in D. Elkind and J. H. Flavell (eds) *Studies in Cognitive Development: Essays in Honour of Jean Piaget*, London: Oxford University Press.

Stevenson, H. W., Stigler, J. W., Lee, S.Y., Lucker, G. W., Kitamura, S. and Hsu, C. C. (1985) 'Cognitive achievement and academic achievement of Japanese, Chinese, and American children', *Child Development* 56: 718–34.

Tudge, J. and Caruso, D. (1988) 'Co-operative problem solving in the classroom: enhancing young children's cognitive development', *Young Children*, November: 46–52.

Wood, D. (1988) *How Children Think and Learn*, Oxford: Basil Blackwell.

Wood, D., Bruner, J. S. and Ross, G. (1976) 'The role of tutoring in problem solving', *Journal of Child Psychology and Psychiatry* 17: 89–100.

Chapter 10

IT, disability and the classroom
A case study

Ian Leech

On 24 November 1972 Daniel was born by caesarean section after a long and trouble-filled confinement. He was near death for some hours and very ill for many days. He showed all the classical symptoms of brain damage, all which proved accurate. Before his first birthday he had been diagnosed as suffering from Athetoid Cerebral Palsy. He would not be able to walk or talk and his arms and hands were in constant movement. His only controlled movement was foot placement.

We, his parents, were left without any knowledge of how all this trauma had affected his intellect. All we could do was wait and search for the milestones of childhood. Many never appeared, or were masked due to his disability. In many ways we were in a limbo of uncertainty, but with our training as teachers we set about enriching his experiences. He could not play normally so we had to provide the opportunities for him to explore the kitchen cupboards and make noises with the pots and pans, an activity that able bodied children would do naturally. Language was also enriched, and after the arrival of our second son, we were beginning to think Daniel might just be educable. He had a sociable look to his eyes, always turning to us for explanations of happenings. The first time he saw a half moon in the night sky, he scanned the rest of the sky for the other half. Before bed we played games involving the use of a Dick Bruna alphabetical frieze. 'Where's the O'? Eye scan soon picked out the octopus and so on.

There was, in our town, a small private nursery school run by the local Spastics Association. Daniel attended there, part-time at first and then full-time. The teachers quickly came to the same conclusions we had reached, that Daniel's brain damage had left his intellect unimpaired. He appeared to have normal intelligence which gave us some hope for his future. What did hurt was the discovery that in a school for disabled children, our son was the most physically disabled. Still he appeared to be making progress; he could put alphabetical bricks together to spell out simple words, and he could indicate his needs with eye pointing and other signals.

We were invited to see a demonstration of an electric typewriter (called PEK) from POSSUM. The expanded keyboard had a guard and the idea was to see if Daniel could use his toes. Off came his socks and he spelt out 'daniel leech'. The man from the suppliers was overjoyed. Daniel was only 2½ but he was far from satisfied. It transpired that no one had shown Daniel how to select upper and lower cases! That confirmed our hopes. We continued to enrich his learning at home while the teachers at the school set about teaching him to read. That in itself was a pedagogic miracle. As he had no speech, new methods of teaching him reading had to be put into place. Work done at school was continued at home in play situations. Communication between school and home was through a small book which was filled in each day, keeping school and home working with the same aims – a *very* important process!

A new machine appeared from POSSUM, this one had a large frame with the alphabet, numerals and other characters displayed in lines. A light shone behind the top left and this could be moved using two foot switches. On landing on a character, it was typed on an electric typewriter. Errors were left there, but Daniel could now read and write.

In 1978 I noticed an invitation in the local newspaper to the annual display put on by members of the Cheltenham Computer Club. I went along out of curiosity. What I saw there changed my life and Daniel's. I stood transfixed, watching some of the tricks these people were able to coax out of those very new devices. A man approached and asked me if I had any questions. I described Daniel's POSSUM screen used at school, and his disability. This man became very excited, took my telephone number and said he would be in touch.

Four weeks later he rang to invite me to his home. There he had rigged up some crude switches to an Acorn Atom (do you remember that?). Using only switches, he managed to write a limerick generated from a matrix of letters. I could see that this was the way to go but did not own a computer. He allowed Daniel to borrow his computer. The next job was to find switches Daniel could use. A visit to a local second-hand shop turned up some beauties, still in use today. They were double switches of a very heavy make-up, designed to be used with an industrial metal cutter. One switch closed the safety gate, the second started the cutter. These had to be rewired to be used independently of each other and mounted on a sloping wooden frame to allow foot control, Daniel's most accurate body movement. I was learning new skills. Daniel was soon creating script with the ability to rub out mistakes, but not able to word process yet. I ordered the brand new BBC model B and taught myself the Basic coding language. When the machine arrived I translated the Atom code to BBC Basic and eventually it worked.

In the mean time, Daniel had been placed in a Local Authority School for disabled pupils at the age of 6. I persuaded the school (eventually, after a demonstration of Daniel's home system) to buy a BBC computer. The program was copied and his teacher trained in its use. I even managed to buy some more double switches. This home/school co-operation proved to be invaluable.

I was then approached by the local teacher training college. They had employed a computer research assistant to develop aids for the disabled. He created a system which I regard as still the fastest way of selecting letters. An 8×8 matrix quartered by colour was displayed. Four switches, each representing one of the quarterings, were foot-mounted. Pressing the appropriate switch eliminated all but the desired quarter. The remaining 4×4 matrix was again quartered by colour and a further selection made. A final 2×2 matrix produced the character or control required. Some areas could produce further matrices. Just three presses of switches to gain the needed character! No waiting for scanning, so the system worked at optimal speed always. If this selection method could be used in the latest systems available today, it would be perfect. Daniel demonstrated the finished system (called QUASAR) at the NADEX exhibition in London's Earls Court where Lord Snowdon took particular interest.

Meanwhile the Warnock Report came out in 1980, followed closely by the 1981 Education Act which gave parents a major voice in the future education of their children. We immediately informed the Local Education Authority that we wanted Daniel considered for placement in a comprehensive school. We were backed by Daniel's school who regarded him as a very bright young man, but we were opposed by the LEA. Although they eventually acceded the legal points, they continued to drag their feet, resulting in Daniel's joining Bournside Comprehensive School half a term late, two weeks before his twelfth birthday. A BBC Master computer and teaching assistants were provided and his secondary schooling began. Success was immediate, gaining top marks for many subjects. The BBC Master computer and QUASAR served him well for two weeks. Then I discovered a ROM chip called ROMULATOR. This placed a scanning matrix within any mode-7 package. So it was perfect to use with Word-wise, which is a semi-commercial word processor. Yes, we lost the speed of the QUASAR selection but gained the use of a standard word processor with all its abilities to full editing. All in all a worthwhile swap. This program saw Daniel through GCSE (nine gained at C grade and above) and A-levels (two C grades). He only sat two subjects (English literature and sociology) owing to the slowness of his writing. The examination board were wonder-ful with their time allowances, but retrospectively, Daniel should have been using more modern technology. He spent hours com-pleting his papers and at the end of the exams was completely exhausted and had no desire to enter university. The level of academic achievement which Daniel attained was wholly due to the very forward-looking school in which he was placed. They liaised with his previous school and arranged visits for staff and children so that transition between the two schools would be smooth. We were consulted at all stages and were able to contact a named teacher at any time. The teacher/helper who was in place became a close family friend. Again an example of the importance of the home–school relationship.

In the mean time POSSUM took over our home for three days and fitted the house with computer controls. Most of the power points can be controlled from one of three screens sited in differ-ent rooms. The front door can be answered and opened, and Daniel has control of his hi-fi and can change channels on his TV – in fact has full 'remote' control. He can also call us from any room in the house.

After a long rest on leaving school, Daniel put himself on a course to learn Desk Top Publishing techniques. He was placed with the Countryside Commission headquarters in Cheltenham where he revamped their large guide to services; a major publication that went out to many other organisations and universities.

I won a 486 (20 SX) PC computer in an exhibition in London and we got in touch with an American software house. Their new (but very expensive) programs (called EZI KEYS and Scanning WSKI) are wonderful and point the way to the future. Scanning is still used but, coupling a portable computer to the desktop computer, Daniel can now select characters using the latest ideas from the USA (available from Cambridge Adaptive Communications). The screen layout looks like this:

Table A					
a	e	i	o	u	q
t	n	d	m	y	b
r	h	c	g	w	k
s	l	f	p	v	j
1	2	3	4	5	6
x	z	_	.	,	'
		s̄h̄	ct	al	X
-	#	F	¶	M

To the right of Table A appears the fast select section:

Table B
1: a
2: I
3: the
4: to
5: in
6: you

In to Table A, the top 4 rows and row 6 select what is shown. Row 5 selects words from Table B. These words are constantly changing. Other functions such as SHIFT (sh) can be utilised from remaining rows and characters, including access to further matrices. The system makes an attempt to guess the word required by displaying words at the side of the scanning matrix.

An example will illustrate the system. If Daniel wants the word 'ILLUSTRATION' he selects 'I'. The following table is displayed:

```
1: I
2: if
3: in

4: is
5: isn't
6: it
```

He now selects 'I' and the offered words change to:

```
1: ill
2: illness
3: illustrate

4: illustration
5: illusion
6: illustrious
```

these being the six most used 'il' words. He now selects '4' from
the matrix and the word is implanted in whatever document is
being run on the desktop computer. The two computers (portable,
running the switch system, and the desk top running any commercial program) are serially linked together and information
is passed, using a program called TTAM (Trace Transferable
Access Module) copyright, to the Trace company in America
(again from CAC). However, the ingenuity does not stop there.
Having selected 'ILLUSTRATION', the system, having been used
for some time, has learned from the user. It has coupled the word
to the last six times that word was used and therefore can offer
another six words which may be required. In this case it displays:

```
1: of
2: by
3: which

4: you
5: to
6: the
```

It is often possible to weave your way through the network of a
complex sentence using numbers only. Notice the second three
are slightly separated from the first three. Research has shown

that this speeds up recognition. All the keys of the PC are accessible from these matrices. Although 6 × 8 (48) is not large enough to
cover all keyboard characters, other depths are accessed to utilise
'f' keys and the control keys.

So now Daniel had full access to the keyboard of his PC but he
still had no ability to use a mouse. There are systems that use
switches to access up, down, left and right, but they are slow,
cumbersome and inaccurate. So we obtained a very large tracker-
ball taken out of an Air Traffic Control System. This worked as if a
mouse was being used. Daniel could not use *double click* even
when slowed up so we provided a second *click* button that sent a
double pulse; and then a third *click* button that stayed down
when pressed and then was released on the second press. This
provided him with a *drag* button. Just to give him more power
than the ordinary mouse user has, two more buttons were fitted.
One that disabled the 'x-axis' and one which disabled the 'y-axis'.
This positive discrimination proves invaluable to the accurate
placement of items. His future needs are access to middle and
right Microsoft mouse buttons.

A local firm donated an older 386 computer which he uses
simply for mass storage of files as he cannot change floppies. The
backing-up of files has to be done when I get home from work.
This Bull computer is serially linked to the main desktop and uses
Laplink to pass files back and forth. Other additions have been a
faster 486 (60DX2), multi-media along with CD-ROM capability, a
top of the range printer (Hewlett Packard Laserjet III Si) which
prints at 16 pages per minute and has a superb output, a Panasonic
flat bed scanner to copy illustrations and an Amstrad FX6000AT
fax/answer telephone which also allows photocopying.

Using the same software, with the addition of a speech capability, a laptop computer is mounted on a wheelchair. The screen is
mounted to the front, with the main part box-mounted on the
rear. Power was brought up from batteries placed under the seat,
complete with charging sockets. A switch was attached to a foot
plate and Daniel now has a voice. It's the same set-up as used by
Dr Steven Hawking and used in the famous BT advertisement
and supplied by Cambridge Adaptive Communications. It also
allows Daniel to use a simple word processor (called Bank Street
Writer) when he is away from his main system. This is an excellent word processor and he can save work which can later be
loaded into Ami Pro for further refinement.

So he was set up with a lovely system but what was he going to do with it? He decided he wanted to run a small desktop publishing business from home. Bank accounts were set up and a family conference decided on Footprint as his trading name. On 4 May 1992 Footprint went into business. The original idea was simple headed notepaper, but it has grown ever since. Leaflets, business cards, wedding stationery, advertising materials, logos and posters are just some of the areas Footprint now deals with. He has Ventura, Ami Pro and CorelDraw 2 and recently he bought CorelDraw 4 complete with CD-ROM capabilities.

This historical perspective could now be viewed as a help to educationalists facing a very disabled person in their class. I am convinced that this sort of success story is not always possible without other, more important qualities being present. Daniel is intelligent, single-minded, determined and mature. He has confidence, drive and is totally self-motivated. His sense of humour and lack of self-pity have all come together along with some far-seeing educators. Also he was lucky in being at the start of the application of the 1981 Education Act. As with all Acts of Parliament, momentum is at its greatest at the beginning. Being one of the first brings with it a determination that placements and experiments will work despite any short-comings. Of course this is offset by the gaining of experience by mainstream teachers who are now better placed to deal with the complexities of disabilities. I had the feeling that Daniel's secondary school was rather proud of him. Young people themselves are far more accepting than many adults and there is a general air of disgust at any attempt to display prejudice against people with any form of disability. Society, through various means has laid down the groundwork towards a much more acceptable future for the handicapped but complacency must not set in. They can, and some will, contribute their best and in doing so will enrich us all.

My advice to any school wishing to give of their best to future Daniels is never to accept yesterday's technology as we did at one point. Always look at the fastest machines, the largest memory systems and try to keep up to date with what is happening in the software market. Innovations undreamed of by us now will allow speed of input to become ever closer to that used by the able bodied, and one day even surpass them. Only then will everybody be using the same system and there will be no differences between the disabled and the able bodied.

However, there are other disabilities which require different approaches. Learning disabilities as opposed to access problems are hard to cope with but computer technology can support the learner to a greater or lesser degree. Recent improvements in software and hardware allow youngsters to carry their own laptop computer into a lesson and take accurate notes using software systems that aid such problems as dyslexia – which regular word processing users out there have not fallen slightly in love with their spell-checker?, even starting from a very low spelling ability which will often fool the spell checker. How do I spell 'belief'? OK try 'beleef', then press ALT-W (using Bank Street Writer), and the answer comes up in a drop-down menu.

Even blind children can be mainstreamed. Consider a system that, through earphones, speaks the individual letters as they are typed in, then the last word when a space is detected, and finally the last sentence when the full stop is in place. Of course, the child has to be taught touch-typing. I have had the extreme pleasure of watching a blind child take notes in a geography lesson in a local comprehensive school using this type of software (available from The Foundation for Communication for the Disabled). With some small adaptation, this program can easily be used with the aphasic (non-speaking) pupil. Liberator not only supply portable kits for aphasics, but run excellent training weekends for users and helpers.

Above all there has to be a strong working partnership between client, school, LEA (if appropriate in these days of opting out) and people who are well versed in the application of computer technology for the disabled. Daniel was lucky again, as in the early days I worked on the same campus of special schools in Gloucester. When he was placed in his secondary school, again I worked on the same campus in Cheltenham. I was on hand when machines started to go wrong. The partnership between school and parent was very strong and extremely practical. It was not just a consultative relationship. Both schools recognised that they needed my help as the technology was in its infancy and neither school had IT expertise in place. We needed their help to a much greater degree than parents of able bodied children. Having a second son (who went to the same secondary school as Daniel) we realised early on that the partnership is two-way in both cases, but is more than just a positive thing when dealing with the disabled, a placement can stand or fall by the structure of that relationship. Homework has to be done and the need was more than the home providing a kitchen table and peace and quiet to do homework. The school technology had to be duplicated at home.

If the reader is starting out from the beginning, then consult the small list at the end of this chapter. Consider contacting NCET in the first instance. Some LEAs still have an advisory teacher for IT who has expertise in the field of disability. This partnership will be vital for the success of integration. Perhaps one day we will be talking about non-segregation instead of integration and our children who have disabilities can have them addressed within the mainstream classroom, can grow up and mature alongside their peers, and society will no longer regard them as something separate. Access to jobs, transport buildings and housing will be regarded as the right of all, not just a concession that fails because of lack of funding. Financing problems always leads to the most vulnerable suffering. Authorities who are capped by central government always have to consider concessionary rights as a rich seam to cut into, to balance their books, as the disabled have been badly protected in law.

USEFUL ADDRESSES

General information

NCET, Milburn Road, Science Park, Coventry CV4 7JJ. Tel.: (01203) 416994.

Assessment and access advice

The National Federation of Access Centres, Bramston Crescent, Pile Hill Road, Coventry CV4 9SW.
CENMAC, Charlton Park School, Charlton Park Road, London SE7 8HX. Tel.: (0181) 3167589.
The Wolfson Centre, Mecklenburgh Square, London, WC1N 2AP. Tel.: (0171) 8377618.
ACE Centre, Ormerod School, Waynflete Road, Headington, Oxford OX3 8DD. Tel.: (01865) 63508.
ACE/ACCESS Centre, Broadbent Place, Oldham, Lancs. OL1 4HU. Tel.: (0161) 6271358.
The CALL Centre, 4 Buccleuch Place, Edinburgh EH8 9CW. Tel.: (0131) 6671438.

Suppliers

Widget Software, 102 Radford Road, Leamington Spa CV31 1LF. Tel.: (01926) 885303.

The Foundation for Communication for the Disabled, 25 High Street, Woking, Surrey GU21 1BW. Tel.: (01483) 727848.

The Concept Keyboard Company, Moorside Road, Winnall Industrial Estate, Winchester, Hants SO23 7RX. Tel.: (01962) 550391.

Liberator Ltd (speech enablers), Whitegates, Swinstead, Lincs. NG33 4PA. Tel.: (01476) 550391.

Quest Enabling Designs Ltd (switches), Ability House, 242 Gosport Road, Fareham, Hants PO16 0SS. Tel.: (01329) 828444.

Research Machines PLC (computers), New Mill House, 183 Milton Park, Abingdon OX14 4SE. Tel.: (01905) 754577.

Cambridge Adaptive Communications, The Mount, Toft, Cambridge CB3 7RL. Tel.: (01223) 264244.

Part V

Whole-school approaches

Part V looks at ways in which schools, as institutions, can pay more attention to the opinions of, and encourage more active involvement by, pupils. Malcolm Hanson discusses the way in which pupils can be encouraged to take more control of their own behaviour through the use of self-monitoring schemes. He presents a detailed account of a self-monitoring scheme which is used with pupils in his own school and discusses its implementation through the use of case studies. Paul Cooper considers the active participation of pupils in the government of schools, and their participation on committees and councils. Despite the fact that legislation sometimes militates against full involvement, he discusses ways in which pupil involvement in decision-making can enhance a sense of community and, in so doing, improve conditions for learning. This theme is then taken up by Philip Garner who recommends ways in which pupils can assume roles in auditing school ethos and determining behaviour (and other) policies within schools.

Chapter 11

Self-management through self-monitoring

Malcolm Hanson

The aim of this chapter is to consider the value of self-monitoring schemes which help pupils to have better control of their own progress. In order to achieve this I will refer to work currently being undertaken within an LEA-controlled Boys' Special School, where I am at present employed.

Allington Boys' School is a school for secondary aged (11–16) students who are considered to have a range of emotional and behavioural disorders. The school is situated on the western out-skirts of a large market town; however, the catchment area for the students is countywide. The school is funded for up to seventy-five boys of whom 25 per cent are residential for the duration of the school week, returning to their homes at weekends. The remainder of the boys are brought in daily by taxi or bus.

The school operates (where possible) teaching groups within the DfE guidelines of one teacher to eight students. Classes are supported by Educational Welfare Assistants (EWOs) and Residential Child Care Officers (RCCOs), all of whom form an integral part of the Behaviour Management Programme.

The school operates a prescriptive Behaviour Management Programme which is allied closely to Assertive Discipline (Cantor and Cantor 1992). The principal feature of the model employed at Allington is the tenet that what can most constructively be done for troubled and troublesome children is to teach them a more appropriate range of responses and skills than they are currently using. Fundamental to the approach is the assumption that most behaviour is learnt and, therefore, can be unlearnt. The school places its main emphasis on the introduction of alternative be-haviours which are better reinforced than the inappropriate be-haviours. This also requires the reduction of those 'reinforcers' which have sustained the inappropriate behaviour. The establishment of clear observable, individual or group objectives which give definition to desired behaviours is an important element in behaviourist programmes. Allington School makes extensive use of individual objectives to provide both precision and focus. The use of explicit behaviour criteria, a token economy, and related methods of recording aspects of pupil behaviour brings a high degree of objectivity to the measurement of change in the pupils' responses.

The assumption is made that any boy who is recommended for admission to Allington School has ceased to behave in a controlled way, within the mainstream school environment. It is the re-establishment of an appropriate level of self-control which is the principal objective of this policy. Initially, control is imposed externally; it is hoped that this will steadily reduce as the pupil regains the motivation of self-direction to the point where control is little more than adult guidance (the handing over of control from teacher to pupil is discussed in more detail by Jones, Charlton and Whittern in Chapter 14).

The aim of Allington's Behaviour Management Programme is twofold. At an organisational level it seeks to ensure that the school provides a safe and secure environment and a calm atmosphere in which the students have freedom and opportunity to learn. On an individual basis the programme seeks to provide students with a structure which will encourage them to reflect on their behaviour and, where appropriate, to adopt alternative behaviour strategies in order that they should be able to develop more acceptable social interaction skills.

The school makes four demands of all the students which are held as fundamental to the establishment and maintenance of a well-ordered school. Students are expected to follow the four rules of respect:

1 to respect and be courteous to all adults;
2 to respect and be courteous towards fellow pupils;
3 to respect and be considerate in their use of school property;
4 to respect themselves.

These expectations are also made of all adults who work in the school.

Central to the school's behaviour modification approach is the notion that *all actions have consequences*. This statement is open to both positive and negative interpretation. The emphasis in the school must be focused predominantly on the maximum reinforcement of all positive actions. Success, even at relatively small gains, is acknowledged and valued. It is considered inappropriate that most negative behaviour produced by pupils should be dealt with through disapproval or being ignored.

The effectiveness of the school's programme is dependent on students perceiving the rewards within the system as being worth while. The need to provide motivation is recognised within the structure. Much of the success in effecting significant change is dependent on the value pupils put on the motivators offered. Since this value changes relatively quickly, a degree of responsiveness to fashion is a necessary component of the overall response.

The principal task in managing the behaviour of students is to establish effective control while at the same time encouraging pupils towards the development of *self-regulation*. The system operated within Allington is organised within three levels, each reflecting pupils' increasing ability to take more responsibility for their own behaviour.

The programme recognises that the individual should serve as his own agent of behaviour change. This notion is also discussed by Temple in Chapter 5 and by Clarizio and McCoy (1983: 572), who note that the 'shift away from reinforcement by others and towards reinforcement by self is central to the child's shift from dependence to independence'.

As stated initially, the aim of this chapter is to look at the constructive use of self-management skills, with a particular emphasis on self-monitoring schemes, including the use of on-report systems. Many of the students at Allington School who present emotional and behavioural disorders lack the personal and social skills to cope with stressful situations. Life Skills and Personal and Social Education programmes are intended to address many of the issues pertinent to the needs of the students. Systems of self-recording and self-monitoring are closely related to the social skills and Behaviour Management Programmes, and are considered to be an extension of behaviour management techniques and can be focused on a targeted behaviour according to individual needs, and form a part of the continuum towards independence and self-regulation.

Topping (1983) describes the on-report process as a system which is utilised by many secondary schools. Disruptive pupils are required to collect signatures and comments of every class teacher on a card during each day. These are then checked, at regular intervals, by a designated person, usually a senior teacher. Parents are also encouraged to take part in this process. Some students will be expected to take home their card which will be signed by their parents before returning it. This method is advocated by Topping (1983) who suggests that in some cases parents may be asked 'to apply domestic rewards and punishments on the basis of the report' (p. 117).

Allington School has utilised the on-report system to facilitate an in-built framework of token/point awards which form a fundamental part of the Behaviour Management Programme. The principal task in managing the behaviour of students is to establish effective external control while at the same time encouraging students towards the development of self-regulation. The system practised at Allington is organised on three levels, each reflecting the pupils' increasing ability to be independent of external factors.

All pupils enter the school at Level One. Since only pupils who have displayed significant behaviour problems are admitted to the school, the assumption is made that all new pupils are unlikely to be reliable, or trustworthy, at first. This assumption establishes a clear starting point. This seeks to be consistent with the school's emphasis on positive progress – the only way a pupil can move in terms of reliability and trustworthiness is forward. Central to the Level One programme is the achievement of Baseline Behaviour Criteria (Figure 1).

A report card system is used to record positive engagement in the school process. The points/tokens awarded during each lesson are used as a main source of objective information to support the working of the criteria. Students are able to gain up to 20 points during a day, these are awarded for behaviour/social skills which have been previously defined as target behaviour. Each pupil carries a report card with him between lessons. While I believe it inappropriate to expand too much on the Assertive Discipline Programme (Cantor and Cantor 1992), which serves to give teachers a range of skills for managing classroom behaviour, it should be noted that it is used to ensure consistency in awarding points. A point is not awarded if the pupil has displayed inappropriate behaviour and has chosen to ignore three warnings given by the teacher or supervising adult. The first warning lets

Baseline behaviour criteria

1 Have you attended school punctually every day?
2 Have you remained within the school boundaries?
3 Has your behaviour endangered yourself or anyone else? This includes having in your possession prohibited materials?
4 Has your self-control of your behaviour been sufficient so that no adult has needed to control you physically?
5 Have you avoided using threatening language or violent actions?

You must be able to answer 'yes' to the above questions for 30 consecutive days

6 Have you remained within the immediate care and supervision of staff?
7 Have you remained within the bounds of acceptable behaviour?
8 Has your use of language been acceptable and respectful?
9 Have you earned 80 token points in each five-day period?
10 Have you earned 16 uniform, lunch and break points in each five-day period?

You must answer 'yes' to questions 6 to 10 for 20 consecutive days

11 Have you carried out a job of responsibility in the correct manner for 15 consecutive days?

If you are able to answer yes to all the questions above, then you have met the basic School Conduct Criteria and should be ready to take on more responsibility.
  This will mean that you will be trusted to behave more sensibly in many situations without close staff supervision. Remember, an increase in freedom and privileges also means an increase in duties and responsibilities.

Figure 1 Baseline behavioural criteria – level one

the student know that the behaviour has been noted; the second warning informs the student that behaviour has consequences, this is the time to make a choice; the third warning tells the student that he has run out of options, and will not achieve his point. The report card is used to record the reason for the pupil's failure to achieve his point(s), this way individual behaviour objectives can be monitored.

  Unlike the traditional 'House Point System' familiar to many of us, the report system is designed to be positive. Points awarded to a student are recognised as student achievement, and under no circumstances can be removed for any breach of the behaviour code.

At the end of each day, or at a time deemed appropriate by the supervising adult, class groups are brought together in small meetings to review their individual cards. The focus of these 'meetings' is to encourage pupils to participate in honest self-appraisal of their actions and re-actions. This aspect of the programme can initially be extremely difficult for some students who find honest self-reflection a stressful issue. However, it is maintained that little true progress in terms of promoting adjustment in social interaction will be achieved without pupils taking on responsibility for their own actions. Rogers (1994) suggests that the techniques of 'mirroring' and 'picture cueing' might help pupils to understand and appreciate the significance of their own behaviours (see Chapter 14).

It is not unknown for some students to fail to acknowledge their levels of inappropriate behaviour or their level of achievement. The report card system, and the recording of comments, again provides material evidence which the teacher or supervising adult can use for discussion with the individual students.

As with any token economy/report system the points must lead to a tangible reward. The importance of this has already been stated. At Allington the Friday afternoon timetable is dedicated to Enrichment Activities. Students are expected to achieve a 70 per cent points threshold during each week. Points over and above this threshold are used to gain access to a wide range of activities. These activities include swimming, roller disco, mountain biking, supervised use of the school's motor bikes, model soldiers, video making. Some students just prefer a quiet walk, with a listening adult, around the school grounds or into the town. For those pupils who do not achieve the 70 per cent threshold, it is recognised that their level of behaviour has been inappropriate and unacceptable. These students continue an academic timetable.

The report card system is further extended when a pupil has been identified as someone who is meeting the Baseline Behaviour Criteria (Figure 1), and has been recommended for progress to Level Two of the Behaviour Management Programme. The initial stages of the report card system are aimed at helping students to achieve consistency, stability and trustworthiness. Once this has been demonstrated and there is evidence that they are capable of sustaining these qualities, it is considered appropriate that they should have the opportunity to test and widen their skills further in a more open atmosphere. Before achieving this, a secondary report card is issued. This is a simple tick sheet that is completed by the student and teacher/supervising adult. The 'ticks' or 'positive marks' reflect achievement of the Baseline Behaviour Criteria. Once this sheet has been completed satisfactorily the student's move to Level Two is facilitated.

Throughout the Level One programme, emphasis is placed on responsibility. Each student is responsible for his report card. If he is unable to produce the card or he destroys it the point is not recorded. This will effectively limit access to activities and progress to Level Two. Students are frequently reminded that behaviour has consequences; this includes failure to produce the report card.

The Allington School system seeks to minimise the notion of punishment in its response to negative behaviours. Much inappropriate behaviour is essentially ignored. However, as pupils progress, the range of opportunities available needs to be significantly increased, while the level of supervision is reduced.

Membership of Level Two is designed to encompass personal and social skills as well as educational requirements. Throughout their time within Level Two the student remains 'on-report'. The Level Two report card has been designed to reflect the extended responsibility and a new Behaviour Baseline Criteria (Figure 2). Points/tokens are substituted for credits and the record card reflects both behaviour and output.

There is also the introduction of a system of discretionary awards and sanctions. Information from the report cards is transferred to a 'status board' in the staff room. This ensures that information is circulated to all staff, thus supporting consistency. The process by which points are awarded is explained within the Level Two Baseline Behaviour Criteria (Figure 2), I therefore do not intend to expand on that any further. However, it should be noted that the principle *that behaviour has consequences* is continued throughout Level Two. Coloured pins or 'spots' on the record card indicate negative behaviour. Unlike Level One, credit balances are reduced when pins are awarded. The amount of credits deducted is consistent with the colour of the pin or spot. A negative credit balance will in the first instance result in the student being placed on a 'special programme' aimed at helping him sustain his membership of Level Two. This involves, once again, the use of an 'on-report' system. Responsibility is placed on the student, while the teacher/supervising adult uses the card to record information about the student's response to the 'special programme'. A review is carried out after one or two weeks. A student who has failed to respond is then returned to Level One.

Baseline behaviour criteria – level two

1 Education
You are required to remain 'on target' in education both in terms of Behaviour and Output. Full engagement in the educational activity of the lesson is an expectation. This target is achieved by scoring a weekly total in excess of 90 points for both Behaviour and Output scores. An acceptable level of performance must be maintained for 4 out of every 5 weeks to remain on target.

There is no requirement that Group 2 pupils will undertake homework. It will, however, be provided if it is requested and collected. Satisfactory completion of each piece of homework will be rewarded.

2 Negative interference
You must avoid negative interference in the programmes of other boys for at least 4 out of every 5 weeks. This means you are expected to prove that you can now control impetuous, aggressive and socially inappropriate behaviours. Young people who continue to engage in intimidation of any form, provocation (trouble stirring), disruption of group sessions, gossip, or any unkindness cannot expect to receive the benefits of group membership.

You will be considered to have been involved in 'negative interference' if the Level 2 director or deputy director receives information that results in the award of an amber or red pin as a result of your attitude or conduct towards other boys. Every effort will be made to help you ensure that your behaviour remains within appropriate boundaries.

3 Self-help skills
During your normal lessons and especially during some of your tutor time, you will be taught some of the skills and knowledge you need, to be able to look after yourself safely and properly.

There are eight components of the self-help syllabus. The Group 2 Director will organise a programme that will deal with one of these topics every two weeks. During the last teaching session in each block, a small test will be given to check that some understanding of the topic has been retained. To remain 'on target', a score in excess of 40 per cent must be achieved in all tests taken.

Self-help syllabus

A Electricity

1 Wire a plug
2 Use and selection of fuses
3 Change bulbs

B First aid

1 A.B.C. (resuscitation)
2 Burns, Scalds, Shock
3 Wounds

C Sewing skills

1 Sew buttons
2 Sew hems
3 Sew tear

D Laundering

1 Use washing machine
    Handwash
2 Fabric care – including interpretation
    about garment care from label
3 Ironing

E Survival

1 Planning a meal
2 Budgeting and buying
3 Cooking a meal – using the oven

F Road safety

1 Highway code
2 Safe riding

G Personal care

1 Basic hygiene
2 Healthy living

H Public transport

1 Reading timetables
2 Personal transport

Where it is possible to arrange it, pupils in years 10 and 11 will be expected to demonstrate their practical ability in arranging their own journey to and from school. It is recognised that this is unlikely to be organisationally possible for all pupils.

Rewards and sanctions
Pupils' positive efforts and success are recognised through the use of a credit system which is the principal objective means by which continuing success can be gauged. The main means by which pupils can earn credits are outlined below. Promotion to Group 2 earns an immediate 20 credits.

	Credits
Weekly school card score in excess of 100 points for both Output and Behaviour	3
Weekly school card score in excess of 120 points for both Output and Behaviour	5
Award of 20 Gold slips in a 10-day period	2
Satisfactory completion of each piece of homework	1

The completion of each phase of the Group 2 Criteria will also be recognised with Credits:

Remaining on target in education for 4 out of 5 weeks	3
Avoiding negative interference for 4 out of 5 weeks	3
Successful completion of each module of the self-help programme	1

Discretionary awards
Any adult may make a recommendation to the Group 2 Director that a specific positive action should be recognised. Credits will only be awarded by the Director or Deputy Director.

Negative behaviour is monitored through the use of a 'status' board which, through the use of coloured pins, is a visual reminder to pupils of the consequences of their behaviour. Different coloured pins signify different levels of inappropriate behaviour. The placing of a pin on the board has the effect of deducting credits, each colour having a different value.

Blue pins are used to signify a relatively minor transgression and constitute no more than a warning. They remain on the board for five school days. Each blue pin removes one credit. Should three blue pins be accumulated within the five-day period, they are exchanged for an amber pin. An amber pin may be placed directly for any behaviour covered in questions 6–8 in the Basic Behaviour Criteria (see Figure 1). Six credits will be removed when an Amber pin is awarded. The placing of an amber pin is accompanied by a reduction in the freedom of operation for that pupil which remains in force for five teaching days. The accumulation of two amber pins within this period will result in a red pin being placed.

A red pin will be placed directly for the following reasons:

• each day of unexcused absence
• conduct which requires staff to intervene physically
• gross misconduct such as bullying or unprovoked assault

- possession of any dangerous materials
- unauthorised absence from the school site

A red pin remains in force for 10 school days during which time pupils will not be able to participate in any out-of-school activity which would normally be available to them.

Group 1 pupils. The Group 2 Director will on the placing of a red pin alert the Senior Tutor. The first red pin will lead to the removal of 10 credits. Should another red pin be placed within 10 school days, 15 credits will be removed. Further red pins within 10 school days of the second red will result in the removal of 20 credits.

When a pupil has no remaining credits, he will be returned to Level One. On the third day, following the return to Level One, the Senior Tutor will make a single attempt to draw up a contract for a quick return to Group 2.

Progression to Level 3
Meet Education Criteria for 15 weeks – treated as three batches of five weeks.

Avoid Negative Interference for 15 weeks – treated as three batches of five weeks.

Pass self-help skills in at least six of the syllabus components.

Transfer to Level Three will take place when the above criteria have been met and a credit balance in excess of 75 credits has been achieved.

Figure 2 Baseline behaviour criteria – level two

A central part of the Level Two Criteria is a Life Skills/Self-Help Programme. Time is set aside for the Level Two students to work on aspects of this work which are outlined in Figure 2. This may be carried out by a range of supervising adults, and for the residential pupils this may be carried out outside of the school day. It is therefore essential that the report card system provides information of student progress in this field. Information can then be transferred to the 'Status Board'.

Level Two students enjoy greater freedom and responsibility within the school. They also experience a wider range of enrichment activities. Once a student has achieved the Behaviour Baseline Criteria – Level Two, then progress to Level Three can be accomplished. Once this has been achieved the report card system is suspended. It is acknowledged that a student who has achieved this status has shown that he is capable of fulfilling the expectations of the Behaviour Management Programme. Such achievement opens the door, where appropriate, to return to mainstream education.

SELF-MONITORING PROGRAMMES

It is not unusual for students familiar with the 'on-report' programme to request an alternative strategy to the report system. For some students, self-monitoring is a natural progression towards independence. These students recognise that they have a particular behaviour problem and want to do something about it. This may be the result of self-recognition or it may come from one-to-one supervision. At Allington it is not unusual for a problem to have been identified within the daily group sessions described in the previous section. Such behaviours tend to be covert like swearing, smoking, inappropriate touching, talking out of turn, or inappropriate noises such as 'burping'.

Self-monitoring in the form of self-recording is also a strategy available to teachers and other supervising adults such as Residential Child Care Officers who are involved in the preparation of Individual Behaviour Plans or Care Plans. Self-recording is of little, or no, benefit unless the student becomes an agent of his own change, and uses the information recorded to facilitate that change. Meichenbaum and Burland (1979) studied the technique of self-recording and found that it was not unusual to find students observing, instructing, rewarding and punishing themselves in an attempt to modify their own behaviour. They indicated that behaviourists have studied and scientific support for self-management techniques.

Central to the use of self-recording techniques is planning. Techniques have to be devised to facilitate the transfer of control from the external agency (the teacher) to the student himself. Part of the ethos of Allington School is the continuing development of relationships between the student and the supervising adults (teachers as well as other staff). The ability to have regular one-to-one sessions provides for the development of both individual and corporate support during the planning stages.

Herbert (1981) suggests that before a child can be taught to reinforce himself for a behaviour pattern he must learn to evaluate his behaviour correctly. In the initial stages of the self-monitoring process, the student at Allington School is helped to judge the level of his own behaviour by collecting baseline information. This is intended to help the student to evaluate the extent of the problem. This information is then used to set a standard by which he can measure the change in his behaviour. Initial discussions will involve the establishment of the method by which baseline information is collected, the need for accurate data, and the building-in of a checking process to ensure accuracy.

CONRAD

Conrad is an extremely difficult 14-year-old. His behaviours are usually attention-seeking and frequently aimed at those who help him the most. Female teachers in particular are the focus of extreme sexual innuendo. Despite extensive counselling there has been little or no improvement in Conrad's behaviour. He is, however, aware of the gravity of the problem.

Following a brief period of exclusion, Conrad expressed sincere concerns about the way he hurt certain teachers on whom he relied for support. He also expressed a wish to do something about it but did not know what he could do. He relied on his own behaviour to draw attention to himself and for personal kudos within the class group. After establishing that Conrad genuinely wanted to improve his behaviour, and his relationships with adults within the school, it was agreed that he would use a blank timetable sheet on which he would collect baseline information. Using each lesson sector, he would record each time he made an inappropriate comment towards a supervising adult. Ticks would be used. Conrad agreed to the support of all the adults he would be in contact with. They in turn were asked to keep a similar record of inappropriate remarks. This data would serve to cross-check Conrad's record. The aim of this was to promote accurate recording.

After one week (25 teaching periods) Conrad's sheet was checked by myself and discussed during a one-to-one session. Conrad's record showed a surprisingly high level of accuracy, suggesting his willingness to want to succeed. The information provided was used to look at the following:

1 The number of occurrences of the usage of inappropriate comments in a one-week period.
2 The average number of occurrences of the use of inappropriate comment per lesson.
3 The average number of occurrences of the use of inappropriate comment during the morning.
4 The average number of occurrences of the use of inappropriate comment during the afternoon.
5 With which teacher did the highest number of occurrences of the use of inappropriate comment take place.
6 With which teacher did the lowest number of occurrences of the use of inappropriate comment take place.

It was agreed between Conrad and myself that in order to use this information effectively there was a need for a second period of data collecting. While this was accepted, I was aware that to prolong the baseline process beyond one more week was likely to result in the client, Conrad, losing interest. However, after one more week it became evident in discussion that there had been an increased level of self-awareness by Conrad brought about by the self-monitoring process.

At the end of the second week, a further analysis of the information collected took place. The self-recorded information provided the following baseline data:

1 During a 25-period week Conrad used inappropriate sexual innuendo/comments on 124 occasions.
2 The average number of occasions during any given teaching period Conrad used such comments was 4.96.
3 The evidence suggested that Conrad was more likely to use inappropriate comments first thing in the morning, and again immediately after lunch. There were an average of 9 occurrences during the first teaching period of each day and 7 occurrences during period five which commenced at 1.30 p.m.
4 The above data also coincided with the time that Conrad was with his class tutor, Mrs 'Y'.

Using this information, Conrad and I worked out a programme to reduce this behaviour. Planning is again fundamental to the process. Behaviour cannot be eliminated completely using the baseline information. The data tell us the frequency with which it occurs and when it is most likely to occur. The initial planning involves reducing the behaviour, not extinguishing it completely. Once this principle has been agreed with the student then planning the 'how' becomes the focus of the programme. It is crucial that the planning at this stage engages the student in a rewards system. Behaviour has consequences, positive behaviour requires positive consequences. Herbert (1981) suggests that the child should be encouraged to reward himself either covertly by engaging in positive self-thoughts, or recording positive self-statements; or overtly by indulging in a favourite activity.

In the first instance it was agreed that Conrad should attempt to reduce his behaviour by 30 per cent during the first week. This was explained to him in simplistic terms, a lesson where he had an average baseline score of 10 should be reduced to 7 or less. Where the behaviour frequency was 6, then a score of 4 or less was required.

Conrad continued to self-record his behaviour. At the end of each lesson he checked his score against the teacher's record for accuracy. If Conrad had achieved his target behaviour he was awarded with a 'special token'. Once he had collected five tokens he became entitled to fifteen minutes of uninterrupted time on a games computer which was in one of the residential houses.

Conrad understood that a programme which offered consequences for positive behaviour must also offer consequences for negative behaviour. Again, during discussions between Conrad and myself, we were able to fix appropriate sanctions if he failed to achieve his new baseline target. Failure to collect a token in a lesson would reflect a high level of inappropriate behaviour. The sanction for this would be a five-minute period of supervised detention at the end of each day. During this time Conrad would be expected to complete an academic task. Failure to collect three tokens in any one day would lead to a fifteen-minute detention and so on.

At the end of the first week, the programme was evaluated. Conrad had achieved 75 per cent of his target behaviour. His recording had been honest and teachers acknowledged that there had been an improvement. During week two a decrease of 50 per cent of the original baseline behaviour was planned using the same criteria. A dispute in the playground which subsequently spilled over into the classroom resulted in the programme temporarily breaking down. However, some counselling helped

Conrad to understand how much he had achieved and he was continuing to achieve. Conrad's new-found self-awareness helped him to acknowledge the better relationships he was establishing with teachers. It was agreed to extend the week two criteria by a further week, before aiming for a 75 per cent reduction of original baseline behaviour.

It is true to say that Conrad's use of inappropriate sexual innuendo has never been fully eliminated. However, the self-monitoring process has led to a significant reduction in the level of occurrences and an improved relationship between himself and adults. There has also been a new self-awareness for Conrad, and a will to succeed.

WESLEY

An important extension of the self-monitoring process at Allington School has been its use to assist students with severe behavioural disorders to achieve better anger management. Wesley is 14 years old and of Afro-Caribbean origin. His domestic life is confused and chaotic. His response to any challenging situation is usually one of extreme anger and occasional violence. He has considerable emotional needs.

During a particularly difficult period for Wesley, in which his anger became extreme and violent, he acknowledged his own need for greater self-control. This allowed his tutor to talk to him about self-monitoring procedures. An extended period of discussion led to the following programme being initiated:

1 That Wesley should record events in which he displays angry and emotional behaviour.
2 He should note down what led up to the event (the antecedents).
3 He should note down his reaction to the situation.
4 How comfortable did he feel in each situation?
5 How satisfied was he with his reaction?
6 How could he have reacted differently?

Acknowledging that Wesley has some learning difficulties, and could react if he was expected to respond to all of the six points on his own, a pro-forma was produced which was to be completed with the help of a 'trusted adult'. Wesley was asked to nominate an adult whom he would like to go to when a problem arose. He elected a particular Residential Child Care Officer with whom he had a positive relationship.

The practice of recording incidents and the opportunity to share the problem with a 'trusted adult' enabled Wesley to consider the antecedents which preceded an outburst and to develop strategies to handle the situation. As a result of his problem sharing, the RCCO was able to offer a refuge in the residential unit to allow Wesley space when he felt that he was going to lose his temper. Arrangements with the teaching staff facilitated access to this refuge when it was considered appropriate, and the teaching staff often advised Wesley to use the facility when the situation deemed this appropriate. Like Conrad, self-recording did not eliminate the problem for Wesley. However, it did enable him to become aware of his behaviour and offer him a strategy for managing his anger.

There is extensive documentation on the effectiveness of the use of self-management programmes in order to support young people with emotional and behavioural disorders. Broden *et al.* (1971) used self-recording techniques with two 14-year-olds who displayed inattentive behaviours. The programme successfully reduced disruptive behaviours, while increasing the level of study behaviour. Topping (1983), notes that there has been no long-term follow-up results to these studies but states that there appears to be little reason why a pupil should not continue to use the programme for as long as is deemed necessary.

The work of Rumsey and Ballard (1985) considered the low levels of on-task writing behaviour of seven primary school students with behavioural difficulties. This manifested itself in high levels of disruptive behaviour and low levels of work produced. The whole class of thirty-four students were introduced to self-recording of work behaviours during story writing. The authors reported an increase in on-task behaviour and a decrease in off-task disruptive behaviour of the targeted children. There was also a considerable increase in the written words by six other students. A number of single case studies have been produced by Lovitt (1973) who considered the use of self-management projects with students who have recognised behavioural disabilities.

The use of self-management techniques to emphasise goal setting, planning and self-instruction is explored by Meichenbaum and Burland (1979). Flexibrod and O'Leary (1973) extended the notion of self-recording to include self-reinforcement. While they found self-reinforcement to be as effective as teacher reinforcement, their work raised concerns about students who reinforced themselves without earning the rewards. Although they suggested that 'honesty' bonuses for truthful recording provide measures which can be taken to guard against such actions, Clarizio and McCoy (1983) ask the question, *'Can we rely on self-control techniques to alter behaviour when the individual has limited willpower to begin with?'*

It is the belief of the staff at Allington School that we should, at all times, have high expectations of the students with whom we work. While we appreciate that some may have limited willpower, we do not consider this a 'block' to the use of self-management techniques. The Behaviour Management Programme discussed extensively throughout this chapter states that trust and reliability have to be demonstrated. Both the school's on-report systems and self-management programmes are intended to develop trust and reliability, and to provide a range of opportunities for the pupil to display these characteristics and to progress accordingly.

The systems and programmes used at Allington and described in this chapter are not the work of any one person. They have been developed through the will of a committed and enthusiastic staff who have elected to work with difficult pupils and who want to offer these young people the best possible opportunity to succeed.

REFERENCES

Broden, M., Hall, R. V. and Mitts, B. (1971) 'The effect on self-recording on the classroom behaviour of two eighth-grade students', *Journal of Applied Behaviour Analysis* 4: 191–9.

Cantor, L. and Cantor, M. (1992) *Assertive Discipline – Positive Behaviour Management for Today's Classroom*, Santa Monica: Lee Cantor & Associates.

Clarizio, H. F. and McCoy, G. F. (1983) *Behaviour Disorders in Children*, New York: Harper Row.

Flexibrod, J. and O'Leary, K. (1973) 'Effects of reinforcement on children's academic behaviour as a function of self-discrimination and externally imposed contingencies', *Journal of Applied Behaviour Analysis* 6: 241–50.

Herbert, M. (1981) *Behavioural Treatment of Problem Children*, London: Academic Press.

Lovitt, T. (1973) 'Self-management projects with children with behavioural disabilities', *Journal of Learning Disabilities* 6: 138–50.

Meichenbaum, D. and Burland, S. (1979) 'Cognitive behaviour modification with children', *School Psychology Digest* 8: 426–33.

Rogers, B. (1994) 'Teaching positive behaviour to behaviourally disordered students in primary schools', *Support for Learning* 9(4): 166–70.

Rumsey, I. and Ballard, K. D. (1985) 'Teaching self-management strategies for independent story writing to children with classroom behavioural difficulties', *Educational Psychology* 5 (2): 147–57.

Topping, K. (1983) *Educational Systems for Disruptive Adolescents*, London: Croom Helm.

Chapter 12

Pupils as partners
Pupils' contributions to the governance of schools

Paul Cooper

INTRODUCTION

> 4.24 It has been suggested to us, from a number of sources, that provision should be made for a school's pupils, or at least some of them, to play a part in the government of the school.
>
> 4.25 We are in no doubt that every effort should be made to draw on pupils' knowledge and ideas for the benefit of the governing body, and we have carefully considered several arguments to the effect that service on governing bodies should be seen as a special exception to the principle set out above that legislation ought expressly to permit pupils below the age of 18 — perhaps those aged 16 or more — to serve as members of school governing bodies in future.
>
> 4.26 ... *We RECOMMEND that the secretaries of State should take definitive advice on whether it is possible to change the law to enable pupils to serve as governors at 16 without opening the whole question of the age of majority and the holding of public office.* In the light of that advice they should consider, as soon as practicable, whether the law should be amended or whether the question should be raised in its wider context. *Meanwhile we RECOMMEND that secondary school pupils should participate in school government to the fullest extent allowed by law until they are eligible for membership.*
>
> (DES 1977)
>
> Within twenty years, I suspect, all secondary schools will have a school council and pupil governors . . .
>
> (Hargreaves 1982: 115)

Unfortunately the visions stated in the above quotations are even further from realisation today than when they were first stated. At the present time the law states that any person serving on the governing body of a maintained school must be over the age of 18. This allows for the exclusion of pupils from the governing bodies of the schools they attend. Pupils over the age of 18 may be co-opted on to governing bodies of schools, but there is no legal requirement that pupils should be represented in this way.

In this chapter, consideration is given to the contribution that *can* be made by pupils to the governance of schools within existing regulations. It will be argued that the achievement of the social and educational purposes of schools will be facilitated if pupils are more fully involved in the decision-making processes that shape the internal structures of our schools. Structures that are appropriate to enable such pupil contributions will be described. Particular emphasis will be placed on the ideas behind this proposed development. Towards the end of the chapter some of the procedures and mechanisms will be considered that will enable this kind of pupil involvement to take place.

Fundamental to this chapter is the argument that the interests of pupils and schools would be better served by changes in the law which would make pupil involvement in governing bodies a statutory requirement.

WHY SHOULD PUPILS BE INVOLVED IN SCHOOL GOVERNANCE?

In this section and the next one, some background issues will be explored. The main thrust of what follows is that there are important social and political reasons why pupils should be involved in the governance of schools. It will be argued that the exclusion of pupils from school governance means that pupils are deprived of important experiences that are of immediate educational benefit as well as being inconsistent with society's need for a population of school leavers who have a sense of the importance of community and their role in helping the community to develop.

Among the most important functions of schooling is the preparation of pupils for an adult life in which they participate in society in productive, active and constructive ways. Few people would argue with this statement. Clearly, without a copious supply of people who are able and willing to identify, confront and solve the often novel technical, social and economic problems that threaten a society, there can be little hope for the future of that society. Such participation requires certain skills and knowledge, such as high levels of literacy and numeracy, and familiarity with scientific and cultural understandings important to society. Of equal importance are certain attitudes and beliefs about the value and possibilities for active participation, as well as knowledge of what makes participation 'constructive'. The simple matter is that in order for people to learn that it is valuable to participate in certain ways, they must experience at first hand positive rewards from this participation. This is a basic educational principle.

When it comes to learning within the confines of the formal curriculum it is the increasingly accepted view of researchers and many teachers that effective learning is dependent to a large extent on the active involvement of the student. Learning is seen increasingly as a 'transactional' process (Bruner 1987, Cooper and McIntyre 1994, 1995) involving collaboration between teacher and learner, rather than simply a transmission process. Effective learning would seem to depend upon creating opportunities for pupils to engage with tasks on their own terms, so that they can make sense of new knowledge in terms of their existing knowledge (see also Chapter 9). Without this opportunity not only is knowledge difficult to assimilate, it has no real meaning to the learner, and therefore is unlikely to be used to its best advantage. Similarly, if pupils are to learn about the value of constructive and active participation in society they must be given access to experiences that enable them to perceive this value.

It is also important to remember, of course, that schools do not only exist to serve the needs of the society in a narrow sense. As Hargreaves (1982) points out:

> An education's system which is entirely determined by its social functions in society will become merely an instrument which furthers the interests of those who determine the content of those prescribed social functions, and the education of the individual will be sacrificed to these social ends.
>
> (p. 89)

It is essential that the education system, as well as stressing the importance of personal involvement in the service of the broader society, also places a high value on the development of the individual. Encouraging pupils in school to develop a high sense of self-esteem and confidence in their individual capacity to make an impact on their world is a vital component of an education system which seeks to encourage pupils to value the needs and rights of others.

Unfortunately, it would seem that the kinds of experience required to educate pupils about the value of participation have often been felt to be absent from the mass of schooling as we know it. There is a strong body of research that described the experience of schooling as dehumanising and destructive for large proportions of children (e.g. Cooper 1993, Keys and Fernandes 1993, Schostak 1983, Sharp and Green 1975). The work of David Hargreaves (1967, 1982) and Hargreaves *et al.* (1975) has been particularly influential in this area. As Hargreaves (1982) points out:

> If the earlier argument that schooling tends to damage dignity is sound, then we might take as our principal aim for secondary education the promotion of dignity. This was defined earlier as 'a sense of being worthy, of possessing creative, inventive and critical capacities, of having the power to achieve personal and social change'. . . . We can make it a little more concrete if the conditions under which dignity is likely to be achieved are specified. First, the person must acquire competencies and a sense of making a valid contribution to the life of the groups and institutions of which he or she is a member. Second, the person must have a sense of being valued by others in the groups or institutions of which he or she is a part.
>
> (pp. 83–4)

It is interesting to note that Hargreaves wrote these words in what he and others experienced as a period of crisis within the education service. It is interesting to reflect that in the thirteen years that have elapsed since this statement was first made, changes have occurred in our education system (and our society in general) that make the conditions of 1982 seem preferable to those of today (Simon and Chitty 1993). In the following sections the issue of student participation in school governance will be discussed in relation to these and other points.

GOVERNANCE, COMMUNITY AND PUPIL DIGNITY

Hargreaves (1982) sees a central problem of the comprehensive school in terms of a failure to place sufficient emphasis on issues of 'community'. The disintegration of community in the broader society is seen to be reflected in the concerns that are aired about some of our schools. Current problems in the broader society that signal the loss of community are: the destruction of industrial communities, the decline of the importance of the church in people's lives, high level of family breakup, increased crime rates, and the widespread perception that neither the law nor our political leaders are effective in addressing these problems. In addition, the decline of Western economies has given rise to the development of a significant 'underclass' that appears to have little stake in the broader society.

The importance of community is that when it is present it helps to give individuals a sense of belonging and sense of purpose. Community is borne out of, and perpetuated by, a set of shared values and purposes. In a healthy community, individuals have a commitment to serving the community, because they gain personal rewards, in the form of positive recognition, status and (to use Hargreaves' term) 'dignity', in return for their service. A healthy community, then, is characterised by the way in which it maintains a healthy balance between, on the one hand, the needs and rights of the individual, and on the other, the obligations and duties of the individual to the community as a whole.

It is suggested that our schools are ideally situated to create within themselves this sense of community. More to the point, the most desirable aims and purposes of schooling will be more effectively achieved when such a sense of community exists. As well as this, some of the most destructive and negative aspects of our schools will be addressed by such an enterprise. It is further suggested that central to the development of community is active and practical involvement of all members of the community in the life of the community. The sharing of responsibility in the decision-making processes that govern the life of the community is a valuable way of integrating members of a community.

THE VALUE OF INVOLVING PUPILS IN SCHOOL GOVERNANCE

It is no coincidence that many of the pioneer workers with 'maladjusted' children (see Bridgeland 1971) saw 'self government' as an essential therapeutic tool in their work with disturbed and disadvantaged youngsters (see also Chapter 2). What these pioneers have to say about their experience of involving pupils in the running of their schools is of great relevance to schools today. Otto Shaw, who was for many years the head of Red Hill School in Kent, made the following comment about what he saw as a key benefit of 'self government' by pupils:

> There are many objects of self government, and among these is an attempt to place the adults in a new and different relationship to pupils which will make it harder for both to feel that they have alien aims and intentions, and therefore easier for them to make their mark as individuals and individual personalities.

(1965:35)

The foundation for any functioning community is a set of shared values, and the cement that holds the community together is comprised of the everyday procedures and interactions that are consistent with these values. Clearly the greatest threat to any community occurs when the differing and sometimes conflicting interests that different groups inevitably have are acted out without opportunities and mechanisms for debate and compromise. When we look at the kinds of aims that schools habitually claim to have for their students, we find little to argue with. For example, consider the set of aims taken from an English secondary school prospectus.

Our aims for *all* our students are:

1 To help them acquire knowledge and skills (both practical and academic), abilities and the motivation to utilise them to their best advantage
2 To help them develop mental, physical and spiritual qualities
3 To help them to appreciate the breadth of human achievement, aspirations and creativity in art, science, mathematics, technology and literature, and, where possible, to give pupils first hand experience of these
4 To help them to understand language and numbers, and to use them effectively
5 To help them to understand the social, economic and political order
6 To help them develop a reasoned set of values and beliefs and to instil in them respect and tolerance for the beliefs and values of other religions, races and ways of life
7 To help them leave our school at 16, 17 or 18, well prepared for the adult world they will meet in their personal and working lives,

and ready to make a full contribution to the local as well as the wider community

8 To help them develop a sense of their own self worth, the ability to be self reliant, to have lively and enquiring minds, to be able to question and argue rationally, while being active and constructive participants in society

9 To help them find pleasure in learning and give them the experience of success and personal achievement.

There is little to argue with in this set of aims. It is highly compatible with the kinds of liberal sentiments that suffuse government documents relating to the National Curriculum and other educational policies. These are aims that the majority of teachers in our schools would agree with and that many of our schools would claim to be pursuing. Furthermore, these aims are highly compatible with what has already beén said about community in schools. These aims are intended for *all* pupils. The most commonly used word in this list is 'help': the school aims to support and nurture all of its pupils in the pursuit of these aims. Furthermore, this intention to be supportive and nurturing is intended to support the individual's personal development, so as to enable each pupil to become 'self-reliant', critical, actively and informedly involved in the society they will enter, so as to maximise each person's access to success and personal achievement.

INVOLVEMENT, EBD AND COMMUNITY

In the case of this particular school, there is evidence to suggest that these aims are being achieved to some considerable extent (see Cooper 1993). What is clear, however, is that although many schools would claim to subscribe to these values many fail to live up to them. This is illustrated by research into pupils' perceptions of schooling (see also Charlton, Chapter 2). As the quotation from Shaw in the previous section suggests, many children, and particularly those who are most at risk of being rejected by schools, would not recognise the aims described here in their first-hand experience of schools. One such group of pupils came up with a list of complaints that indicated they felt alienated from and disregarded by their teachers. According to them, teachers were:

• too formal in their behaviour towards pupils
• too strict

- 'stuck up'
- unfriendly
- intolerant
- humourless
- uninterested in pupils' personal welfare
- not prepared/able to give pupils individual attention
- guilty of labelling some pupils with negative identities
- guilty of treating some pupils unfairly
- guilty of conducting boring lessons
- insufficiently helpful to pupils with learning difficulties.

These pupils felt marginalised and rejected by their schools. Far from being supported, nurtured or 'helped' to achieve personal autonomy and the skills for active and constructive participation in society, these children felt disempowered and helpless. They believed themselves to be victims of forces beyond their control: forces that not only failed to help and support them, but actively undermined and in some cases abused them, leaving them with low self-esteem and not only a sense of failure, but a fear of being unable to face the challenges they must meet in order to develop positively.

The pupils in this study were all pupils who had been referred to special residential schools for boys with emotional and behavioural difficulties. While we should not think of the views of EBD pupils as being necessarily representative of the views of all children, we should think of these views as being of special significance. Such pupils often react to aspects of the school environment that other pupils find aversive but are able to 'put up with'. Rather like the canaries that nineteenth-century miners employed to test the toxicity of the mining environment, EBD pupils can be seen as being particularly sensitive to those aspects of the school environment that are socially and personally 'toxic'. Children who attract the EBD label often experience a wide range of difficulties of a social and personal nature, particularly in their family circumstances (Cooper 1993). These difficulties make them especially vulnerable and sensitive to aversive aspects of their school environments. Children with EBD simply react more graphically than the majority of their peers to environmental circumstances that are experienced as negative by all pupils. They can, therefore, be seen as markers for such negative environmental circumstances. These circumstances need to be brought to light because they are the very circumstances that contribute to the development and maintenance of pupil deviance in schools. Furthermore, we find that their complaints about school are echoed in the views of a much wider range of pupils, as illustrated in research by Schostak (1983) and Keys and Fernandes (1993), and Jones and Charlton in Chapter 1. Both of these studies chart the growing disaffection of pupils as they progress through schooling, indicating that such disaffection is not simply the province of a disgruntled failing minority, but is rather far more widespread and systemic than this.

The argument presented so far, then, suggests that pupils should be seen as a source of knowledge and expertise that should be harnessed in the service of school governance. The particular expertise of pupils lies in their unique knowledge of what it is like to be a pupil in a particular school environment, and inside knowledge of the factors that are experienced as motivators and demotivators. In the case of many of the EBD pupils in the study referred to above, a significant factor in their rehabilitation according to their own accounts was the experience of involvement in the schools to which they were referred (Cooper 1989, 1993). Of particular note was the contrast identified between their experience of powerlessness and victimisation in their mainstream schools and their sense of being valued members of residential communities. In both residential schools, shared responsibility and self-government were important aspects of school organisation. Mechanisms for these features involved group meetings involving staff and pupils as well as more informal systems by which staff consulted pupils on their concerns. Pupils also had access to formal and informal channels which enabled them to express personal and other concerns with a view to influencing the running of their schools. Chapters 2, 3 and 4 discuss other ways in which teachers can help pupils to voice their opinions, interests and concerns.

The issues and concerns that these pupils were able to raise in these circumstances were very wide ranging. Routine institutional matters included the identification of perceived needs for repair and maintenance activities to the fabric of the schools, discussion of decoration requirements, discussion of bed and mealtime arrangements and other rules. Other matters included the discussion of particular issues of concern to the school community, these ranged from incidents of individual conflict between pupils, to problems of theft and vandalism and the needs of individuals for particular dispensations or privileges. In some cases decisions on expenditure were delegated to pupils, for example in relation to the purchase of leisure equipment, and the planned development of some disused buildings on the school site.

The involvement of pupils in decision-making processes has for many years been a common feature of special schools for pupils with EBD (Bridgeland 1971). This is perhaps ironic when we consider that pupils who find their way into such schools are often considered to be uncooperative and a threat to the school communities from where they came. What these schools often demonstrate, however, is the powerful therapeutic effect of self-government and shared responsibility for individual pupils. They achieve these outcomes by helping pupils to develop a sense of belonging and personal value in relation to the school community. They demonstrate that formal and informal arrangements which enable pupils' voices to be heard (and influential in the running of their schools) have the effect of promoting a sense of involvement and commitment to the community: in short, they help to promote the very *sense of community* referred to earlier as being of such importance.

POSITIVE SIGNIFICATION AND RE-SIGNIFICATION

The mechanism at work here has been termed 'positive signification' (Cooper 1993). This describes the process by which pupils come to internalise positive images of themselves and enhanced self-esteem through their experience of being valued members of a community. For some pupils, this is an uphill task, especially when they enter a situation with an already established and internalised negative identity (such as 'disruptive pupils', 'deviant' or 'anti-social'). This was the case with many of the pupils in the study referred to above. In these cases, a process of 're-signification' had to take place (Cooper 1989, 1993), whereby the old negative identity was replaced with a new positive identity. The challenge to the school system is to promote positive signification from the outset, and to prevent negative signification.

The positive effects of pupil involvement on self-esteem and behaviour in mainstream schools have long been noted by researchers. Reynolds and Sullivan (1979) contrast co-optive and coercive school regimes. Coercive regimes are marked by school practices that objectify pupils and make them subject to authoritarian rule structure.

Co-optive schools, on the other hand, are marked by practices that seek to maximise the active involvement of pupils, at the classroom and institutional levels. In co-optive schools, pupils are valued as individuals. The co-optive schools identified by Reynolds and Sullivan tended to have lower levels of behavioural difficulties and higher levels of academic performance than coercive schools. Another study by Cronk (1987) illustrated the ways in which consultative and person-centred teaching strategies increased the levels of commitment of secondary aged pupils. A common feature of effective mainstream schools is the practice of giving pupils real responsibilities and involving them in the running of their schools (Cooper 1993, Cooper et al. 1994).

THE VALUE OF PUPIL EXPERTISE

Clearly, practices which result in the enhancement of pupils' levels of self-esteem are in themselves valuable. Pupils, however, are not the only beneficiaries of the outcomes of pupil involvement. Increasingly, the pupil perspective on the educational process is being seen as a source of expert knowledge that needs to be drawn on in order to maximise effective teaching. Socio-cultural theories of learning, such as those proposed by Bruner (e.g. Bruner and Haste 1987) and Vygotsky (1989), stress the importance of pupil involvement in the learning process, and the need for teachers to contract learning situations that are based on the specific characteristics of learners. Recent research by Cooper and McIntyre (e.g. 1993, 1994, 1995) reveals the possibility that pupils are in possession of a specific form of 'craft knowledge' which they employ in the learning process. The research also indicates that they are able to offer clear and persuasive accounts of their own learning processes and the ways in which these can be aided by particular teaching strategies. It is unclear at the present time to which extent opportunities exist for pupils to share these insights with staff. Clearly one such vehicle might be governance and related processes.

A more pressing reason why pupil knowledge and expertise should be allowed to feed directly into the governance process related to the particular pressures that governing bodies face in the current market economy approach to education. Recent research (Deem *et al.* 1994) suggests that governing bodies, in response to market forces, are neglecting the interests of their current pupils. The researchers conclude:

> Governors, even those closest to the collective rather than the consumer interest end of the value spectrum, spent a great deal of their time considering pupil numbers, school image and marketing strategies. . . . The major emphasis (of governors in their study) was often on who (i.e. pupils) might attend in the future, rather than the quality of schooling offered to existing pupils. Indeed, . . . existing pupils were often subjected to criticism (e.g. for lack of exam success, behaviour, social class, haircuts).
>
> (p. 537)

In these circumstances pupils have little opportunity to defend themselves from such 'criticism'. Currently they rely on others to state their case for them (e.g. teachers, parent governors). This is in spite of the fact that they possess a distinctive perspective on the educational process that is directly related to the central aim of schooling, namely that of education. Something of the nature of this perspective has been illustrated above, and from this it should be clear that there are times when the pupils' perspective may be in conflict with interests of other parties whose concerns may not serve the needs of effective education. Where such conflicts exist, their negative effects on the life of the school community will be exacerbated by the feelings of powerlessness that naturally flow from the lack of involvement in the governance process that pupils, by law, experience.

To look at the issue of conflict from a slightly different prospective, it might well be asserted that the commitment that flows from formal involvement in school life brings with it responsibilities. Where pupils (or anyone else for that matter) have no power, they also have no responsibility for outcomes: they can, in fact, blame those with the power for whatever negative outcomes arise, even when they themselves contribute to such outcomes. The responsibility that comes with power means that blame may sometimes have to be accepted when things go wrong. This factor, it is suggested, can often have the effect of encouraging compromise, conciliation and co-operation in place of hostility and entrenchment. This point is illustrated negatively by a statement given by a disaffected pupil in one of the residential schools referred to earlier. The powerlessness that this boy perceived himself to experience in the school, made it possible for him to make completely unreasonable demands on the school community, and allowed him to avoid taking responsibility for his own behaviour: 'I think they should be more stricter. But if they get it more strict, I'm going to be the one that's breaking all the rules.' This boy's refusal to accept responsibility points to the heart of the problem of excluding pupils from school governance. Only by giving pupils access to power can we help them to develop and demonstrate a sense of responsibility.

THE SHAPE OF PUPIL INVOLVEMENT IN GOVERNANCE

Having argued for the importance and value of pupil involvement in the governance it is important now to consider some of the practicalities involved, and to describe some of the mechanisms by which this form of pupil involvement might be achieved.

At present, the law in England and Wales does not permit persons under the age of 18 to serve on school governing bodies. This is a regrettable situation. Not only would the interests of pupils be better served than they are now by pupil involvement in governance, but, as is shown above, pupils bring with them knowledge and expertise that should be made available to governors. It is necessary that their access be made a legal requirement simply because places where the beneficial effects of increased pupil involvement will be most powerfully felt are those schools which are hives of disaffection characterised by domineering, coercive and discounting practices. In this way the involvement of pupils in governance is analogous with the abolition of corporal punishment. By the time this law was introduced, the majority of schools and teachers had learned the value and importance of non-physical strategies for dealing with pupil misbehaviour. The change in the law acted as the stimulus to the most entrenched and inert finally to seek a new approach to discipline.

However, even under existing law it is permissible for pupils to be present at, and participate in, governors' meetings, at the invitation of the governing body. Clearly, the value of the participation of a small number of pupils serving on a governing body to the school community as a whole depends on the degree to which this group represents the views and concerns of the pupil population as a whole.

SCHOOL COUNCILS

If such representativeness is to be achieved, the pupil representative on the governing body should be related to the pupil population through a system of shared responsibility. This is achieved in some schools through the setting-up of pupil councils. The councils are pupil-run, though they are facilitated by the management of the school with support and advice being made available where necessary. Such councils are comprised of pupils from all classes in the school. The representatives are democratically elected by their peers. The council is then responsible for selecting delegates to the governing body. For such councils to be taken seriously by pupils, however, it is necessary for them to exercise real responsibilities within certain prescribed areas. This should involve some budgetary authority where appropriate. Areas of responsibility can involve the management of tuck shops, newspapers and other commercial enterprises. Other areas of involvement should include input into discipline committees and other school policy initiatives, including working parties set up to inform policy decisions. Councils should be a forum for pupils to express their interests and concerns (including complaints) without fear of reprisal and with the knowledge that their views will be listened to by staff and management. The pupil governors will act as conduits to and from the governing body.

LIAISON SYSTEMS

As an adjunct to school councils, it will be appropriate for particular staff to take the role of staff–student liaison officers. Such liaison officers should be approved by the pupil group, and attend council meetings by invitation to provide support and advice, when required, as well as acting as a channel of communication with other groups (governors and staff). Similarly, where there is no formal pupil representation on governing bodies it would be appropriate for a member of the governing body to take on specific responsibility of liaising with the school council, and to be responsible for representing the views of pupils.

OPENING UP THE AGENDA

As a minimum requirement, the minutes of governors' meetings should be made available and accessible to pupils. Pupils should also be able to table items on the agenda of the governor's meeting, and to request specific information from governors. At the present time, participation of pupils in governance could be further extended by inviting pupils to be observers at meetings, in addition to being invited participants.

CONCLUSION: DO PUPILS CARE ENOUGH?

The disaffection and apathy that appear to characterise some of our pupils, particularly those in the upper years of schooling, might be used to suggest that pupils will not be interested in such involvement. There is a sense in which the alienation that suffuses our society is seen in the disaffection or cynical instrumentalism of school pupils. This is a sad caricature of the young people in our schools. One thing that has been made clear by researchers over the past thirty years is that school pupils (and often those considered to be disaffected, maladjusted or otherwise deviant) are astute and insightful critics of schools and schooling (e.g. Hargreaves 1967, Willis 1977, Schostak 1983, Cronk 1987, Cooper 1993). We ignore their insights to the detriment of our schools, the future of our pupils and the future of our society.

REFERENCES

Bridgeland, M. (1971) *Pioneer Work with Maladjusted Children*, London: Staples.

Bruner, J. (1987) 'The transactional self', in J. Bruner and H. Haste (eds) *Making Sense: the Child's Construction of the World*, Milton Keynes: Open University Press.

Bruner, J. and Haste, H. (eds) (1987) *Making Sense: The Child's Construction of the World*, Milton Keynes: Open University Press.

Cooper, P. (1989) *Respite, Relationships and Re-Signification: A Study of the Effects of Residential Schooling on Pupils with Emotional and Behavioural Difficulties with Particular Reference to the Perceptions of Pupils*, unpublished Ph.D. thesis, University of Birmingham.

Cooper, P. (1993) *Effective Schools for Disaffected Students: Integration and Segregation*, London: Routledge.

Cooper, P. and McIntyre, D. (1993) 'Commonality in teachers' and pupils' perceptions of effective classroom learning', *British Journal of Educational Psychology* 63: 381–99.

Cooper, P. and McIntyre, D. (1994) 'Patterns of interaction between teachers' and students' classroom thinking, and their implications for the provision of learning opportunities', *Teaching and Teacher Education* 10 (6): 633–46.

Cooper, P. and McIntyre, D. (1995) 'The crafts of the classroom: the knowledge underpinning effective teaching and learning in classrooms', *Research Papers in Education* 10 (2): 181–216.

Cooper, P., Smith, C. J. and Upton, G. (1994) *Emotional and Behavioural Difficulties: From Theory to Practice*, London: Routledge.

Cronk, K. (1987) *Teacher–Pupil Conflict in Secondary Schools*, Lewes: Falmer Press.

Deem, R., Brehony, K. and Heath, S. (1994) 'Governors, schools and the miasma of the market', *British Educational Research Journal* 20 (5): 535–50.

DES and Welsh Office (1977) *A New Partnership for Our Schools*: Report for the Commission of Enquiry jointly appointed by the Secretary of State for Education and Science and the Secretary of State for Wales under the Chairmanship of Mr Tom Taylor, CBE, London: HMSO.

Hargreaves, D. (1967) *Social Relations in a Secondary School*, London: RKP.

Hargreaves, D. (1982) *The Challenge for the Comprehensive School: Culture, Curriculum and Community*, London: Routledge.

Hargreaves, D., Hester, S. and Mellor, F. (1975) *Deviance in Classrooms*, London: Routledge.

Keys, W. and Fernandes, C. (1993) *What do Students Think of School?*, Slough: NFER.

Reynolds, D. and Sullivan, M. (1979) 'Bringing schools back in', in L. Barton and T. Meigham (eds) *Schools, Pupils and Disaffection*, Driffield: Nafferton.

Schostak, J. (1983) *Maladjusted Schooling*, Lewes: Falmer.

Sharp, R. and Green, A. (1975) *Education and Social Control*, London: RKP.

Shaw, O. (1965) *Maladjusted Boys*, London: Allen & Unwin.

Simon and Chitty (1993) *Save our Schools*, London: Lawrence & Wishart.

Vygotsky, L. (1989) *The Collected Works of L. S. Vygotsky*, vol. 1, ed. R. Reiber and A. Carlton, London: Plenum.

Willis, P. (1977) *Learning to Labour*, London: Saxon.

Chapter 13

Involving pupils in policy development

Philip Garner

The Code of Practice relating to special needs (DfE 1994) affirms that 'special educational provision will be most effective when those responsible take into account the ascertainable wishes of the child concerned'. While this statement should not be regarded as unproblematic, it nevertheless presents an indication that, at national level, there is now a recognition that the views of those who have special needs can be of positive benefit to schools in policy development. In consequence, cold water will only be poured over this egalitarian principle in a brief concluding section to this chapter. Meanwhile, sufficient evidence has already been presented in this book to suggest that, with the wind of official recognition in the sails of 'pupil involvement', an opportunity now exists to consider the practicalities of using the views of pupils in policy-making.

Some school policies frequently come under criticism from the 'ordinary' teachers who have to implement them because they are seen as the products of deliberations by a small group of senior managers, their contents being viewed as directives. Such policies, whatever they may relate to, are treated with justifiable resentment by the workers who have not been invited to participate in their formulation. They exist on paper, and seem to be removed from the reality of classroom life (Palmer *et al.* 1994). They are also indicative of an hierarchical approach to school organisation and management. 'Ownership', to coin a popular and politically correct term, is missing.

The same can be said of school policies which do not involve pupils. As with some teachers, certain pupils become alienated from the school's aims or mission if they have not been allowed to participate in some of its day-to-day decision-making (Booth and

Coulby 1987). They will also become cynical, detached and non-participative if they are only allowed to have a say in that policy-making which is non-threatening to teachers. This is what I refer to as the 'tuck shop committee syndrome'. Giving pupils 'power' to decide what flavours of crisps should be sold at break-times is not real power. Invariably, this and other kinds of spurious empowerment are quickly uncovered by pupils as rhetoric (Garner 1993). Nowhere is this feeling more apparent than in the case of those pupils who have special needs associated with 'problem behaviour'.

The Code of Practice focuses mainly upon the identification and assessment of special needs. Its recommendation to schools that they should involve pupils in decision-making processes needs to be given wider currency, so that it covers more general whole-school matters, including policies relating to discipline, curriculum, school organisation and so on. Pupils are the bedrock for determining 'ethos', and it is my contention that this should develop *from them*, rather than given *to them*, as 'helpings' of what is good for them. The resultant sense of 'belonging', or sense of 'community' (see Chapter 12), felt by pupils is an important determinant of a positive ethos (Mongon and Hart 1989).

Circular 8/94, entitled 'Pupil Behaviour and Discipline' (DfE 1994), tacitly reaffirms the official view that pupils should be involved in the development of schools' behaviour policies. In stating that 'they should be worked out co-operatively', the circular is reinforcing the advice promoted by the Elton Report (Dept. of Ed. and Sci. 1989) that the views of pupils should be taken into account in matters relating to school discipline.

All three official documents (the Elton Report, the Code of Practice and Circular 8/94) stop somewhere short of directly recommending that pupils should, as a matter of course, be involved in helping to make decisions about school policy. There can be little doubt that these publications do represent a step forward in seeing children who have special needs not as 'fixed', uni-dimensional individuals but as active agents in their own school lives.

A gradual change of attitude is occurring and, as schools come under increasing scrutiny through more regular inspection, the ways in which pupil opinion is sought, assimilated and acted upon may become an important indicator of school effectiveness. This is signalled, for example, in Framework 4 of the current school inspection manual, which uses the question 'Do the school's arrangements encourage all pupils to contribute to school life and to exercise responsibility?' (OFSTED 1993). Immediately, then, both principle and pragmatism form the rationale for measures designed to incorporate the views of pupils in helping to develop policies.

This having been said, there are particular problems associated with pupil involvement in policy-making, particularly where some of those who need to be involved are seen as 'problems'. Pupils who have learning difficulties associated with 'problem behaviour' frequently conjure up negative feelings in many teachers (Hargreaves *et al.* 1975). This is understandable. Being a teacher is not easy at a time when undue emphasis is placed on outputs, measured by normative indicators such as examination success, exclusion and truancy rates, measurable progress from one National Curriculum attainment target to the next, and so on. The pressure on teachers to 'perform' may mean that they are less inclined to accommodate the demands of pupils with behaviour problems. Put simply, if Billy Worrall and his mates in Year 8 are making my job difficult, so that I spend most of my time trying to establish order in the classroom, I am not inclined to be sympathetic to any moves which I think provide them with an official platform to promote or rationalise their misbehaviour. Doesn't the involvement of the likes of Billy in policy-making enable them to dictate how I should do my job? It becomes a threat to my status and position as a teacher and it can therefore be a risky undertaking.

Pupil participation in policy-making involves a strategic decision in three areas. First, a school climate has to be created in which co-operation between pupils and teachers is seen as routine rather than exceptional. Developing this requires an examination of existing attitudes within the school, especially those management practices which affect the way teachers do their job. Next, the pupils themselves need to be given the skills and strategies necessary to enable them to present their views of school in a rational and objective way, so that they may be able to participate in a more democratically run school. Finally, everyone in the school needs to take part in a review of its policies and resultant organisational procedures (whether these be whole policies, teaching and learning activities across the subject range, day-to-day arrangements and specific areas of concern like support teaching, discipline policy and pastoral care and guidance arrangements). In each case, the *whole* school should subsequently determine (a) the extent to which pupils are currently involved, (b) potential areas for involving pupils in the future and (c) a long-term strategic plan to take account of pupil opinion when constructing whole-school policies.

DEVELOPING A CLIMATE FOR PUPIL INVOLVEMENT IN POLICY-MAKING

Teachers in England and Wales work in a culture within which 'control' in the classroom is seen as a crucial indicator of what comprises a 'good' practitioner (see also Charlton, Chapter 2). A major emphasis in current initial teacher training courses, for example, is placed on the ability (or competence) of students to keep good order (McNamara 1992). Applicants for a new teaching post are often asked a question beginning 'what would you do if . . .', subsequent reference invariably being made to a dilemma involving pupil misconduct. Current inspection arrangements for schools (OFSTED 1993) similarly place considerable emphasis upon classroom management, implicitly suggesting that classroom noise and movement are the attributes of the teacher who lacks control. The belief systems which underpin these values are deep-seated in teaching. The teacher knows best, and children are traditionally the recipients of what goes on in school. In order that curriculum and social values are effectively 'delivered', classroom teachers have to maintain a role of dominance.

Part of the perceived 'threat' felt by classroom teachers originates from the hierarchical nature of many schools. In seeking to promote pupil involvement, therefore, senior management teams need to ask themselves whether 'ordinary' teachers occupy a similar position to those pupils who feel disaffected, who do not share the school's values and who tend, in consequence, to engage in inappropriate behaviour. Do teachers themselves feel removed from, or alienated by, policies and policy-making? To what extent are they given a set of 'rules' relating to school policy to which they have had only nominal input? What protocols exist within the organisation of the school which enable every member of the teaching and support staff to participate in policy-making?

Responses to these questions may help build up a true picture of the school as either an 'open' or 'closed' institution. If the latter is the case, it is unlikely that classroom teachers will be receptive to initiatives which seek to promote pupil involvement. Teachers, in this situation, are 'humiliated by the power of children and by the power of headteachers, and feel degraded and brutalised by exercising power themselves' (Musgrove 1964: 165). Their sense of isolation and marginalisation has to be dealt with before, or at least alongside, any measures to begin or increase pupil participation. Elliot-Kemp (1986) summarises the dangers of lack of consultation, stating that 'An imposed system will, at best, gain compliance; at worst resistance and sabotage', while making the point that 'when teachers really believe in something they will make it work' (p. 5).

A considerable amount of literature now exists which recommends the involvement of all teachers in whole-school policy development. The Code of Practice is explicit, stating that, in relation to an institutional SEN policy, 'the school as a whole should be involved in its development' (p. 8). The requisite climate for this may be generated by the development of a 'participatory management ethos' (Hewton 1988). This demands that equal consideration is given to the views of all teachers. A number of initiatives can help to promote this, including:

- all teachers being asked to chair meetings, in rotation
- senior management meetings being 'open' meetings
- all senior managers teaching in classrooms
- all committees, working parties and groups being open to all teachers
- delegation of traditional senior management tasks
- paired-professional activities where possible (e.g. NQT/ Deputy Head)
- open agenda-setting for all meetings
- heads/deputies 'clinics'
- in-service training (e.g. running meetings, making decisions)
- all decisions being agreed by staff, who are collectively responsible for outcomes.

Immediately there may be resistance. Resources may be stretched, contingencies may interrupt a scheduled meeting, and some teachers may not want to be involved whatever opportunities are provided. Ultimately, however, the school as a collective has to decide whether it wishes to become a truly 'inclusive' school, in which everyone feels able to participate. Nor is such inclusivity to be won easily, or over a short period of time: there should be an assumption, according to Fullan (1982), that effective change will take time.

For both senior managers and for classroom teachers there must be the underlying realisation, promoted from the outset and reinforced repeatedly, that teachers who feel empowered are less inclined to feel the need to control. Such teachers will view the prospect of pupil involvement with far less trepidation, and will be more inclined to listen to the views of those they have previously discounted. Such 'climate-building' should therefore be regarded as the foundation for pupil participation. The general benefit of this approach is neatly summarised by Rogers (1992). He states that 'if we can provide a certain type of relationship, the other person can discover within himself the capacity to use that relationship for growth, and change and personal development will occur' (p. 33).

SKILLS FOR PUPIL PARTICIPATION

Children who have special educational needs associated with problem behaviour are often described as lacking in social skills. As a result they frequently get into trouble with teachers and other pupils because they respond inappropriately in certain social situations (Rogers 1992). They are unfamiliar with many of the sophisticated codes and protocols which govern life in schools. This in turn may militate against their successful involvement in new processes designed to secure their involvement.

It is therefore necessary to provide all pupils, and especially those who have learning difficulties associated with problem behaviour, with the ability to negotiate successfully with their teachers and peers. Broadly speaking, negotiation involves such skills as listening, managing conflict, assertiveness training, taking risks, accepting responsibility and dealing with feelings, as well as the creation of conditions under which such collaboration can take place (see Chapters 3 and 4).

Many pupils who have learning difficulty find these skills very challenging, for a variety of reasons. Many will be pupils who will find it very difficult to accept responsibility for their actions, even when they may clearly be the perpetrators ('it wasn't me, Miss . . .'). Others may have a very low self-opinion, and consequently believe that there is little point in stating a point of view. Still more may be so accustomed to failure that they may be unwilling to participate in anything which might expose their weaknesses. In the most extreme cases, several of these may overlap, contributing to the child being either excessively withdrawn or aggressive.

Additionally, just as it has been noted that teachers occupy roles which are dictated by tradition, so too many children in schools (and especially those with special educational needs) see themselves as parts of a system over which they have no real control. Building up the confidence and trust, so that participation in rule-making and policy matters is seen as an axiomatic of being in school. As with the process of creating a 'climate' in which pupil participation will flourish, it does not happen by itself.

The importance, therefore, of social skills programmes is immense, and is recognised by the huge body of curriculum material currently available in this area. If a school wishes to promote pupil participation, so that there is a unilateral benefit in teaching and learning to everyone in the school, such programmes need a high priority. Part of the risk-taking on the part of senior management teams is that such programmes should be maintained at all costs, irrespective of National Curriculum requirements or other pressures. Subsequently the enhancement of pupils' learning and teachers' teaching can far outweigh the time 'lost' in promoting these co-operative strategies.

PARTICIPATION BY DISRUPTIVE PUPILS: A PRACTICAL EXAMPLE

Pupils who are regarded as 'disruptive' adolescents are seen as amongst the most difficult to deal with in school. Invariably boys, they can be unlovable and aggressive to those around them. Their behaviour frequently touches on the delinquent, and their hostile attitude to authority figures can ignite classroom and whole-school disputes which leads to their exclusion. This is the almost universally accepted deficit-view. Strategies can be developed, however, which seek to tackle the alienation that this group of pupils feel: one way is to involve them more actively in school decision-making.

Cragbank School is a mixed, 11–16 comprehensive school of 700 pupils and 48 teaching staff. Its catchment area is mainly urban, including two estates which have been designated as 'high priority' by social services on account of their high number of single-parent families, unemployment, delinquency figures and overcrowded accommodation. The school occupies a site to the east of the town centre, with buildings dating mainly from the late 1960s.

The school is organised on traditional lines, with headteacher, two deputies and heads of subject departments. Pastoral arrangements are overseen by one of the deputies, who has the support of five heads of year.

Following the appointment in 1989 of a new headteacher and deputy headteacher, the school began a series of initiatives designed to improve its local reputation, which had declined in competition with two grant-maintained schools and a selective 'grammar' school. On the completion of a school review, an institutional development plan was drafted, part of which was designed to address the problem of non-attendance and what was termed as 'anti-social behaviour' by some pupils, both within and outside the school. In particular, teachers were concerned about the gradual alienation of pupils as they moved up the school, feeling that the situation was at its worst in Year 10. The intervention, described below, is an adaptation of a model described elsewhere (Garner 1992).

A number of pastoral staff at the school took the view that at least part of the problem could be traced to the lack of involvement in decision-making felt by a group of boys who were in Year 10. A survey, conducted by their head of year, had revealed that almost a third of pupils felt they did not have a say in making curriculum choices or in the development of the school's Code of Conduct. Moreover, the pupils believed that certain subjects, and certain teachers, were boring, resulting in both non-attendance and in-class misbehaviour, or 'having a laugh', according to Woods (1979).

Consultation with one member of the local authority support services (an educational social worker) and a university teacher (acting as an adviser to the initiative) resulted in the formation of a voluntary working group within the school. This developed a plan which sought (a) to establish the opinions of Year 10 about Cragbank (the AUDIT STAGE) and (b) to arrange a series of structured discussions between pupils and teachers, leading to a set of strategies designed to include the pupils in policy decisions (the ACTION STAGE).

The 'audit' of Year 10 pupils began by using a second questionnaire, which focused on four aspects of school activity: the pupils were asked for their views on the curriculum, school organisation, teachers and teaching and discipline. The questionnaires were simplified for those pupils with reading or other learning difficulties and were completed independently by all pupils in Year 10 during form periods. Eventually a return of 98 per cent was recorded, providing both a valuable insight into what the pupils thought of Cragbank and a basis for the next stage of the exercise.

The returns from the questionnaire were then analysed by the professional team. The views of the pupils indicated a number of things which confirmed many of the widely held beliefs about adolescent school pupils. Amongst these were that many pupils in the school were conscious of the status of individual teachers and they recognised the professional qualities of those who appeared to work hard and were well prepared for lessons. Teachers who 'treated us with respect' and had a sense of humour were more highly regarded by these pupils. Firm but fair discipline, where sanctions were explained to the recipient, was seen to be an essential teacher quality.

The responses of the pupils formed the basis of two staff-development sessions. Although the use of pupil feedback concerning the professional qualities of teachers is in its infancy, the comments made by this group of Year 10 pupils show great insight, fairness and maturity. Over 60 per cent of the responses were positive about the school's provision in each of the four areas under consideration. The first lesson to the teachers at Cragbank, therefore, was that the views of pupils can enhance, rather than threaten, their position.

The next stage of the initiative involved a target group of pupils whose behaviour, for whatever reason, was frequently poor. These were selected by asking all staff to identify confidentially those pupils who were felt to be 'disruptive'. No explanation of this term was given since it was widely accepted that such a definition is based on individual perceptions of what comprises 'disruptive' behaviour (Hargreaves *et al.* 1975). A total of thirty-seven names were provided, and from these the working group selected the twelve who were named most frequently. Significantly, all were boys. They were each approached individually, in order to ascertain their willingness to participate in discussion groups with certain teachers, the purposes of which was 'Making Cragbank School a better place to teach and learn'. The parents of the boys were then approached, and once their agreement had been secured the whole group was introduced to the school at a special assembly.

A request was then made for teacher-volunteers, who would be willing to take part in a number of discussion groups, comprising teachers and the 'disruptive' pupils. Nine teachers responded (one deputy headteacher, two heads of year, two heads of subject departments, three MPG teachers and one part-time support teacher); of these, five were male and four female. Each discussion group comprised three pupils who had been identified as 'disruptive' and three adults selected from the teachers and the initial working party.

A total of six meetings were timetabled to take place during the subsequent term: this constituted the 'action' stage of the initiative. The first meeting allowed a set of ground rules for the conduct of the pupil–teacher discussions to be established. It was accepted, for instance, that no individual teachers or pupils would be identified by name, when accounts were given of classroom events. It was also agreed that only one person should speak at any one time, and that the pupils should have an equal right to state opinions as the teachers. A set of aims were then agreed, and four core teams were formed to consider one each of either the curriculum, school organisation, teachers and teaching and discipline.

During the next four meetings the boys and the teachers based their discussions on what the pupils had written in their questionnaires. The purpose of this was to use what the pupils had said about the school, whether positive or negative, to help identify areas in which the school as a whole could improve. In the curriculum group, for example, much discussion focused upon the lack of choice in teaching and learning styles provided by certain teachers. Elsewhere, the group considering discipline agreed that the school's Code of Conduct included far too many sanctions and placed virtually all responsibility on the pupils to behave well, irrespective of the attitude shown to them by a teacher.

A final meeting involved discussions with all members of the senior management team and two school governors. Subsequently, eleven recommendations from the groups were included, after discussions with the whole staff (in which the boys did not participate), in revised school policies. These were:

- lunchtime supervision arrangements to be reviewed
- all supply teachers to be interviewed prior to employment
- discontinuation of 'prefects' in Year 11
- removal of certain sanctions deemed ineffective from the Discipline Code
- increase in use of suggested 'effective' sanctions
- School Council's terms of reference to be reviewed by a core team
- continuation and expansion of core teams
- all teachers to provide opportunity for whole-class appraisal
- disputes relating to discipline to include a 'neutral' person (either pupil or teacher), identified by the pupil in dispute
- teaching and learning agreements between teachers and classes to be considered
- pupils to assist in periodic review of school organisation and policy.

At this stage it is too early to assess the long-term impact of this school's approach to pupil involvement. An early setback was encountered when two of the pupils decided they did not wish to continue with the discussion groups. They were replaced by two other pupils, who were given independent instructions on the conduct of the groups prior to joining. Another pupil was excluded, and in consequence missed three of his group meetings. He was not replaced. On the teaching-staff side, one of the MPG teachers was absent because of illness at times when her group was due to meet.

In spite of these difficulties the initial feedback from the participants was encouraging. Seven of the boys felt that the exercise had been 'very good' and, of these, five said that they were willing to continue their involvement in Year 11. Of the teaching staff, eight felt that the discussion groups had been worth while and, of these, six indicated a willingness to be involved in similar initiatives. Elsewhere in the school, four new teachers asked to be involved in future schemes. Finally, there was a widely held belief that the school, to quote one teacher, had 'taken the bull by the horns ... so that we are now talking face to face with kids we couldn't even reach'.

A LITTLE COLD WATER

An optimistic note for the prospects of pupil participation has been struck in many recent official documents concerning special needs and 'problem children'. There now exist many examples of pupil participation in school lives at both primary and secondary levels, as illustrated in this book (see also Coulby and Coulby 1989, Ingram and Worrall 1993). But to what extent do these recommendations in respect of so-called disruptive pupils exist as pious hopes? In the 1990s the involvement of 'difficult' children in policy-making sits uneasily alongside the demands made on schools by central government and by society at large. Such children should be punished after all. The last fifteen years have witnessed an era of unprecedented blame-allocation in education and, in spite of the impact of the 1981 and 1989 Acts and the SEN Code of Practice, the pupil who has special needs associated with problem behaviour is usually on the receiving end of much of this.

The UN Convention on the Rights of the Child (1989) is, for the children who need it most (whether 'disruptive' or destitute), a figment of the fertile imagination of political ad-men. Official recommendations that pupils should be actively involved in shaping their own educational destiny should be treated with equal cynicism. The keyhole of opportunity leading to pupil participation had been ambiguously provided by official rhetoric and legislation. Teachers, in particular, now need to be prepared to pick the lock to enable real opportunities for co-operative policy development to become a reality.

REFERENCES

Booth, T. and Coulby, D. (eds) (1987) *Producing and Reducing Disaffection*, Milton Keynes: Open University Press.
Coulby, J. and Coulby, D. (1989) 'Intervening in junior classrooms', in J. Docking (ed.) *Education and Alienation in the Junior School*, London: Falmer.
Department for Education (1994) Circular 8/94.
Department for Education (1994) *Code of Practice*.
Department of Education and Science (1989) *Inquiry into Discipline in Schools* (The Elton Report), London: HMSO.

Elliott-Kemp, J. (1986) *SIGMA – A Process Based Approach to Staff Development*, Sheffield City Polytechnic: Pavic Publications.

Fullan, M. (1982)*The Meaning of Educational Change*, New York: Teachers College Press.

Garner, P. (1992) 'Involving disruptive students in school discipline structures', *Pastoral Care in Education* 10: 3, pp. 13–19.

Garner, P. (1993) 'A Comparative Study of the Views of Disruptive Students in England and the United States', unpublished Ph.D. thesis, University of London: Institute of Education.

Hargreaves, D., Hestor, S. and Mellor, F. (1975) *Deviance in Classrooms*, London: Routledge & Kegan Paul.

Hewton, E. (1988) *School Focused Staff Development*, Lewes: Falmer Press.

Ingram, J. and Worrall, N. (1993) *Teacher–Child Partnership: The Negotiating Classroom*, London: David Fulton.

McNamara, D. (1992) 'The reform of teacher education in England and Wales: teacher competence, panacea or rhetoric?', *Journal of Education for Teaching* 18: 3, pp. 273–85.

Mongon, D. and Hart, S.(1989) *Improving Classroom Behaviour: New Directions for Teachers and Pupils*, London: Cassell.

Musgrove, F. (1964) *Youth and Social Order*, London: Routledge & Kegan Paul.

Office of Standards in Education (OFSTED) (1993), *School Inspection Handbook*, London: HMSO.

Palmer, C., Redfern, R. and Smith, K. (1994) 'The four P's of policy', *British Journal of Special Education* 21: 1, pp. 4–6.

Rogers, W. (1992) 'Students who want the last word', *Support for Learning* 7: 4, pp. 166–70.

United Nations (1989) *Convention on the Rights of the Child*, New York: United Nations.

Woods, P. (1979) *The Divided School*, London: Routledge & Kegan Paul.

Part VI

Enhancing pupils' involvement in schools

In this final section the editors are joined by Rebecca Whittern in discussing the quality of different levels of partnership with pupils. The thoughts and practices outlined in the prior sections are drawn together in order to assemble a checklist of practices which individual teachers could use in order:

- to assess the extent to which they provide opportunities for pupils to become involved in their schooling; and
- to make arrangements to enhance opportunities for this type of involvement to take place.

Chapter 14

Enhancing and auditing partnership with pupils

Kevin Jones, Tony Charlton and Rebecca Whittern

'Partnerships' with pupils can be acted out in many different ways. Some teachers give pupils a minor role in activities which lie at the fringe of partnership, while others involve them in teamwork, in which the balance of power is more equitably shared between all members of the group. In Chapter 13, Garner refers to an example of token partnership, whereby pupils are allowed to make decisions about minor issues, such as what flavours of crisps are sold at break-times, but denied membership of more important policy-making groups. In contrast, and in other settings, the knowledge, insights and advice of pupils have been utilised in the governance of schools (see Cooper, Chapter 12). The rich variety of working practices, which have been described in preceding chapters, illustrates the many different shades and qualities of partnership which can be developed between teachers and pupils.

Teacher–pupil partnerships can be categorised according to the balance of power which exists within them. A similar type of categorisation was used by Cunningham and Davis (1985) to explain different kinds of relationships between parents, teachers and other professionals. They identified three types of working relationship, which they describe in their 'expert', 'transplant' and 'consumer' models. These models form the foundations upon which three 'levels' of teacher–pupil partnership are described below.

LEVEL 1: TEACHER-DOMINATED PARTNERSHIPS

Learning relationships which are dominated by teachers (such as those described by Charlton at the beginning of Chapter 2) are, at best, at the fringe of partnership. While some of these 'token partnerships' might signal the beginnings of, or preparation for, a more active involvement and empowerment of pupils, others might mitigate against learning.

Many teachers, who, with very good intentions, try to 'help' pupils who experience learning and behaviour problems, inadvertently run the risk of creating new barriers to learning. In Chapter 8, Jones, Bill and Quah suggest that this is due to the fact that when people encounter someone who is in difficulty, the natural inclination is to do things for them, rather than helping them to confront problems for themselves. With similar sentiment teachers can easily take over the task of learning *for* their pupils, rather than helping them to develop their own learning and problem-solving skills.

For example, in their haste to help failing children, many teachers put a lot of time and effort into devising 'worksheets' and other activities which maximise the possibility that they will produce correct answers, thus minimising the likelihood of further failure. Many such worksheets provide pupils with a series of simple clues which nudge them into making appropriate responses. There is little doubt that such fail-safe activities can boost pupils' confidence, thus providing a useful foundation for future learning. However, despite the fact that structured worksheets can help them to produce correct answers and remain on-task in the classroom, many restrict pupil 'learning' to the revision and recall of already known facts. Very few worksheets teach failing pupils *how* to learn. This is a pity, because many of these pupils are badly in need of such help. They need to be introduced to strategies which will help them to approach new learning and subsequently retrieve and apply newly acquired knowledge and skills. If they are restricted to a diet of simple worksheets, which limit them to 'recall' type activities, they will continue to encounter difficulties in learning.

Pupils should not only be introduced to learning strategies; they should also be given control over them. Unfortunately those who encounter difficulties in learning are given very few opportunities to think about, or apply, strategies for themselves. For example, many teachers attempt to teach children *how* to learn to spell by introducing them to strategies such as the Look-Cover-Write-Check procedure (Cripps 1983). Briefly, the Look-Cover-Write-Check procedure requires that pupils:

- LOOK at the word carefully in such a way that they will re-member what they have seen;
- COVER the word so that they cannot see it;
- WRITE the word from memory, saying it softly to themselves as they are writing;
- CHECK what they have written. If they have not written the word correctly they do not alter it, but instead go back and repeat all the above steps again.

While this procedure can help children to focus upon the visual characteristics of words, thus helping them to develop cues for the recall of spellings, its potential impact will be reduced if it is controlled by the teacher, rather than the learner. In the case of failing children, many teachers (and parents), who want to 'help' as much as they possibly can, dutifully remember the procedure *for* their pupils and remind them what to do at each and every stage. These children don't have to remember the strategy for themselves. There is always someone there to help them. They don't have to remember how to LOOK at words, think about their characteristics, COVER them, WRITE or CHECK their own attempts to spell them, because they can depend upon someone else to do it for them. What's more, if they show signs that they are in difficulty their 'carer' is likely to do even more for them! So, with the very best of intentions, many teachers and parents who attempt to help their pupils by doing lots of things *for* them inadvertently create more barriers to learning.

Teacher-dominated partnerships can also have a detrimental effect upon the development of *thinking skills*. Ingram and Worrall (1993) are critical of the fact that thinking skills are not promoted in many 'traditional' classrooms, where the teacher does most of the learning, in terms of hunting out information books, prepara-tory reading, thinking through and reflecting on how best to transmit and organise the children's experiences or knowledge; all skills that children themselves are capable of learning and ap-plying, which will probably be important to them in their future lives (see Chapters 8 and 9). This theme is also taken up by Jones and Quah (in press) who claim that traditional, teacher-dominated learning 'partnerships', in which children are required to give set answers to closed questions, are unlikely to help chil-dren to achieve the kinds of learning which are embedded in recently stated curricular aims, such as those for the mathematics curriculum which require that children:

- use number, algebra and measures in practical tasks, in real-life problem solving and to investigate within mathematics itself
- estimate and approximate
- look for patterns and relationships
- make generalisations
- select, interpret and use appropriate data
- interpret results.

The appropriateness and effectiveness of teacher-dominated learning is also questioned by Galton (1994) who draws attention to the fact that, in the name of 'individualised' programmed learning, many children who encounter learning difficulties are consigned to endless hours of solitary activity, such as the completion of worksheets. Galton (see Chapter 8) questions the relevance of such teacher-led and teacher-focused activities to the future lives of pupils and recommends that children should be encouraged to develop the skills of co-operative learning:

> Given the rapid changes in the global economy, promoting a need for greater inter-dependence between states, future generations of pupils will need to extend their social and intellectual skills so that they can solve complex problems, often as members of multi-national teams. Children, therefore, from an early age need to learn and value the skills that come from working together in this way.
>
> (p. 2)

Westwood (1993) is critical of teachers who encourage pupils to be dependent upon them, for another reason. He fears that *dependent relationships* will reinforce pupils' beliefs that they must rely upon the support of others (an external locus of control belief) rather than realising that their performance is also attributable to their own actions (an internal locus of control belief). This theme is developed in more detail by Jones, Bill and Quah, in Chapter 8.

Similarly, in Chapter 5, Temple claims that just 'telling' *troubled children* how they should behave in a certain situation, will not necessarily help them to behave appropriately in all other situations. She suggests that, at best, it provides an answer for that occasion and explains that, 'because each human situation is always slightly different, what might work in one, won't necessarily work in the next'. Teacher-dominated, crisis-management, approaches to behaviour management tell pupils that a particular behaviour is wrong in a particular setting. They do not encourage *pupils* to reflect upon the situational appropriateness and acceptability of different types of behaviour. Children need to learn, for example, that a behaviour which is 'acceptable' in the privacy of their own room might not be appropriate in a public place. In schools they need to develop even finer skills of discrimination, in order that *they* can distinguish between behaviours which are acceptable to some teachers, but not others. They are unlikely to develop these skills in teacher-dominated partnerships, in which the teacher, acting as 'expert' (Cunningham and Davis 1985) merely *dictates* rules and punishes infringements of them.

In summary, teacher-dominated relationships, in which teachers do much of the thinking *for* their pupils, can create even greater barriers to learning for those pupils who have already encountered problems. By adopting the role of 'expert' (Cunningham and Davis 1985) teachers can unwittingly increase the child's dependence upon adult help, thus reinforcing external locus of control beliefs. If teachers do not ensure that they develop efficient strategies which can help them to control their own learning, their pupils will be unable to decide, for themselves, which academic and social behaviours are appropriate in particular settings. They are also unlikely to have the chance to develop the thinking skills and co-operative working strategies which are likely to feature prominently in their future lives.

LEVEL 2: PUPIL-EMPOWERING PARTNERSHIPS

While teachers still play a dominant role in Level 2 partnerships their main aim is to help pupils to develop the skills, knowledge and attitudes which will allow them to take a more active part in the management of their own learning, decision-making and community life. Within these Level 2 pupil-empowering partnerships, teachers pass on, or 'transplant' (Cunningham and Davis 1985), some of their skills, knowledge and 'control' to their pupils. There are several ways in which this can be done, some of which are discussed below.

Teachers can help pupils to unshackle themselves from high dependence on external support by helping them to cultivate *self-management skills*. In Chapter 8, Jones, Bill and Quah, referring to Charlton (1992) and Westwood (1993), suggest that pupils are most likely to develop such skills if their teachers use strategies such as those listed below:

- develop simple contracts with pupils (see Brown, Chapter 7)
- use positive reinforcement judiciously, making it clear what behaviours are being rewarded
- use WAIT TIME when orally questioning pupils in order to give them ample opportunity to reply
- encourage pupils to practise analysing problem situations, in order to make them aware of the influence of people's behaviour upon their outcomes and experiences.

The majority of these strategies do not call for major changes in teaching practices. Teachers can help pupils to develop and control efficient strategies for learning through subtle changes in their own behaviour. For example, teachers (or parents) can help failing children to internalise and use the Look-Cover-Write-Check strategy (referred to earlier) through a subtle change in prompting. Instead of *telling* the child what to do at each stage, they could encourage the child to think about the learning process, for themselves, as illustrated in the following dialogue:

Pupil	I can't remember how to spell 'station'
Teacher	How could you find out?
Pupil	Um . . . find the word in my spelling bank and use Look, Cover to write it.
Teacher	Yes, we use that method because if we just glance at words we don't really notice particular patterns in them. The Look, Cover, Write, Check technique helps us to look at words carefully so that we notice patterns. That helps us to remember them. So, what do you do first?
Pupil	Find the word then look at it to see if there are any patterns I already know . . .

The learning partnership illustrated in this example puts the responsibility for remembering and applying the procedure firmly in the hands of the pupil. The teacher encourages the child to think through the process. The only explanation which is offered concerns the reasons behind the procedure, which further helps the pupil to understand and take control over their own learning.

Similarly in the teaching of reading, teachers can either organise activities so that pupils become dependent upon them, or they can provide activities which give them control over the 'learning to read' process. An adaptation of a procedure which was developed by Brennan (1978) can be particularly effective in helping failing readers to overcome their difficulties. This strategy uses a language-experience approach, in which the child's own interests and vocabulary are used to generate material for reading and writing. The main stages of this approach are described below:

1 Within general group activity in the classroom the teacher introduces topics and guides activities towards the point where the pupil is required to choose a topic for the beginning of 'interest' book work. Discussion and conversation establish and exercise the vocabulary which will be converted into writing when the work starts.

2 Pupils begin work on their interest book (of appropriate format). Classroom material is searched for appropriate illustrations which are pasted into the book. Teacher–pupil interaction and discussion continues to concentrate on appropriate vocabulary. At the appropriate time the pupil offers a sentence about the illustration which the teacher writes in plain, clear script below the illustration. Once this is done, discussion continues, establishing and reinforcing its connection with the illustration and its context. The object is to relate the words and the illustration in order to provide as many cues to recall as possible.

During this phase, pupils will read the sentence written by the teacher (by repeating it after him/her). Skilful teachers can work the repetition into the discussion, so avoiding 'say it after me'. The 'reading' is immediately reinforced by praise. This so-called 'reading' should help to establish an efficient, correct response to the written word.

3 Pupils now firmly establish their 'reading' of the sentence by tracing over the teacher's copy, copying the sentence onto separate papers, copying it in different colours and so on, with frequent attempts to write the sentence by recall without copying.

After each activity, the pupil must attempt to read the sentence to the teacher, with praise for a good attempt and positive support for failed attempts. The work, at all times, must be surrounded by continuous discussion which keeps the sentence rooted in meaning and in its richly cued context.

4 Further illustrations are now used to secure the repetition of basic words.

5 The pupil can now 'read' with reasonable accuracy a number of sentences which are directly related to the illustrations. Paper is stapled over the illustration and the pupil now 'reads' without the former cues. This should be presented as a stimulating challenge. If the child cannot read it, the teacher encourages them to look for relevant 'cues' (e.g. to uncover the illustration to reveal the picture cues). In other words, the teacher encourages the child to take more personal control over the 'learning to read' process.

6 When the sentence is 'read' successfully without the help of the illustration, the teacher prepares a sentence card, which is kept by the pupil in a suitable box or file. Pupils now attempt to read the sentence strips, a situation still further removed from the original presentation. Reinforcement can also occur by copying the sentences.

7 Once the child can read sentences independently of illustrations, another process begins. It is introduced at failure point. When pupils fail to read a sentence strip they go back to their interest book and, by matching, find the sentence there. If, despite the cues offered they still fail to 'read' it, the teacher encourages them to go back through the various 'cue' levels.

8 At this stage supplementary activities, such as matching games, are introduced.

9 The teacher now prepares duplicate sentence strips, which the pupil reads and then cuts into individual words. Lots of matching type activities are introduced, using the child's stock of words. If pupils are unable to read any of the words the teacher should ask them how they could find out. Hopefully pupils will begin to learn that they can go through the matching stages, as outlined in the previous phases, until they find sufficient cues.

This particular approach to the teaching of reading introduces learners to various types of cues which can help them to read (pictorial, grapho-phonetic, semantic and syntactic). By encouraging them to search independently for cues when they are 'stuck', the teacher gradually hands more and more control for the 'learning to read' process to the child.

Pupils can also *help each other* to develop more control over their own learning. In Chapter 6, Charlton and Jones refer to a project undertaken by James *et al.* (1992) in which 12-year-old secondary school students (N = 12) were provided with counselling facilities by older students (befrienders). An interesting feature of this particular project was the fact that, whenever practicable, the 'counsellors' were encouraged to inculcate within the youngsters feelings of responsibility for future outcomes, thus helping them to develop more internal locus of control. For example, when the younger pupils made comments such as 'I'm no good at reading', their befrienders might respond, 'I know what you mean. I used to be poor at maths, but I kept trying and I'm quite good at it now'. This project, which ran for a period of twenty weeks, brought about a noticeable improvement in the pupils' control over their own learning, as well as improved academic performance.

Some teachers try to help pupils to exercise greater self-control over their social behaviour by involving them in the *formulation of rules*. In this respect, a strategy referred to as 'Rules, Praise and Ignoring' (RPI) has been extensively used, with good effect, as a positive classroom management procedure. RPI was originally devised in the United States by Madsen *et al.* (1968). In brief, it requires the teacher to negotiate a set of three to four short, positively phrased rules, covering acceptable classroom behaviours. These often take the form of simple declarations of intent such as 'we try to get on with our work quietly', or 'we put up our hands when we want to ask a question'. Rules act as a kind of prompt and teachers are encouraged to draw attention to them regularly, preferably when pupils are clearly keeping, rather than infringing them. Teachers are required to praise pupils for keeping the rules and ignore infractions of them. Praise may be addressed to the whole class or to individuals, but should refer specifically to their behaviour in keeping the rules.

While research has shown that the RPI strategy can help teachers to create a classroom atmosphere which is more conducive to learning, it should only be considered as a starting point in the process of helping children to achieve control over their own behaviours. Despite the fact that pupils are encouraged to participate in the setting of appropriate rules, the teacher still plays a very dominant role through the management of a positive reward strategy. If the eventual aim is to help pupils to self-regulate their behaviour, teachers will need to pass even more control to them by allowing them to monitor and judge the appropriateness of their own actions (see also Chapter 11).

Rogers (1994) gives good practical advice about ways in which teachers can begin to help pupils to *monitor and self-regulate their actions* by helping children to see what their current disordered behaviour looks and sounds like and how it affects their peers (and their long-suffering teacher). He shows how teachers can do this through the use of *picture cues* and *mirroring*. In *picture cues* the child's inappropriate behaviour (e.g. calling out, not sitting with others) is illustrated on an A4-sized card. It depicts, pictorially, what the off-task behaviour looks like. In the background the faces and actions of socially disapproving peers and teachers can be seen. Rogers recommends that, in a one-to-one session, the teachers should refer to the card with questions such as, 'Who is this person here?', 'That's right, it's you, Jarrod', 'What are you doing here?', 'What can you tell me about the faces of the other children?', 'Why do they look so upset?'

Mirroring aims to show the student what a behaviour looks and sounds like in as concrete a way as possible. For example, children who are inappropriately loud in calling out (and in discussion time at their table) can be shown 'how' loud they sound by the teacher mirroring it, during a private one-to-one session. Rogers (1994) indicates that some children are quite surprised (some will laugh nervously) at what they see of themselves in the teacher's mirror. The session is concluded by the teacher saying, 'That's what it sounds like in class when you . . .'. The teacher refrains from passing judgement upon, and exploring reasons for, the behaviour. The aim is to raise the child's awareness of the behaviour and its effects and to help the child to plan alternative behaviours which will increase social approval. By using such strategies teachers can help pupils to reflect upon the appropriateness of their own behaviours, thus encouraging them to take responsibility for their own actions. While they might still require adult guidance, they are, nevertheless, being empowered to think and make decisions for themselves.

Also consistent with this theme is Brown's advice, in Chapter 7, concerning the establishment of 'contracts' which aim to modify problematic behaviours. Brown recommends that pupils should be actively involved in the formulation of contracts for two reasons. First, when contracts are drawn up *prior to* interviews with pupils and their parents or guardians, it is likely to be construed as imposed, thus causing the children to feel persecuted and controlled. Such contracts seem doomed to failure because the control has been further removed from the children, rather than helping them to take responsibility for their own actions. Second, when pupils are actively involved in the drawing-up of a contract, they have to reflect upon the 'problematic' nature of particular behaviours and their appropriateness in particular settings, thus enabling them to make more informed judgements about the desirability of their own actions.

In the course of discussion many pupils indicate that a behaviour which is problematic to teachers is also problematic to them (e.g. because of peer pressure to act in a certain way). Once the problematic nature of the behaviour(s) has been established, pupils can work with their teachers in order to try to establish conditions under which appropriate alternative behaviour can be established. This will result in the pupil being handed much more 'control', the likelihood of the contract succeeding is much greater and the pupil is more likely to transfer the learning to other situations.

As pupils develop more 'internal' control for their own learning and actions, teachers can increasingly 'let go' of their control, thus further empowering pupils to utilise their new-found self-management skills. For example, pupils can be taught to monitor their own academic and social behaviour, make judgements about its acceptability (in relation to their previous performance) and decide whether it is worthy of praise. When the relationship develops towards this level it is approaching, what is referred to below as, a Level 3 partnership, within which learning is founded upon teamwork between pupils and teachers.

LEVEL 3: PARTNERSHIPS FOUNDED UPON 'TEAMWORK'

Teacher–pupil partnerships which fall into the Level 3 category are characterised by 'teamwork' which contains some of the qualities referred to by Lacey and Lomas (1993: 4) such as:

- each person respects the expertise and individual viewpoints of all other members of the group
- the group holds a common purpose

- members collaborate in order to make plans, determine actions and future directions.

There is a growing awareness that teacher–pupil partnerships which are founded on good teamwork can help pupils to overcome, or circumvent, learning difficulties and problem behaviours (see Chapter 8). Pupils, as 'consumers' of education are in a unique position to make visible sources of problems which might otherwise be overlooked by their teachers. Their perspective upon the effectiveness and *appropriateness of teaching and learning activities and classroom conditions* is different from that of their teacher (Carnell 1983). As Cooper (Chapter 12) points out, they have knowledge about what it is like to be a pupil in a particular school environment and an inside awareness of factors which contribute to learning and behaviour problems. If, within the spirit of teamwork, their opinions are sought, it is likely that they will be able to provide valuable information on a whole range of issues, including the appropriateness of the curriculum to their learning needs, the clarity of instructions and explanations, the effectiveness of 'support' (including peer support) and the extent to which they perceive learning activities to be purposeful and relevant to their lives, to name but a few. When all members of the teaching-learning team (teachers, pupils, parents and associated professionals) pool information about the causes of learning and/or behaviour problems, they will be in a much better position to plan *lasting* responses to the range of factors which cause learning and/or behaviour problems (see Chapter 1).

In Chapter 8, Jones, Bill and Quah refer to research which indicates that insightful comments made by pupils provide a good foundation from which simple changes can be made to overcome, or circumvent, the difficulties which they are experiencing. For example, they cite the case of a pupil who was easily able to trace the source of a learning difficulty in mathematics (in particular 'measurement') to poorly displayed calibrations on a set of callipers, with which he was trying to measure the diameter of a tree. The pupil was able to recommend a simple, effective solution to the problem which involved the selection of a similar, but less complex, measuring device and the support of peers (see Chapter 6 for further examples of peer support strategies).

For many pupils, the effectiveness of the learning environment will depend upon certain 'teacher qualities' which they deem to be important. Within the spirit of teamwork, and with the intention of improving conditions for learning within the classroom, Whittern examined primary aged pupils' perceptions of the qualities of good teachers. The research, which was based on a questionnaire survey, elicited the views of 85 Year 5 pupils in an urban school which caters for 385 children aged 7–11 years. The questionnaire was constructed by first soliciting Year 5 children's (N = 31) views about teachers, during circle time. The children were asked to discuss what made a good or bad teacher, based upon their experiences. The resultant statements were used to develop a fifty-item questionnaire which was administered simultaneously with three classes by their own teachers. Children were given instructions which included, 'think about the sort of teacher you would like to have'. The questionnaires were completed in confidence and children were asked to respond to the questions on a five-point scale, ranging from 'strongly agree' to 'strongly disagree'.

The teacher quality most favoured by the children was that of 'explaining things clearly'. This attribute was also rated top by pupils in Wragg and Wood's (1983) survey of secondary school pupils. Being cheerful was rated second in importance. Interestingly the third most popular attribute of a 'good teacher', which does not appear in the extant literature, is that of 'forgiveness' if children admit doing wrong. It is clear that children value the sort of respectful and trusting relationships they may have with teachers whereby it is 'safe to tell'. Mutual respect was noted by Kutnick and Jules (1993) as desired more by pupils than an appropriate curriculum. The most disliked teacher behaviour in Whittern's study was that of 'punishing the whole class when one person does wrong'. This was closely followed by the personality traits of 'being grumpy' and 'moaning'. Whittern presented the results of the survey to her pupils who were then asked to suggest ways in which the learning environment could be improved to further facilitate learning.

Other studies have elicited comments from children who encounter learning and/or behaviour problems. In Chapter 12, Cooper argues that such pupils, who are especially vulnerable and sensitive to aversive aspects of their school environments are often able to describe graphically conditions which have an important influence upon learning. Similarly, Tattum's (1992) study of 29 special school pupils (18 boys and 11 girls) over a three-year period found that pupils had five motives for misbehaviour:

- ineffective teaching which was unable to occupy and interest them
- preservation of self in response to daily onslaught of their identity
- inconsistent rule application
- having favourites and picking on people
- having a laugh.

These, and other studies, reinforce the fact that certain teacher attributes (e.g. respectfulness, humour, cheerfulness, being firm, trusting, forgiving) create conditions in which children feel able to learn, while other qualities (e.g. being grumpy, moaning, unjust, bossy, unfriendly, intolerant, humourless, uninterested in pupil welfare, unfair) create conditions which could block learning for pupils. These factors, which influence the affective state of learners should be taken into account when special educational provision is being planned. The above mentioned studies indicate that this can be achieved through 'teamwork'.

Partnerships which are founded on teamwork also acknowledge the fact that the planning and giving of 'support' is not the sole province of teachers. Other members of the teaching-learning team (especially pupils) can also play a very effective role in the design and development of learning activities and support strategies (see Chapter 8), the support of their peers (see Chapters 6 and 8) and the creation, implementation and amendment of school policies (see Chapters 12 and 13).

For example, when certain aspects of the curriculum are negotiated between teachers and pupils, it is likely that learning activities will be more meaningful and purposeful (see also Chapter 8). A number of writers (e.g. Ainscow 1994, Wade and Moore 1993) are critical of traditional forms of practice whereby children are given boring, repetitive work in order to ensure that the 'basics' are being learnt, claiming that effective learning is only likely to be achieved when activities are meaningful to pupils.

A negotiated partnership is interactive, continuous and involves both partners in an active role (Ingram and Worrall 1993). Children's opinions are valued and they are given an active role which is reflected in the teacher's own behaviour and attitudes. Ingram and Worrall (1993) discuss five basic principles of a good, negotiated partnership (see also Hincks 1986):

1 teacher and child seen to be equal
2 teacher and child interests to be explicitly valued
3 direct speaking and active listening to be emphasised
4 learning activities to be planned, with clear objectives and two-way feedback between child and teacher
5 children's self-directed learning to be preferable to teacher-directed learning.

Furthermore, Ingram and Worrall (1993: 53–5) state that the partnership should be developed over time, in order that 'a range of mutual skills that include communication, agreeing objectives, planning application and feedback can be developed'. Feedback involves the child and teacher sharing honest comments of various aspects of the activity such as problems that have been met, or whether an activity is beginning to meet the negotiated learning aims.

Another example of Level 3 partnership can be found in Chapter 12, in which Cooper discusses the advantages which have been derived from teamwork involving pupils and teachers in special school settings. Pupils who were considered to be uncooperative and a threat to the school community from which they were referred showed that they could responsibly participate in the governance of their own schools. They were able to discuss a whole range of issues with their peers and teachers, including routine maintenance matters, rules and the discussion of particular incidents which were of wider concern to the whole community. Rather than being placed in a situation in which they wanted to rebel against imposed rules, pupils were able to help to establish procedures and interactions by which *their* community could work (see also Chapter 13).

The above analysis has shown the impact which different types of pupil–teacher partnerships can have upon the quality of the learning environment. Teacher-dominated (Level 1) partnerships can create more barriers to learning for those who are already encountering difficulties, whereas pupil-empowering relationships (Level 2) can help pupils to learn to take more responsibility for their own action and thus begin to overcome the difficulties which they face. Eventually, some partnerships evolve into teamwork (Level 3), within which teachers and pupils work closely together in order to improve conditions for learning in the classroom and the school.

AUDITING PARTNERSHIP WITH PUPILS

Foregoing chapters have shown the potential for overcoming learning and behaviour problems through partnership with pupils. Some of the main ideas have been compiled into the following checklist which summarises what can be achieved. This listing might help teachers, in partnership with pupils, to audit current practice in their own schools, in order that they can plan future developments.

---

1 Pupils can be consulted about the likely causes of learning and behaviour problems and their impact upon learning. In particular they can help to 'make visible' the influence of causal factors within:

	refer to Chapter	Comments
• themselves (e.g. poor hearing, sensory processing difficulties)	1	
• the curriculum (e.g. the extent to which tasks are matched to their prior knowledge, skills and experience, their understanding of learning processes, whether they perceive learning tasks to be meaningful and purposeful)	1	
• the learning environment (e.g. physical aspects, organisation of lessons, clarity of instructions, quality of feedback, peer and parental support)	1	

2 Through observation and/or consultation, teachers can try to ensure that learning activities are in tune with the *ways* in which individual pupils think and learn. In particular they can try to ensure that:

	refer to Chapter	Comments
• pupils are clear about task requirements	1, 9	
• classroom discourse is not dominated by teachers and children are given plenty of opportunity to talk about and reflect upon their learning	2, 6, 9	
• pupils are given adequate opportunities to respond to	8	

---

tasks and questions (e.g. through the use of 'WAIT TIME')	8
• learning activities encourage pupils to develop and apply personal problem-solving strategies	9,12, 14
• teaching resources are adapted according to the child's individual learning requirements	10
• computer technology is utilised and adapted according to the child's needs	10
• activities encourage independence in learning	9,10

3 Pupils can be helped to face up to, and overcome, learning and behaviour problems by:

	refer to Chapter	Comments
• developing their own self-management skills (e.g. how to organise their own materials, knowing when to seek help and how to check their own work)	8	
• learning to monitor their own progress through the use of self-instructing materials	8	
• being encouraged to take control over learning processes	14	
• controlling the learning to read process	14	
• analysing problem situations	8	
• seeking solutions to problems (with peers)	6,8	
• devising school rules	2	
• suggesting and implementing methods by which behaviour (e.g. playground behaviour) can be improved	2	
• negotiating curriculum content and/or the design of specific learning activities	8	
• being involved in 'review' meetings, in order that they can specify areas in which they feel they need support	8	

4 Pupils can gain more control over their own behaviour through the use of contracting and self-monitoring schemes if:

	refer to Chapter	*Comments*
• the scheme operates in a calm, safe and secure environment	7, 11	
• their involvement is carefully negotiated at the outset	7, 11	
• they are involved in the specification of problem and target behaviours	7, 11	
• the end result is negotiated with them and perceived to be rewarding	7, 11	
• they monitor and record progress	7, 11	
• teachers help pupils to develop skills of self-appraisal	11, 14	
• they appraise their own actions and reactions	7, 11	
• adjustments to the scheme are negotiated with them	7, 11	
• agreements are signed by all parties	7	

5 Pupils can help their peers to overcome learning and behaviour problems by:

	refer to Chapter	*Comments*
• learning collaboratively with them	6, 8	
• providing sympathetic support to someone who is encountering difficulty in adjusting to the demands of school (e.g. on school transfer)	2, 6	
• attending to them while they talk about their personal problems	6	
• establishing 'bully-lines'	2	
• acting as 'peer tutors' (e.g. through shared reading, teaching a particular topic in mathematics)	6,8	
• non-directive counselling	6	
• bereavement counselling	1	

6 Pupils can participate in the development and governance of the school community by:

	refer to Chapter	Comments
• living in a school community which encourages co-operation between teachers and pupils as a matter of routine	13	
• developing positive images of themselves as valued members of a school community	12	
• participating in the development of a set of shared values, purposes and policies that form the foundations of a community	12, 13	
• helping to identify, confront and solve often novel, technical, social and economic problems that threaten a community	12	
• joining school councils, or making their views known to such bodies	12	
• having a voice on governing bodies	12	
• receiving feedback on their views (e.g. from the governing body through the publication of minutes)	12	
• take part in the review of policies and resultant organisational procedures	13	
• achieving recognition, status and dignity in return for their service to the community	1	

7 Teachers can enhance children's ability to participate in the process of overcoming learning and behaviour problems by training them to:

	refer to Chapter	Comments
• develop skills and strategies which enable them to present their views of school in a rational and objective way (e.g. negotiation skills of listening, managing conflict, assertiveness training, taking risks)	13	
• make decisions (e.g. through communication, data collection, problem solving)	6	

• use specific methods to support their peers (e.g. the use of the 'pause, prompt and praise' technique)	6
• to understand issues which affect their peers (e.g. the effects of peer pressure, homework, sexuality, school transfer)	6
• to be good listeners (i.e. refrain from interrupting, to react appropriately to silence and emotion and to be able to paraphrase)	6
• to develop appropriate body language	6

This book has shown that the above mentioned achievements are only likely to occur in a climate within which teachers are prepared to listen to children with respect. Trusting partnerships need to be built up over time, and teachers' actions must confirm that pupils' involvement is *really* needed and appreciated. The authors of Chapters 2–5 provide detailed advice about how such relationships can be built up in order that learning and behaviour difficulties can be overcome through activities such as those listed above.

REFERENCES

Ainscow, M. (1994) *Special Needs in the Classroom*, Paris, UNESCO Publishing.

Blishen, E. (1969) *The School I'd Like*, Harmondsworth: Penguin.

Brennan, W. K. (1978) *Reading for Slow Learners: A Curriculum Guide*, London: Evans/Methuen for Schools Council.

Carnell, C. (1983) 'Disturbed pupils' perceptions of the personality characteristics of their teachers', *Maladjustment and Therapeutic Education* 1 (1): 22–5.

Charlton, T. (1992) 'Giving access to the National Curriculum', in K. Jones and T. Charlton (eds) *Learning Difficulties in Primary Classrooms: Delivering the Whole Curriculum*, London: Routledge.

Cooper, P. W. (1989) 'Exploring pupils' perceptions of the effects of residential schooling on children with emotional and behavioural difficulties', *Maladjustment and Therapeutic Education* 7 (3): 178–85.

Cripps, C. (1983) *The Teaching of Spelling*, NARE Insets, Stafford: NARE.

Cunningham, C. and Davis, H. (1985) *Working with Parents: Frameworks for Collaboration*, Milton Keynes: Open University Press.

Davie, R. (1993) 'Listen to the child: a time for change', *The Psychologist* 6 (2): 252–7.

Dawson, R. L. (1980) *Schools Council Research Studies, Special Provision for Disturbed Pupils: A University of Aston Survey*, London: Macmillan Education.

Dawson, R. L. (1984) 'Disturbed pupils' perceptions of their teachers' support and strictness', *Maladjustment and Therapeutic Education* 2 (1): 24–7.

Dawson, R. L. (1984) 'Disturbed pupils' perceptions of the behaviour and friendliness of other pupils, their school work and school satisfaction', *Maladjustment and Therapeutic Education* 2 (1): 21–5.

Department for Education (1993) *Pupils with Problems: Draft Circular*, London: DfE Publication Centre.

Entwhistle, N., Kozeki, B. and Tait, M. (1989) 'Pupils' perceptions of schools and teachers', *British Journal of Educational Psychology* 59: 326–50.

Evans, K. M. (1962) *Sociometry and Education*, London: Routledge.

Furlong, V. (1976) 'Interaction sets in the classroom', in M. Shebbs and S. Delamont (eds) *Explorations in Classroom Observation*, London: Wiley.

Galloway, D. (1990) 'Disruptive behaviour in school: implications for teachers and other professionals', *Links* 15 (2): 29–33.

Galton, M. (1994) *Meeting the Challenge of Diversity through Collaborative Learning*. Paper presented at the 8th annual conference of the Singapore Educational Research Association, Singapore: National Institute of Education.

Hammersley, M. and Woods, P. (eds) (1976) *The Process of Schooling*, London: Routledge and Open University Press.

Hincks, T. (1986) 'Students' rights: negotiation and participation at Countesthorpe College', *World Studies Journal* 6: 16–20.

HMI (1992) *Using Ethos Indicators in Primary School Evaluation*, Glasgow: Scottish Office Education Department.

Ingram, J. and Worrall, N. (1993) *Teacher–Child Partnership: The Negotiating Classroom*, London: David Fulton.

James, J., Charlton, T., Leo, E. and Indoe, D. (1992) 'A peer to listen', *Support for Learning* 6 (4): 165–9.

Jones, K. and Quah, M. L. (in press) 'How children learn', in K. David and T. Charlton (eds) *Pastoral Care Matters: in Primary and Middle Schools*, London: Routledge.

Keys, W. and Fernandes, C. (1993) *What do Students Think about School: A Report of the National Commission on Education*, Slough: NFER-Nelson.

Kutnick, P. and Jules, V. (1993) 'Pupils' perspectives of a good teacher: a developmental perspective from Trinidad and Tobago', *British Journal of Educational Psychology* 64: 400–13.

Lacey, P. and Lomas, J. (1993) *Support Services and the Curriculum*, London: David Fulton.

Lang, P. (1983) 'How pupils see it: looking at how pupils perceive care', *Pastoral Care in Education* 1: 164–74.

Lubbe, T. (1985) 'Some disturbed pupils' perceptions of their teachers: a psychotherapist's viewpoint', *Maladjustment and Therapeutic Education* 4 (1): 29–35.

Madsen, C. H., Becker, W. C. and Thomas, D. R. (1968) 'Rules, praise and ignoring: elements of elementary classroom control', *Journal of Applied Behaviour Analysis* 10: 465–78.

Nash, R. (1976) 'Pupils' expectations of their teachers', in M. Stubbs and S. Delamont (eds) *Explorations in Classroom Observation*, London: Wiley.

National Commission on Education (1993) *Learning to Succeed*, London: Heinemann.

Pumfrey, P. D. and Ward, J. (1976) 'Adjustment from primary to secondary school', *Education Research* 19: 25–34.

Rogers, B. (1994) 'Teaching positive behaviour to behaviourally disordered students in primary schools, *Support for Learning* 9 (4): 166–70.

Scarlett, P. (1989) 'Discipline: pupil and teacher perceptions', *Maladjustment and Therapeutic Education* 7 (3): 169–77.

Stubbs, M. and Delamont, S. (eds) (1976) *Explorations in Classroom Observation*, London: Wiley.

Tattum, D. (1992) *Disruptive Pupils in Schools and Units*, Chichester: Wiley.

Taylor, P. H. (1962) 'Children's evaluations of the characteristics of a good teacher', *British Journal of Educational Psychology* 32: 258–66.

Wade, B. and Moore, M. (1993) *Experiencing Special Education*, Buckingham: Open University Press.

Westwood, P. (1993) *Commonsense Methods for Children with Special Educational Needs*, London: Routledge.

Wheldall, K. and Merrett, F. (1994) 'The attitude of British primary school pupils to praise, rewards, punishment and reprimands', *British Journal of Educational Psychology* 64: 91–103.

Woods, P. (1976) 'Having a laugh: an antidote to schooling', in M. Hammersley and P. Woods (eds) *The Process of Schooling*, London: Routledge and Open University Press.

Wragg, E. C. (ed.) (1984) *Classroom Teaching Skills*, London: Croom Helm.

Wragg, E. C. and Woods, E. K. (1983) 'Pupil appraisals of teaching', in E. C. Wragg (ed.) *Classroom Teaching Skills*, London: Croom Helm.

Youngman, M. B. (1978) 'Six reactions to school transfer', *British Journal of Educational Psychology* 38 (3): 280–9.

Index